The Battle to Stay in America

The Battle to Stay in America

Immigration's Hidden Front Line

By Michael Kagan

UNIVERSITY OF NEVADA PRESS *Reno & Las Vegas*

University of Nevada Press, Reno, Nevada 89557 USA
Copyright © 2020 by Michael Kagan
All rights reserved
Manufactured in the United States of America

Library of Congress Cataloging-in-Publication Data
Names: Kagan, Michael, J.D., author.
Title: The battle to stay in America : immigration's hidden front line / Michael Kagan.
Description: Reno; Las Vegas : University of Nevada Press, 2020. | Includes bibliographical
    references and index. | Summary: "The Battle to Stay in America is the story of a
    community learning to defend itself from the U.S. federal government's crackdown on
    immigrants. Told through the eyes of a lawyer on the front line, the book offers an
    introduction to a broken legal system"— Provided by publisher.
Identifiers: LCCN 2020016910 (print) | LCCN 2020016911 (ebook) |
    ISBN 9781948908504 (hardcover) | ISBN 9781948908511 (ebook)
Subjects: LCSH: Emigration and immigration law—United States. | Immigration
    enforcement—United States. | Immigrants—Nevada—Las Vegas—Social conditions. |
    Immigrants—Nevada—Las Vegas—Anecdotes. | Immigration lawyers—Nevada—Las
    Vegas—Biography. | United States—Emigration and immigration—Government policy. |
    United States—Emigration and immigration—Social aspects. | Las Vegas (Nev.)—
    Emigration and immigration.
Classification: LCC KF4819 .K255 2020 (print) | LCC KF4819 (ebook) |
    DDC 342.7308/2—dc23
LC record available at https://lccn.loc.gov/2020016910
LC ebook record available at https://lccn.loc.gov/2020016911

The paper used in this book is a recycled stock made from 30 percent post-consumer waste
    materials, certified by FSC, and meets the requirements of American National Standard
    for Information Sciences—Permanence of Paper for Printed Library Materials, ANSI/
    NISO Z39.48-1992 (R2002). Binding materials were selected for strength and durability.

First Printing
29 28 27 26 25 24 23 22 21 20   5 4 3 2 1

In honor of my great-grandparents, my children,
and all those who make the journey

Contents

Preface

A Note About Word Choice

WE ARE SO DIVIDED ON immigration that I cannot even say who or what this book is about without invoking some controversial vocabulary. The best I can do is to offer a quick guide to some of the more contentious words I use, and why I use them. (Immigration policy also involves an array of legal and bureaucratic terminology, and many different government officials. If you get confused, for example, by the difference between CBP, DHS, and ICE, there is a glossary at the end of the book to help.)

Immigrant: I use the term "immigrant" to mean a person who was not originally a U.S. citizen who came to the United States to stay and establish a home here. However, in the Immigration and Nationality Act, an "immigrant" has a narrow meaning: a person who receives legal permanent residency. In the law, a "non-immigrant" is a non-citizen who is in the country ostensibly temporarily. That could be a business visitor in Las Vegas for a week for the Consumer Electronics Show, a tourist visiting Yellowstone National Park for a few days, or someone on a student visa here for five years. In this book, I'll try to be clear when I am using the strictly legal concept, but most of the time I am using the broader, non-legal meaning.[1]

Alien: The unfortunate and archaic word used in the Immigration and Nationality Act for any person who is not a United States citizen or national. I use "alien" when quoting the law or another person. I never use it otherwise. Some people take pleasure in using the term "aliens" to describe immigrants because it is dehumanizing, but it is also in the statute books, which confers some legitimacy. I think we can see what they're doing. Most of us don't use archaic legal terms when we can avoid them. For example, most of us say, "I bought a house." We don't say, "I acquired a tenancy in an estate-in-land."[2]

Illegal: I use this word, but carefully. Merriam-Webster's first definition for this word refers to something that is "not according to or authorized by law." I'm fine with using the word "illegal" that way. I have gotten tickets for parking my car illegally, for example. We've all probably done at least a small illegal act in our lives. There's no shame in admitting that. That is why I am comfortable talking about "illegal immigration," if the term is used in the same way someone might talk about "illegal parking" on Fremont Street. People do cross borders illegally, and people do overstay visas in violation of the law. However, Merriam-Webster's second definition is a problem: "a *person* who enters or lives in a country without the documentation required for legal entry or residence." As in "an illegal," or "illegals." The dictionary correctly notes that this definition is "sometimes disparaging + offensive." Very. Homicide is illegal. But we do not even call a murderer "an illegal."[3]

An act can be illegal, but a person can never be illegal. This is why I will sometimes say that a person crossed the border illegally, but I avoid labeling a person an "illegal immigrant." I also avoid this term because many undocumented immigrants have been living in the United States for many years. For many undocumented people, the border crossing (legal or illegal) may have been more than a decade ago, which makes it problematic to make that act the defining characteristic of their identity.

I have even more serious problems with the term "illegal alien." This phrase combines two dehumanizing words to make a doubly dehumanizing phrase. That's the point. Using this term—just like saying "the illegals"—says, in effect, "I don't like these people. I don't see them as equal to me. They are *different* (alien). They are *wrong* (illegal)." That's not how I talk about other human beings.

Undocumented immigrant: The term most generally favored by immigrant advocates, and the phrase I use, to describe immigrants who are unlawfully present in the United States. As typically used, and as I use it in this book, it includes both people who crossed the border illegally and those who entered legally but overstayed their visas. Although I use "undocumented immigrant" for lack of a better and commonly understood alternative, I do not love this phrase. Most "undocumented immigrants" have plenty of documentation proving *who* they are. The problem is their lack of legal authorization to be *where* they are.

The Battle to Stay in America

Introduction

MY DAUGHTER WOULD prefer I not tell this story, but I think it is important. On election night in 2016, she was terrified. She was in fifth grade at the time. Already at that age, the early signs of tweeny drama were upon us. The sound of slamming doors had become common in our house, as had marginally inappropriate music played at extremely high volumes. She did not like to concede that she had to answer to us, or needed anything from us other than transportation and money. Except when it became clear that Donald Trump had won. Suddenly, on the sofa in our home in central Las Vegas, in front of the TV, she sobbed. Not dramatic tears. I'd become accustomed to those. She was really crying. It seemed like her body had become smaller; her knees were bent and her elbows were holding them close to her chest. This was my daughter genuinely, deeply upset.

"Daddy," Maya said, "they're going to deport me now, right?"

I was shocked. To be clear, we are a very politically aware family, progressive in our commitments, and we found Donald Trump's candidacy at once shocking and outrageous from the start. But my wife and I are well-educated, white, upper-middle-class. We were angry and confused by the election, just like many other Americans. But I could not conceive of a way in which Trump would directly hurt *us*.

On the other hand, both our children were born in Ethiopia. They were adopted. It had never really occurred to me that my older daughter would feel at risk. There are no legal problems with their adoptions. I know, legally, that there should be no danger. So I tried to reassure her. I told her she was a United States citizen. I am a professor of law, and I teach immigration law. I am supposed to know about these things. I asked her to trust me. I told Maya, with as much authority and confidence as I could, "You cannot be deported. They cannot do that." But she would not be consoled.

"But Daddy, I'm an immigrant."

"Yes, but you are a citizen. They cannot take that away."

"Yes, he can," she said.

I told her that I knew she needed a hug, and to be close, but I asked her for permission to get up. I had something I wanted to show her. I ran upstairs to our filing closet. I pulled down my daughter's file and retrieved her original certificate of citizenship. It had been issued to her when she was still an infant. I still remember taking the oath on her behalf, renouncing any allegiances to foreign princes and potentates with her sitting on my knee in a Department of Homeland Security office. Her baby picture is stapled to the corner, with an embossed U.S. government stamp. The document is printed with a great deal of blue script on expensive stationery. It is soft to the touch, not like regular paper. It feels expensive, and it looks very official. It *is* very official.

I ran back downstairs. I told Maya to look at it. She had calmed a bit but was still breathing heavily. I thought the certificate would put her at ease. "See, look! This is you. You are a citizen. They cannot take this away. They cannot deport you. See? Trust me."

She burst into sobs again. She seemed more upset than before. Her small shoulders shook. "Daddy," she cried, "it's just a piece of paper. That doesn't even matter. It's just a piece of paper!"

In the time since that night, I have been immersed in immigrant defense in my adopted home of Las Vegas. My daughter's tears have echoed in my mind almost every day. In part, I have been angry that the man who became president terrified my daughter so thoroughly. A father does not forget that easily. But that's really a side matter. Children have fears. I have never for a moment worried that she, or anyone else in my family, was directly at risk from the Trump administration. I personally know many people who are really in danger, and I do not pretend for a minute that my family or I share their burden.

What sticks with me are the words she used: *It's just a piece of paper.* That is a profound indictment. A basic statement of no confidence in the rule of law in the United States of America. After all, my daughter's certificate of citizenship *is* just a piece of paper. A careless child could tear it up, which is why I keep it secured up high in the closet. If determined government agents burst through the door, this paper could not *physically* stop them. That is my daughter's fear, at base. The entire theory of constitutional democracy is that a piece of paper can somehow control the government's infinite capacity for brute force. I am a lawyer, a law professor, and my entire profession is based on this idea. Yet for my daughter in her darkest hour, it could not comfort her. In fact, for a child afraid that government agents would take her from her family, the concept of rule of law is absurd.

My daughter did not identify with that piece of paper. It has her name and her baby picture, and it's very fancy. But the photo was taken when she was less than six months old. It could be any baby, really. It's just one of many papers her dad keeps filed away in the closet, one shelf away from the electricity and cable bills. Why should that paper represent her any more than those utility bills represent me? It's just paper. It's not who a person *is*.

But in immigration law, papers are everything. We talk about "show me your papers" laws. To gain legal status, immigrants must fill out forms, on paper. Immigrants who are in the country without authorization are called "undocumented"—they lack the right papers. Why do these papers matter so much?

I thought the piece of paper mattered because it was a certificate of welcome, a gesture of inclusion, and a form of protection. It means that she is American, and that's final. But my daughter sensed that, to the incoming president, at a far more fundamental level, being welcomed in America might be provisional. Because she is an immigrant. Because she is black.

Indeed, within his first three years in office, the new president referred to immigrants from Africa and Haiti as coming from "shithole" countries, said he could issue an executive order to suspend the Fourteenth Amendment's citizenship guarantee, claimed that "our country is full," and told armed border guards that "if judges give you trouble, just say, 'sorry, judge, I can't do it.'" The Department of Justice started a new initiative to aggressively strip naturalized immigrants of their citizenship if they could find errors in their original applications. Then, in the summer of 2019, the president said that four women of color who serve in the House of Representatives and who criticize him regularly should "go back" to the "crime-infested places from which they came." At a campaign rally in Greenville, North Carolina, three days later, he brought up Rep. Ilhan Omar, who came from Somalia as a refugee. His supporters began chanting, "Send her back! Send her back!" The president of the United States basked in the call of the crowd and appeared to smile.

In May and June 2018, federal agents took thousands of children away from their parents when they crossed the border. Most of them were Central Americans, trying to flee rampant gang violence by seeking asylum in the United States. Some of the children may have been separated permanently. Then they continued to take children from their parents even after a court told them to stop. In most cases, the justification for such separation was that families had not crossed the border at an official port of entry, and parents were to be prosecuted criminally for misdemeanors. But a journalist found earlier cases of fathers whose children were taken from them when they tried to seek asylum at legal entry points, after U.S. officials did not accept the Salvadoran birth certificates they carried. For an adoptive father like me, this is terrifying. My kids don't look like me. In a pinch, I can't take a DNA test to prove we belong together. For most of my daughters' lives, the only documentation we had that they belonged in our family were Ethiopian-issued certificates listing my wife and me as adoptive parents. These papers are printed on yellow card stock. I know they are genuine because I was there when government clerks in Addis Ababa produced them. But I also know that I could make pretty close duplicates with supplies purchased at the Office Depot around the corner from my house.[1]

So much depends on cheap paper.

When I think about it, there have been many times in American history when people could not rely on their papers for protection against the United States government. American immigration law as we know it today began with a case in 1889 in which the government gave a Chinese immigrant a paper promising to let him back into the country after a trip, then reneged. The Supreme Court said that was fine. That is my daughter's fear. Such things have happened before.

It's not just a nineteenth-century concern. In the 1930s, people who looked Mexican were rounded up in public parks in Southern California, detained, and then placed onto trains that took them by force to Mexico. It was part of President Herbert Hoover's response to the Great Depression. "American jobs for real Americans," he called it. Those are words that echo our current president. By the end of Hoover's campaign, 1.8 million people were deported to Mexico, and the majority of them were actually American citizens.[2]

In August 2018, the *Washington Post* reported that the State Department was denying passports to some Mexican Americans born along the Texas-Mexico border because of vague doubts about the validity of decades-old birth records. The *Post* reported:

> In some cases, passport applicants with official U.S. birth certificates are being jailed in immigration detention centers and entered into deportation proceedings. In others, they are stuck in Mexico, their passports suddenly revoked when they tried to reenter the United States.

When I read this, I thought immediately about my kids' adoption papers from Ethiopia. I don't think there's any legal problem with their documents. But how difficult would it really be for someone in the government to raise vague doubts about them?

In 2019, Customs and Border Protection detained at least two children who were U.S. citizens. They detained Francisco Galicia, an eighteen-year-old high school student, when he tried to pass through a checkpoint in Texas on his way to a soccer event. He carried his American birth certificate with him, but immigration officials said he gave them conflicting information. They also detained a girl who was going through a border crossing on her way to school. Despite the fact that the girl carried a U.S. passport, federal officials blamed her for giving "inconsistent information." She was nine. At the time, my younger daughter, Tesi, was the same age.[3]

Maybe Maya's fears on election night were not so irrational. Maybe not much has changed since the 1880s. Maybe I was the one who was naive.

It is more important than ever for informed Americans to understand how our laws regulate the lives of immigrants. Part of my purpose in writing this book is to provide an accessible taste of immigration law, without it being a lawyer's reference book. I don't want to spend too many pages on waivers of inadmissibility, bars to consular processing, or the other technicalities of immigration practice. Can I sponsor my brother? Which form do you file if you need a waiver for a marijuana conviction? Why could my neighbor sponsor his wife, but my cleaning lady can't get papers? These things matter for people. A lot. But the rules and the application procedures constantly change. They are in many ways tedious and, in the end, arbitrary. They miss the big questions: Why should so much depend on these arcane procedures? In a democracy, what rights should depend on having a piece of paper, versus on just being a person?

I am a law professor, and normally I write law review articles about deep problems in immigration law. But this book is far more personal. I will try to tell a story about people I know in Las Vegas, and what it has been like to try to defend immigrants here these last few years. Las Vegas is an iconic, familiar place to many Americans, but it is also a place where real people live, work, and go to school. In the American war over immigration, Las Vegas is the front line. In fact, in fiscal year 2018, Immigration and Customs Enforcement (ICE) would make about as many arrests in the Las Vegas area as in Manhattan or Chicago. More than one in five residents of the Las Vegas metropolitan area was born in a foreign country. Per capita, more people in this state are undocumented than anywhere else in the country. More than in California. More than in Texas. More than in New York—although these places are where the national media usually turn when journalists want to do a feature on immigration. Las Vegas stands out even more among big cities in another way: it has only recently become so diverse. All of America has been growing in diversity, of course. According to data compiled by *USA Today*, the chances that two random people in Las Vegas will be of a different race are about the same as they are in Los Angeles or Brooklyn—about seven in ten. But Las Vegas is different because this is new. The racial diversity of Las Vegas has increased 80 percent in the last thirty years.[4]

I know all this today, but I was blind to it for a long time. For my first four years in Las Vegas, we lived in the suburb of Henderson, in an upper-middle-class neighborhood where only 6 percent of residents were not U.S. citizens. My faculty biography said that I worked on immigration law, but in truth I had little real contact with immigrants. Or, to be more accurate, I was not as aware as I should have been of the immigrants that I interacted with every day. The 2016 election shocked me awake to the realities with which my neighbors had been living for a long time.

I tell this story with hesitation. I am not an immigrant. It might be better to hear about the immigrant experience from one of the thousands of immigrants who work on the Las Vegas Strip and now find themselves targets of the federal government. Or to hear from students at Nevada colleges who work their way through school, help their parents buy houses, and now must worry it will all be taken away. Or from someone who has spent months detained by ICE. However, I know that the cruelty Donald Trump has unleashed has awakened many reasonable Americans who were shocked and confused to discover that such callousness was even possible in our country. Many of these Americans are, like me, outsiders to the world of immigrants. I started this book with the thought that, because I've seen glimpses of the struggle that immigrants face and because I have professional knowledge of how this area of law works, I might be a useful guide for concerned citizens who are in a position to push back and to say no to cruelty. More than that, I hoped I might be able to clarify issues for Americans hungry for a better way to govern immigration, one that does not offend basic American values, one that incorporates principles of fairness, balance, and proportionality.

I have worked on this book while the federal government's anti-immigrant policies have escalated, and as the community around me has struggled to respond. None of what I report in this book would tell any immigration lawyer or scholar anything they do not already know. I make no attempt here to offer any novel legal ideas, nor to summarize everything legal scholars know about immigration law before and after Trump. But I do hope to draw much more attention to the people affected by the policy. We all have a responsibility to learn about the struggles of our neighbors, because we do not really live separately. We need to stand by them. We cannot allow them to be invisible. I hope this book is a contribution to that effort.

Through these last few years, I have had to grapple with what my own role should be. My position as a lawyer, and as a secure, well-paid, highly educated, white law professor, encourages me to think that I can play hero. Maybe I can win the big case, or design the perfect piece of legislation. Some of the highest-profile moments in Trump-era immigration policy encourage this kind of thinking, because lawyers have indeed often been front and center. But in this struggle and others, lawyers acting alone have usually lost in the long run. The courts have eventually allowed many anti-immigrant policies to stand, or the government has found its way around narrow rulings. What I have learned, more than anything, is that the only way to defend a community is through a coalition of everyone in the community. The strongest leaders are people who are most affected by the threat, but everyone has a role.

Most important, this is a story that is not yet finished. By the end of this book, I hope you will understand how immigration law works in real people's lives and get to know some remarkable people who grapple with it every day. I hope you will understand the attack that is under way against people and families who are as much a part of our country as me and my children. More than anything, I hope you will understand that this battle is only just beginning. It is difficult and frightening, but we are not helpless.

PART I
THE TARGETS

1

The Graveyards of Nevada

THE HIGHEST HOURLY wage Fernando Gonzalez ever earned in Las Vegas was $16.54 an hour, and that didn't last long.* For that, he picked cucumbers at a hothouse on the northern frontier of Las Vegas's urban sprawl, somewhere in between the Stratosphere and Nellis Air Force Base, where the desert meets the city.

"The cucumbers got infected," he told me. That was the end of that job.

But Fernando didn't come to Las Vegas for the money. I tried to get him to tell me a story of misery from Guatemala, where he came from. Something that would place him in a standard immigrant narrative. Some details about extreme poverty. Maybe some violence. But Fernando wouldn't bite.

"All my family was here. My mom wanted us to be together." At age twenty-three, he walked across the desert in Arizona and came to live with his mom and dad in a rented house just north of Route 95.

Fernando is undocumented, which seems a bit out of place in his family. His parents are legal permanent residents. His youngest sister is a U.S. citizen. He also has a brother, who came here with his parents as a boy; he's a citizen. This all might seem weird, to have three different statuses in one family, but it is common. Many undocumented immigrants live in mixed families. This is probably why Fernando tends to just shrug if you ask him why he is one thing and his mom and dad are something else. These are the cards you're dealt.

---

* Like most undocumented people in this book, this is not Fernando's real name. I have also fictionalized the names of the family members of most undocumented people in this book. But everything else is true.

That's life. What matters, his mom told him, is that they are all here together. All in one place. That's what she wanted.

Fernando had been in Las Vegas for thirteen years when I met him, twice as long as me. Along the way, he had a daughter, who was eight when I talked to him. She was the product of a relationship that was long in his past, but his daughter still lived with him for part of the year. She may be the only person who ever made Fernando cry. But that came later in this story.

For the first few years in Las Vegas, he worked for an employment agency for minimum wage. The agency had him doing a bit of everything. Sometimes cleaning, sometimes unloading trucks, sometimes stacking pallets for delivery. Whatever was needed, for not much money. "I was trying to do my best. I was good at any job they sent me to," he said. He was initially happy with the transition to the hothouse vegetable business because the money was much better. But, of course, the vegetables did not cooperate.

After the cucumbers died, the pastor from Fernando's church told him that he knew a guy who could give him some work as a painter. It did not pay as well—just $12 an hour. But Fernando sees it as a turning point in his life. It started him in the field of construction and handyman work. As a result of this job, which he got in 2013, he now does house repairs and remodeling. Painting, drywall, electricity. At each of the several meetings I had with him, his pickup truck was filled with a slightly different mix of supplies. Sometimes paint, sometimes plasterboard. Whatever the suburban homeowners in Southern Highlands or Summerlin need. It's not hard to imagine why a homeowner would trust Fernando. His face is soft, and he doesn't frown or smile much. His answers to questions are simple and concrete. No embellishment. He seems like someone who will tell you things as they are and will do whatever he says he will do. And that's how he sells himself.

The homeowners who hire Fernando often know that he is undocumented. It's hardly a secret, he said. He doesn't think it's ever cost him a job. "They feel kind of sorry for me because I don't have the status," he said. "I'm a nice guy. I like to help people." Of greater difficulty, potentially at least, is the fact that Fernando doesn't have a contractor's license. Technically, therefore, he shouldn't do much more than painting. He was interested in getting a license, but he wasn't allowed to for most of his time in Las Vegas because he wasn't in the country legally.

You might think that keeping undocumented people from getting a contractor's license makes sense in terms of restricting them from working. But that's not really what happens. My wife and I own a home in Las Vegas. When we hired a licensed contractor to do some remodeling, we shook hands with, and wrote a check to, a white man. He came to our house, drew some sketches, gave us an estimate, and told us when the work would begin. And on that appointed day, when the actual workers arrive, they were people like Fernando.

Fernando prefers to just work for himself. And it is his truck that makes that possible. Oh, the truck. It looks like just an old pickup. But it's much more than that. Much like the man who owns it, it's nothing fancy, but it does what it needs to do. It's a Chevy. It's white, or it used to be. Now it's merely dirty. The body of the truck is marked, dented in some places, and just bruised in others. It's worn and battered, but it gets Fernando where he needs to go, with his supplies and tools in the back. He bought it in March 2017. He paid $1,800. "A great, great price," he said. It was a big improvement over his previous truck, which he said had engine problems and bad gas mileage. Owning a truck lets him work for himself.

As his work got better, Fernando's life turned upward in other ways, too. In early 2017, he was on Facebook and—as one does on Facebook—he ran into someone from a long time ago. Reina, a girl he'd known in Guatemala since they were two years old. It had been a while. Somehow, after all this time, she'd ended up in Minnesota, where she worked as a manager at a Chipotle restaurant. She found Fernando. As Elvis said, so it goes—some things are meant to be. Fernando and Reina started exchanging messages. They started talking on the phone. Then they decided that Reina should move to Las Vegas. By early 2018, she was pregnant.

Now, let's be clear. Fernando had problems. Working for himself, going from job to job, can be unstable. He had to keep his truck working, but he couldn't always afford to fix the little things. He neglected to replace a broken brake light. And in April 2018, a cop gave him a ticket. But Fernando didn't worry. It was just a brake light. He did not quite understand that in Nevada, minor traffic infractions like broken brake lights are criminal offenses. "Stop Lamps Req (Misdemeanor)," it says on the municipal court docket. That remains, to this day, the most serious criminal conduct for which he has ever been charged. The police officer gave Fernando a lecture about it, too, and so Fernando did the right thing: he spent some money fixing the light. It works now. However, Fernando readily admits that there was one thing he did not do. He did not go to court for the ticket. At the time, he didn't really understand what that meant. He did know that he had to pay the ticket eventually. "I was having some financial problems," he said. He saw the ticket as a debt he was having trouble paying, like a credit card or a utility bill. Sometimes, when money was short, he was late to pay those, too. But he always pays people back, eventually, if you give him enough time.

Things were not perfect, but Fernando was happy. Fernando had a girl. He loved her and she loved him. They had a small, decent place to live. They were starting a family together, and he was working for himself. It was never about the money with him anyway. So long as his truck kept working, so long as the jobs kept coming, he and Reina and their baby-to-be would be fine. He would find work and pay the bills. He always did. Like his mom wanted, they would be together.

That was how it all seemed, right through the summer of 2018. But this is no fairy tale. That broken brake light had changed everything.

* * *

My first experience of what it's like to be a resident of Las Vegas was in the Seattle-Tacoma airport in the fall of 2010. I had my laptop open in the Southwest Airlines departure lounge, and I was studying my notes. The two men and a woman next to me were already drunk. I probably projected some level of annoyance.

"You going to Vegas alone, hon?" the woman said. "Where are you staying? You'll see a show?"

"I'm going to a job interview," I said.

"A what?"

The three of them stared at me for a moment. One of the men laughed awkwardly. "I didn't see that coming," he said. A few minutes later the three of them moved away from me. I was no fun.

The job I was applying for was at the University of Nevada, Las Vegas. I moved my family to Las Vegas in 2011. Since then, I've gotten used to the reality that many people find it surprising that there are around 2 million people who actually live in Las Vegas, and that they do normal things like go to job interviews or take their kids to gymnastics.

I was hired to teach immigration law, and to co-direct the UNLV Immigration Clinic. In reality, I didn't know as much as I should have about American immigration or how it impacted Las Vegas. I had been working with refugees in the Middle East for the first ten years of my career. In December 2000, when I took my last law school exam, I got on an airplane to join my wife in London, and from there we moved on to Egypt. By the time I got the UNLV job, we were in our thirties and had two kids, but Las Vegas was the first American city where my wife and I lived in our post-student phase of life. We bought our first house here and learned how to take out an American auto loan here. I got myself a Hyundai Elantra and excitedly ordered a pro-diversity license plate frame on Amazon. It was a political statement on the back of my car. I could never do something like that in Cairo or Beirut.

Although I knew many fundamental concepts of American immigration law, it seemed to me that American immigration lawyers talked in code, using government form numbers rather than, you know, words. People didn't apply for asylum; they filed an I-589. Family members didn't sponsor each other; they had a pending I-130. I didn't understand what they were talking about, because I had never practiced immigration law in the United States. It was a real problem, and one I had to keep on the down-low as much as possible.

I was saved in my first few years because until the spring of 2016 I had a co-director at the clinic, Fatma Marouf, who had an encyclopedic knowledge of immigration rules. So did Angela Morrison, who for my first few years at UNLV ran an immigration program out of the clinic offices. In meetings, Fatma or Angela would say something like, "We need to do an I-601A" for a client and I would try to discreetly check Google on my iPhone to find out what in God's name that was. And then I would smile and nod.

These forms have been the focus of immigration law for a very long time. Almost every immigration category created by Congress becomes a form. Most of these forms have to be mailed off on paper, so it is literally papers required to get papers. For each of these forms there are lists of criteria and exclusions. For many exclusions, there are waivers. For each waiver, there are specific requirements, and another form. And on and on.

All this paperwork can make immigration law blind to real life. The government should recognize that children who have survived abuse and neglect need special protection. But immigration lawyers might instead say, "She has an approved I-360." Perhaps this is part of why immigration policy can become so rigid and so cruel. It's just about papers, not people. Perhaps this is part of why the public is so confused about how American immigration law actually works. It does seem like the right lawyer might know the right form for any situation, so why doesn't every immigrant just follow the law and send in an application? Still, while it always bothered me that immigration lawyers talk this way, I tried to become conversant in the lingo. To an extent, that was a necessity in my line of work. It made me feel less insecure around other immigration lawyers. I liked being able to be the one throwing the form numbers around. Like I knew what I was doing.

Suffice it to say that for my first few years in Las Vegas, despite the progressive language on my Elantra's license plate frame, despite my title as co-director of one of the only programs in the entire state offering free legal assistance to immigrants, I didn't have much real contact with the immigrant residents of my city.

In 2014, cable news was gripped by a migrant crisis at the southern border—an influx of unaccompanied children. The kids were teenagers and some younger children. They had come from El Salvador and some from Honduras and Guatemala, and they had horrendous stories of abuse by criminal gangs. Many of the girls were rape victims, or had been told they had to become gang "girlfriends." Boys told stories of gang members from MS-13 interrupting middle school classes to tell them they had to join the gangs. They had walked through Mexico, sometimes hitching a ride on a notorious train called "La Bestia" (the beast).

The Obama administration found this influx to be most inconvenient. At the time, there was still a faint hope of immigration reform moving in Congress, and these kids made it look like there was chaos at the border when it would have been better to have cable news focus on the improving economy or the normalization of relations with Cuba. Instead, there were awful photos of children crowded shoulder to shoulder, sleeping on the floor under shiny metallic blankets. The Obama administration responded schizophrenically. Officials made grave threats that the migrants would all be deported quickly. Parents who had traveled with their children were locked up in remote detention centers. A frequently reproduced photograph from the time shows a boy, maybe six or seven years old, in jeans and a gray T-shirt, standing on polished concrete in the middle of some kind of warehouse that had been divided by tall chain-link fencing. A bored officer in a green uniform stands over the boy, his thumbs on his utility belt, while the boy stares up at a television mounted high on the fencing that surrounded him. The boy was watching a cartoon while locked in a makeshift prison. America was putting children in cages. That was before Trump even announced he was running for president.

I did nothing—although, fortunately, others stepped up. The kids who came alone across the borders were supposed to be locked up only for a brief period, after which they were to be sent to live with sponsors, if the government could find a relative living in the United States. That is why some of these kids began arriving in Las Vegas. The attorney general at the time, Eric Holder, started a program to provide lawyers to the kids in some of the places where they ended up. Two of my colleagues, Fatma and Anne Traum, applied to participate. I thought the program was poorly thought out and unsustainable— I'm pretty sure I used that phrasing at the time, although on paper I was part of the grant. In Las Vegas, the kids would have to fight deportation in court. Anne and Fatma hired two recent graduates, Katelyn Leese and Alissa Cooley, to defend children in these deportation cases. They began attracting local attention for their work. Nominally I was co-director of the clinic, and so I started getting compliments on their work, too. It was a nice feeling, I'll be honest, even though had it been up to me, we never would have taken part in this program at all.

Many of the kids had viable asylum claims, and others were eligible for something I had known little about previously: Special Immigrant Juvenile Status, or SIJS. If a child in the United States has been the victim of abuse, abandonment, or neglect as defined by state law, and if it is not in the child's best interest to be reunited with a parent and sent home to her country of origin, she may be eligible to stay in the United States. By early 2016—against the confident statements made by government officials—Katelyn and Alissa had begun winning legal residency for some of these kids.

Katelyn and Alissa earned approximately $25,000 a year each for their work as AmeriCorps fellows. They told dark jokes about surviving on ramen. As they began attracting more media attention, one article highlighted their poverty wages, and the fact that one of them could not afford to fix the air-conditioning in her car, which she drove to court hearings in the summer, with temperatures over 105 degrees every day. Of course, not everyone loved what they were doing. Someone wrote a comment below the article that they must be "bottom dwelling lawyers" because they'd taken a job making so little money. Katelyn and Alissa joked about it, but it clearly stung.

Katelyn and Alissa shared an office across from mine in the UNLV Immigration Clinic. They had a whiteboard where they tracked all of their cases. Before they came in 2014, the clinic rarely had as many as thirty cases at a time. Now, a year out of law school, they had increased our client roster to more than a hundred. I remember one day noticing that colorful handprints had started appearing on their office wall. When their first child clients received legal permanent residency, they bought small canvases and tempera paint in primary colors from a craft store. Whenever a child won asylum or legal residency, Katelyn and Alissa took the kid's handprint and wrote his or her name on the back of the canvas. The handprints were colorful wall decor for an office that had no windows. Each one meant at least one child would stay safe.

Meanwhile, my own kids had more contact with immigrants than I did. That should not have been a surprise to me, given the demographics of Las Vegas. But that was not something I thought about at the time. What my wife and I wanted was to send them to a good school, and we eventually ended up at Sandy Miller Academy, an award-winning magnet elementary. It had a renowned, dynamic principal, Anne Grisham—known to everyone as

Dr. Grish. That's what we thought about as parents. But it was through this decision that I eventually faced the reality of Las Vegas.

Sandy Miller Academy occupies a modern brick building surrounded on three sides by vacant lots. Where I grew up in upstate New York, a vacant lot is a green space—an overgrown field that, after enough time, turns into woods. But here, a vacant lot is just rock and light gray dirt, the color of blank newsprint. If no one builds on it, it stays that way. The hard, hot, dusty blocks around the school accentuate the fact that it sits, from one point of view, in the middle of nowhere. However, Sandy Miller Academy occupies a pivotal place in American society today, in the middle of one of the largest immigrant communities in this country. This school and the surrounding dust are in the heart of East Las Vegas, in the middle of a zip code that is home to more than 11,000 people who are not American citizens, out of roughly 59,000 residents. Its student body is 65 percent Hispanic and only 17 percent white.[1]

Through my daughters' friends and through other parents at the school, it gradually became impossible for me to avoid the fact that my community was now an immigrant community, and many of my neighbors were in a great deal of danger. The people who would be targeted in an anti-immigrant crackdown would be the same parents who hosted my older daughter for sleepovers, the same parents who waited with me in the line of cars to drop off our children early in the morning, the same parents who volunteered to help organize games for the kids on Field Day, the same parents who helped the teachers when the kids got to go on an excursion off campus.

Every spring, the fourth grade at Sandy Miller takes a three-day, two-night field trip to Carson City, the state capital. In 2016, I was a chaperone for my daughter Maya. Traveling in rented buses north through the high desert, fueled by cheese sandwiches, bags of chips bought in bulk from Costco, and Capri Sun, we stopped at the Tonopah Historic Mining Park on the site of the old Mizpah Mine, where miners took more than $1 billion in silver (in today's currency) out of a hillside. And then back in the buses, onward to Carson City. The first night, after the kids arrived exhausted, they got pizza and bowling. I sat with other, equally exhausted parent volunteers and marveled at how well behaved the kids were.

In the morning, we drove into the hills, up to Virginia City. It was not clear to me how many fourth graders were interested in the Comstock Lode, the silver strike that made this a late nineteenth-century boomtown. But the school had been doing this trip for years and had it down to a science. They knew how to keep the kids interested. We went to the cemetery. We talked about dead people.

Dr. Grish eventually gathered everyone together for a teachable moment.

"Look at these headstones," Dr. Grish told the kids as we all stood around the broken and faded stone markers. "What do they tell us?"

"Their names!" a child shouted.

"What else?"

It took the kids a while to figure out what Dr. Grish was getting at. But eventually the answer came: "They all have a city!"

"Yes," Dr. Grish said. "They said where these people came from, and people came from very far away to live here in Virginia City." It's true. It's not just that American migrants who were born in the East went west to try to get rich in Nevada. The exploitation of the Comstock Lode in Virginia City depended on immigrants from the British Isles who had experience in a similar type of mining.

We went to the Fourth Ward School Museum, a Victorian schoolhouse where we sat at old wooden desks to learn about how kids in the late nineteenth century got their grades and went outside for recess. The guide explained how a flawed building design creates a massive fire hazard, which is why the school was eventually closed. The Sandy Miller fourth graders found the thought that we might all suddenly burst into flames very exciting. The best part of the museum is the display case showing scraps of papers found below the floorboards during renovations. They included notes that the schoolkids passed to each other, and a neatly folded paper airplane. It's easy to imagine kids quickly slipping their contraband through gaps in the wood floors to escape being detected by a suspicious schoolteacher, items that wouldn't be seen again until the historic building was restored a century later. There's something thrilling about seeing tangible evidence that the children of nineteenth-century silver miners weren't too different from children in twenty-first-century East Las Vegas. Across geography and time, people are people.

Unfortunately for the kids roaming the old schoolhouse, Virginia City offered darker warnings of dangers that before too long would impact some of their own families. In a back corner of the museum, there was a small display that no one brought up to the fourth graders. But a few of them found it, including my daughter Maya. It was about nineteenth-century demonstrations in Virginia City against Chinese immigration. This was something I knew about, because Chinese exclusion is usually the first topic in a law school course on immigration law. This dark era of racism and xenophobia established a legal doctrine known as "plenary power." That doctrine, which has never been repudiated by the Supreme Court, means that immigrants have much less legal protection than other people, because the president and the Congress have especially broad authority over them.

The Chinese exclusion story is not consistent with the story Nevada likes to tell about itself—an open land where people from all over can come and make a go of it, if only they work hard. It was also not completely consistent with the message Dr. Grish tried to communicate to the kids at the cemetery. Yes, people came from all over to build Virginia City, including immigrants from England, but they did not get always get along, and some were more welcome than others. With the discovery of the Comstock Lode, Chinese immigrants flocked to Virginia City just like other people. But unlike English immigrants, they did not work inside the mines. They were not allowed to.

Back in the nineteenth century, Nevadans, like other Americans of the time, expressed their animosity against the Chinese partly through political mobilization and partly through menacing violence. In 1870, Nevada senator William Morris Stewart told the United States Senate that Congress must restrict Chinese immigration, or ethnic violence would erupt: "Do you want to have the Chinese slaughtered on the Pacific Coast? Do you want extermination?" In August 1878, the Chinese quarter of Reno was burned by a fire on the same day the Workingmen's Party held a public meeting about "the Chinese Question." Violence like this was sweeping the West in the 1870s and 1880s. In 1871, a mob in Los Angeles lynched seventeen Chinese men. In early November 1885, a mob of several hundred white men armed with guns and clubs marched through Tacoma, Washington, rounding up Chinese residents until there were none left in the town.[2]

In the 1880 election, the Nevada ballot featured a question about Chinese immigration. It was a straw poll presenting voters with two choices: "for Chinese immigration" or "against Chinese immigration." That November, 17,259 voters chose "against." Only 183 voted "for."

And yet Nevada is a study in contradictions. In November 1880, the anti-Chinese measure was Question 4 on the ballot. Question 3 was quite different. It proposed an amendment to the Nevada state constitution that would remove the word "white" from the provision granting the right to vote. This also passed overwhelmingly: 14,215 to 353. This meant that thousands of white male voters chose to approve allowing non-white men to vote. Then a moment later they moved on to the next question and expressed overwhelming hostility to Chinese immigration. Herein lies the conflict at the heart of American immigration policy: many Americans at many points in history have seen no tension between supporting American values of democracy and non-discrimination while simultaneously expressing fervent hostility toward immigrants and immigration. Virginia City contains all the warnings anyone should need that this can happen in this country. But my trip to Virginia City was in May 2016. I wasn't worried at the time.

In the meantime, I had more immediate shocks to deal with. At the end of the spring semester, Fatma Marouf, on whom I had depended to compensate for my lack of experience in American immigration law, left UNLV. Angela Morrison had left, too. I now had no one to hide behind. Looking toward the fall, I would have to be the sole director of the immigration clinic for the first time. Later that summer, Alissa Cooley and Katelyn Leese, who had launched our work defending kids fleeing violence, announced they were leaving. They had worked for two years with little support or guidance (especially from me) and even less pay. It was a real question whether we would even keep their program going. After wavering for a few months, we hired another Ameri-Corps fellow, Laura Barrera, who had just graduated from law school in Michigan, and she arrived in Las Vegas a few days before the 2016 election. I thought she seemed really quiet. She told me that she worried Michigan would be a problem in the election, and that Donald Trump might win. I thought she was paranoid.

* * *

In the months immediately after the 2016 election, we tried to mobilize. Lawyers and students from my clinic at UNLV spoke at community forums around Las Vegas for nervous immigrants. Many community groups organized similar events. The Legal Aid Center of Southern Nevada did ask-a-lawyer consultation sessions. We trained more than thirty lawyers who said they were willing to take asylum cases pro bono, a first for Las Vegas. We had PowerPoint presentations prepared in English and Spanish to tell immigrants about their rights. There was talk about developing a roster of rapid-response teams, in case of mass roundups by Immigration and Customs Enforcement, also known as ICE.

If I'm being honest, it was a dark but also pretty exciting time to be a professor of immigration law. Within a week of the election, I was on an hour-long call-in show on the local NPR station. That was more exposure than I'd had before. When major legal challenges to Trump policies were in court, I had local and national journalists calling my cellphone. That was new. Immigration law has not historically been very prestigious, and it is famously complicated and convoluted. For attorneys, immigration law is like tax law, but without the money. Some law schools do not even have an immigration spe-cialist on their full-time faculty. I had met prominent Las Vegas attorneys who, upon learning my specialty, would say, "Oh, I don't touch that."

Now, though, immigration law was *the* thing. In those early days, when the first version of President Trump's travel ban blocking entry for nationals of seven Muslim-majority countries was stopped in court, it was easy for lawyers to feel like we were in the center of things. Even for a lawyer like me, who wasn't actually involved in the high-profile cases, there was an adrenaline high from the sheer rate of phone calls and emails. But that does not mean that I had grappled with what this new administration meant for people in my own community. Not really.

Not long after the inauguration of Donald Trump in January 2017, Lynn Tyrell, a teacher at Sandy Miller Academy, sent me a text message. She asked me if I could do a know-your-rights presentation for parents about immigra-tion. I was proud that my kids' school was doing this. We scheduled a morning session, set to begin just after the first bell. This allowed parents to drop their kids off and then go to a classroom to hear about immigrants' rights.

It's always a little funny when adults hold a meeting in an elementary school classroom, because they have to cram their grown-up bodies into the child-sized chairs. But for this meeting, there weren't enough of those little chairs. People stood around the back and leaned on top of desks. Sandy Miller Acad-emy is named for Sandy Searles Miller, a former Nevada first lady, the wife of Bob Miller, the longest-serving governor in state history. She was there, along with her elderly mother, who was an icon to the kids at the school. They called her "Mama Searles." A teacher acted as my interpreter for Spanish.

The PowerPoint that I used was one I had presented before. The slides in-cluded advice about what to do if ICE knocks on the door. (Don't let them in.) What if they say they have a warrant? (Make sure it has a real judge's signa-ture; most ICE warrants don't). If ICE gives you papers and tells you that you have to sign them, don't. If ICE arrests you, make sure to get a lawyer.

I had given this spiel before. The idea of these presentations was to reassure people: Know your rights, because knowledge is power. If you know your rights, the government can't abuse you as easily. That's the idea. But from the start, the session at my daughters' school went much worse than others. Maybe I was starting to lose faith in what I had to say, as the cruelty and anti-immigrant aggression of the Trump administration began to take shape. Maybe it was because people were more comfortable in this setting, in a class-room at their own children's school, than in others, and were willing to ask me tougher questions. Questions that I couldn't answer.

Questions like this:

> You said get a lawyer. What if we don't have enough money for a lawyer?
> Where can I go to get a free lawyer if they try to deport me? (*In Las
> Vegas, nowhere, really.*)
> How am I supposed to know what a real warrant is? I'm not a lawyer.
> (*Even experienced criminal lawyers get confused by the fact that ICE
> doesn't use real arrest warrants. That's a fair point.*)
> There's a lot of crime in my neighborhood. Can I call 911 if I need to, or
> will the police give me over to ICE? (*There are no guarantees about this
> from the Las Vegas police. Sorry.*)
> If I'm alone with my baby, will they still arrest me? (*God, I hope not.
> But I honestly don't know.*)

It went on like this for about two hours. Then, finally, a woman asked me: "If I'm taken, who will pick my son up after school?" I remember the question especially clearly because I recognized the woman who asked it. I didn't actually know her name. But I recalled her face. She had been a chaperone with me on the field trip to Virginia City. On the long bus ride, she sat in front of me, about three rows up on the left. Then, she had been laughing, playing games with her son and other kids. She ate pizza with the rest of us, and she cheered the kids as they went bowling.

"My son needs a lot of help with his homework," she said now. "He needs someone to sit with him. I sit with him every day."

On this day, in early 2017, she looked different than she had in Virginia City. Her shoulder-length hair was pulled back the same way, tied in a neat ponytail. But her face was tight. It wasn't just that she did not smile; I thought it looked like she was forcefully holding her facial features tightly in place, as if she could no long allow herself to show any emotion. When offered an immigration law expert at her son's school who was willing to answer questions, she didn't ask to save herself. She asked a practical question, about after-school pickup. The kind of problems all parents face every day, except she was contemplating being taken away by federal agents. She was a responsible parent. She was planning for worst-case scenarios. But it was also so much more. She might as well have asked: *Who will be my son's mother after they take me?* It was love, practical and terrified.

I didn't know the answer to her question. How could I? I stammered something about going to Legal Aid to set up a guardianship. There were forms that she could fill out. I felt nauseated as the words passed my lips. One of the school's administrators offered some advice about filling out a permission slip with the school to authorize a friend to pick her son up. More forms, in other words. Teachers looked at each other. I heard one of them say, "What would we do?"

You can't just fill out a form to replace someone's mother.

In the first months after Donald Trump's election, there had been a flurry of activity, and it felt satisfying to "do something," as they say. We had held some trainings and a lot of information sessions. But there was still almost no real capacity to defend real people when they needed us. We would not have been able to find enough pro bono lawyers in Las Vegas to serve the immigrants in just one zip code of the city. Maybe not even the parents in one elementary school.

How could a person with limited English, little money, and no lawyer defend herself? I don't know. In Las Vegas, three out of four people detained by ICE never find a lawyer, and they are nearly all deported.

Sure, there had been some victories in court at the national level. In early 2017, the first versions of Trump's travel ban were stopped. But that policy never mattered much in East Las Vegas. Even during the Obama administration, there were complaints that ICE officers abused people physically, shouted racist epithets, tried to force them to sign papers against their will. Thanks to the Chinese exclusion case, the courts had long accepted that the executive branch has extremely wide power over immigrants. Now a man who said Mexicans are rapists, a man who said Mexican Americans should not be federal judges, a man who called for "a total and complete shutdown of Muslims entering the United States," had plenary power. Nearly unfettered power.

At the end of the session, Sandy Miller gave me a hug, and so did Mama Searles. Some of the parents shook my hand. In truth, I don't really know if the session helped them at all. I only know that I felt suddenly dirty and useless. I walked quickly out of the classroom, past the library, past the secretaries at the front desk, and found my car in the front parking lot. I opened the door, collapsed in the driver's seat, and gripped the steering wheel of my Hyundai Elantra. I did not turn on the engine. I sat there for several minutes before I felt composed enough to drive. I had chaperoned field trips with these parents, and I'd been brought here as an expert, but I didn't know how to keep them together with their own children. Instead, all I could say was: *Please fill out a form, ma'am. Turn in your paper.*

It's always about the papers. I had been blind to the people who had been right in front of my eyes every day.

2

Plan B

L ET ME TELL YOU A STORY. It is a story about two bloody feet, and how the sight of them changed a young couple's plans. It's also a story about a Snickers bar that kept a man going in difficult times. It's a story about luck, but also a story about hard work. It's about fine dining, a bicycle, burritos at midnight, and a girl who dreamed of being a dancer. This is a Las Vegas story.

But first, Agua Prieta. In January 2001, Olivero and Manuela arrived in this northern Sonoran town by bus from Mexico City with Adelina, their five-year-old daughter. Adelina was closer to her dad than her mom back then, because for around a year, Olivero had been unemployed while Manuela worked, and Olivero had spent all of that time with his little daughter. He had eventually found work, and on paper was doing well. In fact, he had two jobs. In the morning he worked for a delivery company based at the Mexico City airport. He also worked for another delivery company for the rest of the day. He had started as just a laborer, and by the time he went north, he was a supervisor. Still, even with promotions and multiple jobs, the couple didn't have enough money for a young family in a big city. Especially not enough to pay for the kind of schooling that a girl like Adelina deserved. That's why Manuela's sister told them to come to Las Vegas.

Olivero was wary of the trip. He'd seen it portrayed in Mexican movies, which made it look scary, and for good reason. Since the late 1990s, more than 7,000 people have died trying to enter the United States from Mexico. But Manuela's sister in Las Vegas said it would be easy, and not to worry. "Everybody's coming here," she said. She arranged for a coyote (smuggler), and they were grateful. Olivero and Manuela sold all that they owned, which wasn't much, and paid for a one-way bus ride for the three of them from Mexico City up to this town on the border with eastern Arizona.[1]

In Agua Prieta, the guesthouses were full of people like them, ready to make the journey north for the first time. They were also full of people who had failed—people who had been caught by *la migra* (slang for immigration authorities, in this case the U.S. Border Patrol) and who had come back to Agua Prieta. Many of them over and over again, until one day they didn't come back. Which meant either that they made it or that they were dead somewhere in the desert.

There was indeed much to worry about, but the coyote Manuela's sister had hired was a salesman. Sometimes people get sent back, he said. But everybody crosses. Don't worry. He had fourteen years of experience, he said.

Olivero might have gone along with this, except for one woman he saw with no shoes on. She had been caught and sent back, and her feet were bloody. Two weeks of walking in the desert. She had nearly died before finally being put into a border patrol truck.

And that was it.

"I made a decision," Olivero said. Two decisions, actually. First, he would not take Manuela, his wife, and definitely not his daughter, Adelina. "She was a little kid," he said. Second, he would only try once. "The first time, if I'm taken by immigration and sent back, I was never going to try again."

Agua Prieta shares the international border with Douglas, Arizona. Like many border towns, Agua Prieta and Douglas are in a sense one town with a line through the middle, not unlike Scottsdale and Phoenix. People with the right papers can commute across the border on Route 191 through a crossing just south of an O'Reilly Auto Parts store. But Olivero did not have papers, so he and his group had to walk out deep into the Sonoran Desert.

For a fee of $800, the coyote put Olivero in a group of eleven men and one woman. They began early in the morning, and within an hour they were robbed. Five guys with handguns in the hills made the group stand by a tall cluster of bushes while the bandits searched them for cash and valuables. "Everybody come here," said the gunmen. But then, Olivero remembers, they said, "Relax!" This was just a day's work. The gang made them take their clothes off to be searched for cash. And they all complied—except for the coyote, who conveniently seemed to know what would happen and had made himself scarce right at the key moment.

The coyote's omniscience about the robbers in the desert worked out well for Olivero. Before they'd started out, the coyote had told Olivero, "Hey, give me all your money. I will save it for you." Olivero had agreed. It was hardly an act of generosity; the coyote would have to be paid for this service. But it meant that when the gunmen made Olivero strip his clothes off, he had no money on him. The one thing Olivero had was a Snickers bar. He had just one, because the coyote said they would be walking for just one day. The bandits let him keep it, and sent the group back on its way.

"We just follow the electricity poles. When they finish, that's the USA!" the coyote told his customers. Olivero planned to eat the Snickers as a reward when the walking was done. But it was not just a one-day walk. "It felt like the electric poles never ended," Olivero said.

They walked until 6 or 7 p.m. In the distance he could see the lights of cars driving between the United States and Mexico at an official border crossing. It was cold in the desert at night, and they slept in an empty abandoned gasoline tank. Olivero remembers that it wasn't too bad inside. It didn't smell of gas and it was big enough for them all to sleep. But it was scary, because if anyone had closed the door, they would have suffocated, which is something that has happened to migrants in this desert. "You hear lots of stories," Olivero said. For some of the people in his group of twelve, this was their second or third time trying to cross. They told him not to worry.

The next day, they began walking again. Suddenly the coyote yelled, "Immigration is watching!" They ran and hid in the trees. They trusted the coyote. They had no choice. And, he kept reminding them, he had fourteen years of experience. Often he heard helicopters above them, and they hid again. They found a group of fifteen other migrants nearby. They had lost their coyote, and others in their group had been caught by immigration. Now twenty-seven in total, they walked onward.

Besides his Snickers bar, Olivero had a one-gallon container of water, and he had layered five shirts on his body. The shirts kept him warm. He felt he was better off than most of his companions. Late on the second day, they crossed a farm, and the coyote told them to drink from water left by the farmer for his livestock. It smelled awful. Olivero did not drink it, though, because he had been saving his water, as well as his Snickers bar. Not all the people had water left, and they had no choice but to drink from the smelly trough.

The second night they slept outside.

"The coyote is a liar. He said it was only one night walking," Olivero said. He thought more and more about the Snickers bar. "That was the one thing I was looking forward to." But he refused to eat it. He hadn't made it yet.

On the third night, they slept in a drainage pipe under a remote desert road. They waited there until late afternoon the next day. A U-Haul truck pulled over on the road above them, and they loaded onto it, running out of the pipe two at a time so as to not draw attention. They pulled the back of the truck closed, and the U-Haul drove them to an apartment building in Phoenix. Again moving two by two, they went upstairs. More than two dozen people filled two rooms.

In a technical sense, the migrants were now being held hostage, as human collateral until the smugglers were paid. But Olivero does not remember being at all worried at this point. They had made it to America. They were beyond the border. Their hosts provided them food while they waited. This was a simple piece of business. As payments began to arrive, the people who had made the journey with Olivero began to depart. He remembers some left for the Carolinas, and one went to Utah. Olivero's sister-in-law sent the $800 for his coyote's fee, and his brother-in-law picked him up in a car. Olivero got in, opened the wrapper of his Snickers bar, and began the drive to Las Vegas.

Because this is a book about people, and also about immigration policy, let us be clear: Olivero broke the law. What he did was a crime: *improper entry by an alien*. It is not a capital offense, so we should be realistic. Many things are illegal. On first offense, improper entry is a misdemeanor, punishable by up to six months in prison. In Nevada, coming to a rolling stop at a stop sign is also a misdemeanor, theoretically also punishable by up to six months in jail, just like what Olivero did.

Olivero's choice to cross the border is often misunderstood in American politics. In October 2018, Secretary of Homeland Security Kirstjen Nielsen said of journeys like Olivero's: "There is a right way to immigrate to the United States, and this is not it." If it were true that a legal route to immigration was available, it would indeed be easy to judge Olivero harshly for choosing instead to pay a criminal to smuggle him into the country. But that is not the choice that Olivero made. His real choice was to stay in Mexico or come to America by crossing the border on foot through Arizona. There was no legal option.

The State Department lists all of the legal visas that are available to foreigners on a website. Just Google "State Department Directory of Visa Categories." There are thirty-one commonly used types of visas for permanent immigration, and around forty forms of temporary entry to the United States. But most of these are incredibly narrowly defined, like "Australian professional specialty." There are several for exceptional athletes and artists. That's how baseball players from Venezuela and acrobats in Cirque du Soleil shows come to the United States. But there is essentially no visa category for people who lack formal education but who are smart, disciplined, hardworking, and dreaming of a better life for their children.

In theory, people like Olivero and Manuela might be able to immigrate legally through family sponsorship. Manuela did have a sister in Las Vegas. This would be valuable for immigration—if her sister was a U.S. citizen (she wasn't). But we can ignore that detail for the moment. Even if Olivero and Manuela had a sponsor, there is a quota on family-based immigration to the United States—226,000 per year. That means there are long waits, because there are far more eligible families than that.

And then there is the per-country limit. No more than 7 percent of the quota can be used for nationals of any one country. This makes Mexicans, Chinese, Filipinos, and Indians wait longer than other people, because those four countries are large in population and already have significant numbers of people with deep family ties in the United States. Mexicans have to wait an especially long period of time for family-based immigration.

The visa for brothers and sisters of U.S. citizens is known as F4. For a Mexican to have received this visa in January 2001—when Olivero, Manuela, and Adelina first arrived in Agua Prieta—she would have had to have filed an application *twelve years* earlier. Today, the wait is even worse. For a Mexican sister of an American citizen to get a legal visa in July 2019, she would have needed to file an application more than twenty-two years ago. *Twenty-two years.*

Now you know why Olivero crossed the border illegally.

Back to our story.

After Olivero began his journey across the border, Manuela and Adelina had to go back to Mexico City. They went to live with Manuela's parents. For the moment, they had nothing. They would now be dependent on Olivero earning money in the United States and sending it back to them.

Up north in Las Vegas, Olivero's first possession was a bicycle. He began riding around looking for jobs. He got multiple offers immediately. He started working for a few weeks as a repairman at apartment complexes. But his brother-in-law worked as a cook and got him a job as a dishwasher. He lived with his brother and sister-in-law in Spring Valley, in central Las Vegas. Nearly immediately he began sending money back to Mexico City, which allowed Adelina to go to a good preschool. This had always been what he wanted—but not this way.

It is common among migrants for one parent to come to the United States to work and to send money back home to support their children. But Olivero and Manuela never were willing to accept that. Manuela remembers mainly that Adelina cried for her father constantly. So Olivero saved. After a year, he had enough money to send for Manuela and Adelina. But Olivero remained worried about their safety. He could not imagine his little Adelina sleeping in a fuel tank or drinking water left for animals. So he paid for a higher grade of coyote, at a price of $2,500 for each of them, much more than the $800 his sister-in-law had paid a year earlier for him.

This time it was a female coyote who ran the show. Manuela and Adelina stayed in Agua Prieta for around two days. Then the only really frightening part: she and Adelina, who was now six, had to be separated. Manuela briefly protested. "I was scared," Manuela told me. "This is my daughter." The entire purpose of this journey was for the whole family to be together again. But to make this happen, Manuela had to put her child in the care of organized criminals.

The coyote addressed her fears with the cold logic of a smuggler who was focused on a simple, successful business model. She was paid to deliver people to the other side, not to keep them. "I'm not interested in your kid," she said.

Still, Manuela negotiated the details. The plan was for Adelina to ride in a car through the legal, official border crossing at nighttime, with a family that had their own kids, and also proper papers—maybe even American citizenship. Manuela doesn't know to this day exactly how they did it. Typically, the kids who were being smuggled would be drugged so that they would sleep. The idea is to get the border guards to wave the car through without waking a sleeping six-year-old, who might blurt out something unfortunate. Manuela begged the coyote: "Don't give her the 'candy.' She's smart. Just tell her what to do." They settled on this plan.

Meanwhile, Manuela went with a different woman on foot. But her walk was nothing like her husband's had been a year earlier. They didn't walk deep into the desert. She remembers walking for less than an hour, from central Agua Prieta across the fence to a Walmart Supercenter, which is on the edge of the town of Douglas. Manuela has no idea how the smugglers managed to make it seem so easy. The location where she crossed is so close to the border patrol that it raises questions about whether the smugglers had extremely good intelligence or whether some kind of corruption was involved. If you walk out of that Walmart, turn right, pass the Little Caesar's, and turn right again, the legal border crossing on Route 191 would be right in front of you. But, of course, this is why Olivero had paid a premium. He wanted it to be easier on his wife and daughter.

The coyote told Manuela to just walk into the Walmart as if she were shopping. There she met a second woman, who took her to a truck, which drove them to a trailer on the outskirts of town. The next day, "Adelina came back to me," she says. Safe and sound. The smugglers were true to their word and did not drug her. As a result, Adelina still remembers her arrival in the United States. It wasn't exciting. She just sat quietly in a car with some other kids and drove right in. Adelina had followed directions perfectly.

The smugglers gave Manuela a fake ID and put the two of them on a bus to Phoenix. And then it nearly all came to an end. A couple of hours into the journey, immigration officers pulled the bus over and began checking all of the passengers' identification. They checked Manuela's, too—and then let the bus continue on. Perhaps the ID was a high-quality fake. But Manuela thinks they made it through for a different reason: some other passengers with kids on the bus complained about the delay, "so they didn't check the IDs very well."

Manuela and Adelina got off just before Phoenix, were taken to another house, and then got a ride to Las Vegas, where Olivero was waiting for them. They have lived together in Spring Valley, in the middle of Las Vegas, ever since.

Migration specialists monitor the rate of border crossings by watching the number who fail—those who are caught by American border guards. In February and March 2000, more than 200,000 people were caught at the Mexican border *each month*. We know that in fiscal year 2000, 1.6 million people were caught at the southwest border. In 2001, when Olivero came, American border guards caught just under 1.2 million people trying to do the same thing. It is hard to know exactly how many Mexicans relocated to the United States from the mid-1990s until the Great Recession, because they moved clandestinely—and when they were successful, they were by definition not counted. The Department of Homeland Security (DHS) estimates that today it catches around 70 percent of the people who try to cross the southern border, a result of massive investment in the Border Patrol by Congress and successive administrations. But back then, DHS estimates, they caught only about 35 to 40 percent. So if they *caught* 1.6 million in a year, well, it is fair to say that Manuela, Olivero, and Adelina were part of a mass migration of several million people.[2]

This was also a time when Las Vegas was booming.

In fact, what sets Las Vegas apart from most other large American cities is its rapid growth over the last three decades. The population of Clark County today is about 2 million. The City of Las Vegas is much smaller, with around 645,000 people and very odd boundaries. Because of the odd boundaries, it is more informative to think of Clark County if one wants a gauge of the size of Las Vegas as an urban community. Most important: The population of Clark County more than doubled from 1990 to 2010. When Olivero came, jobs were easy to come by. Las Vegas needed him, and many more like him.

I heard Olivero and Manuela's story sitting around the family's kitchen table. In the zip code where Olivero and Manuela live in Spring Valley, 36 percent of residents were born outside the United States. It is because of families like Olivero and Manuela's, and neighborhoods like Spring Valley, that Nevada has a higher percentage of undocumented people among its long-term residents than any other state. In Nevada one person out of every 13 residents is undocumented, according to a 2018 Pew Research Center report.[3]

When I sat down with Olivero and Manuela to hear their story, they brought donuts and coffee for me. By 2018, when I met them, Adelina was in her twenties and was trying to get herself ready to apply for law school. Manuela and Olivero had had two more children, Natalia and Ana, both teenagers, both born in Las Vegas. The kids all sat around the table with their parents as they talked to me. It was very clear that the kids all knew their parents' story of their journey north, because the kids liked to interrupt their parents and finish the story for them. Especially Adelina, who was there. Manuela occasionally corrected her daughters on some details. But Olivero often just leaned back in his chair and smiled as his teenage daughters put words in his mouth.

Today, Manuela and Olivero both work in the restaurant industry. In 2018, Olivero was promoted to kitchen manager at a restaurant on the Las Vegas Strip. "It's the first time I've had only one job," he said. Manuela's first job was making sandwiches at Subway. Today she is a prep chef at a five-star steakhouse at a well-known resort. She has worked at a series of well-known restaurants in Las Vegas. I won't name them because it would make Manuela too easy to identify. But I can tell you that if you've eaten an expensive meal on the Strip over the last decade, there is a reasonable chance that she has cooked for you.

I asked her how many non-immigrants work in Las Vegas kitchens, and she just laughed. Eighty or 90 percent of the people in the kitchens are immigrants, she said. She said that head chefs like to work with her because she has learned English, which means she can teach the recipes to the rest of the kitchen staff. "When the chef wants to tell the people something, he looks for me," she said. Sometimes, though, the chef calls her over when someone else gets in trouble. She doesn't like being part of that. What Manuela loves to do is cook. Her daughter Natalia told me: "She comes home with all this food, and she practices and practices. And we get to try it. It's *amazing!*"

While both Olivero and Manuela have advanced in their careers, they cannot go any farther because of their immigration status. "The problem is that sometimes you have better opportunities, but you don't have the documents," Olivero said. "I never felt that I stole a job from anyone," Manuela said. "I've worked for all of [my jobs]."

I asked them what they would do if they had legal permission to work.

Manuela didn't hesitate: "I'd open my own restaurant." She fell into cooking because it is a field open to undocumented immigrants, but now she wouldn't want to do anything else.

"Oh, my God, it would be incredible," said Ana, who was thirteen. Natalia bragged about how her mom is learning to cook gourmet Asian food.

Olivero was a bit more hesitant. He told me that if he got papers, he would quit the restaurant business. What he'd really love to do, he said, is work for the school district as a PE teacher so that he could be a soccer coach. And once he said this, it became immediately obvious why he held back.

"Nooooo!" said Natalia, who was fifteen. "He's actually the best cook. He loves to cook. He just doesn't admit it."

Olivero shook his head and smiled.

"Yes, you are, Dad!"

He shook his head some more.

"Sometimes, he works late until the restaurant closes, and comes home at midnight, and we're asleep," Natalia said. "And he knocks on the door and he's so excited. He says, 'Wake up, we're having burritos!' And he has all the ingredients and he makes the most incredible burritos. All fresh. It's so worth it to wake up."

Adelina's first job as a teenager was at a casual (but still pretty pricey) restaurant at a mall on the Strip. Both her mom and dad worked there at the time, and that's how she got the job. This one struck me, because the establishment where they were working was my own kids' favorite restaurant on the Strip, and one of the few to which we will occasionally take them. But for Adelina, the kitchen was an awkward place to work. She was just a high school student trying to earn spending money. "The kitchen was full of adults with families to raise," she said.

Adelina is undocumented. Just like her parents, she crossed the border illegally, and the law takes no pity on her for the fact that she was only six at the time. She is part of the generation of young immigrants, known as Dreamers, who came to the United States as children and who grew up as Americans in every way except for not having the proper paperwork. According to the Immigration and Nationality Act, Adelina, and every other person like her, could be arrested and detained by ICE, and she could be deported.

The plight of the Dreamers has gotten a lot of attention in public and in Congress. In 2001, Sen. Dick Durbin of Illinois and Sen. Orrin Hatch of Utah introduced the DREAM (Development, Relief, and Education for Alien Minors) Act, which would make legal immigration available to Dreamers. It has never passed. The closest it came was in 2010, when it passed the House of

Representatives and received 56 votes in the Senate—not enough to overcome a filibuster. With congressional action stalled, in 2012, President Obama started the DACA program—Deferred Action for Childhood Arrivals.

DACA is not a law. Not really. It's a policy established by a memorandum at the Department of Homeland Security. As an immigration lawyer, I cringe a little when people say that someone has "DACA status," because it is not really a status at all. "Deferred action" literally means that the government could take action against the person if it wanted. It could start deportation proceedings. But instead, it "defers action" against them. It's a form of prosecutorial discretion. Under a regulation in place since the Reagan administration, beneficiaries of deferred action may receive employment authorization. The deferred action and the employment authorization last two years at a time and then have to be renewed. Each renewal comes with a fee: $495 in 2019. That's a month's rent for many people. But the benefits are huge.

Adelina qualified for DACA, and it gave her work authorization, which she used to get a job at Wing Stop. That job lets her work with other teenagers and college students, instead of with parents sweating in a kitchen to support their own kids. Wing Stop offers college scholarships to its employees, which is how Adelina paid tuition at UNLV.

Adelina has taken it upon herself to make sure her younger sister Natalia takes the right advanced classes to get into college. Natalia, who was born here, will be eligible to vote in the 2022 midterm elections. Meanwhile, Ana earned a competitive scholarship from the Nevada Ballet and trains as a dancer after school five days a week. She says that's what she wants to do when she grows up. Day and night, all she thinks about is ballet.

The five members of Adelina's family represent three different immigration situations, all under one roof. The parents are undocumented. Their oldest child has DACA. The future of her legal status is extremely unclear. The two youngest children are U.S. citizens because they were born in Las Vegas. This kind of mixed family is extremely common. In Nevada, one in seven schoolchildren has at least one undocumented parent at home. Most of those children, like Ana and Natalia, are probably citizens.[4]

This is who is at stake as America debates immigration policy. Any day, ICE could carry out a raid on one of the restaurants where Manuela and Olivero work. Or the Trump administration could succeed in ending Adelina's DACA protection, which it is trying to do. Nevertheless, on the surface, everything seemed fine when I met them. Olivero had gotten his promotion. Manuela was mastering new cuisines. Adelina was looking at law school. Natalia had her AP classes, and Ana her ballet.

Inside the United States, away from the border, the main change in immigration enforcement in the early years of the Trump administration has been an increase in arrests of immigrants with no criminal record. People like Manuela and Olivero. In June 2017, the acting director of ICE told Congress that all undocumented immigrants "should be afraid."[5]

When I asked if the Trump administration scared them, Manuela and Olivero sat up straight.

"No," they said.

I asked if they knew anyone else who had problems with ICE.

They denied knowing anyone who did.

At that stage, their daughters interrupted. They reminded their parents about someone the family knows who had been caught by ICE. Manuela and Olivero did not dispute it. A family friend had neglected to pay a traffic ticket, and he was taken by ICE. Natalia said she knows her parents have talked about fearing ICE. She basically told me that her parents were lying to me, pretending not to be worried.

Ana, the thirteen-year-old, said: "They don't like to talk about it in front of us. They hide it. But I know they worry."

Finally Manuela changed her tune. "We have a plan B," she said.

In fact, they had talked about what they would do if the worst happens. "We have a friend," Manuela said. She said the children know that if their parents are ever taken, they are to go to a certain friend's house.

And what then?

Manuela claims that plan B calls for their friend, who is a U.S. citizen, to help them sell all of their belongings and to send Adelina, Natalia, and Ana to Mexico if their parents are deported. When she finally laid all this out, I was in disbelief. Natalia will be applying for colleges before too long. Adelina was finishing college when I met them and was preparing for law school. Would they really rip all that apart? But Manuela was emphatic: under any circumstances, the family must stay together. Her daughters nodded in agreement. I confess that I wondered: Is that really the choice they would make? Is it even possible for them to really know what they would do until they are actually faced with the choice? And for the rest of us: Would our community or our country really be better if we force a family like this to leave or split up?

Much as Manuela and Olivero struggled to talk about this situation with their children, we struggle as a country to talk about them. Olivero and Manuela are immigrants, but they've lived in Las Vegas much longer than I have, and they have much stronger roots here than I do. They came here because Manuela's sister was here before them. Technically, the trouble that Manuela and Olivero have is that they are "unlawfully present." Under the law as it stands, there is virtually nothing Olivero and Manuela could do to gain legal status in the United States. Theoretically, since Natalia is a U.S. citizen, she could claim her parents as immediate relatives as soon as she turns twenty-one. When I met her she was only fifteen. That's a long time to wait—but it's not even the main problem.

The biggest problem for this family is that American immigration law will not forgive Olivero and Manuela for coming into the country illegally so long ago. Because of this, their status cannot be adjusted from inside the United States (with very narrow exceptions), even if they had a relative who could sponsor them. They *entered without inspection*, and so they are what immigration lawyers call EWI (pronounced "eewee"). Even Adelina is stuck in this situation. She is in her early twenties. She could fall in love and marry an American citizen, but that wouldn't help her adjust her status in the United States either. She, too, is EWI, even though she entered the country when she was just six years old. Immigration law will not forgive her, either.

If Manuela and Olivero went back to Mexico, they would be barred from being legally admitted to the United States for ten years. This is because they spent more than a year living unlawfully in the United States. On paper, immigration law wants them to leave—to try to apply to come legally—but immigration law would also punish them if they tried to comply with the law. If an immigrant stays unlawfully for six months, she is barred from reentering for three years. If she stays a year, she is barred for ten.

The result of all this is a stalemate. Olivero and Manuela have never been arrested. Their worst criminal offense was entering the United States, a misdemeanor, and that was nearly two decades ago. They've raised three children who are brimming with potential. But none of that counts for much of anything. Herein lies the central problem of American immigration law. This family embodies so many values that we Americans say we hold dear: discipline, hard work, love of children, sacrifice, deferral of gratification, family. They plan for the future. They make hard choices. They take care of each other, they don't hurt anyone else, and they pay taxes. And yet, the only thing the law offers them is deportation.

* * *

Just a few months after Olivero ate his Snickers bar, while Manuela and Adelina were still waiting back in Mexico City, a sixteen-year-old girl arrived in Las Vegas. She would eventually figure prominently in trying to protect people like Olivero and his family, but back then, Cecia Alvarado did not even want to come to the United States. "I was really forced to move here. I was not part of the decision," she told me. She grew up in a middle-class family in Costa Rica, and the reason her father decided to send her to the United States remains, it seems, a source of confusion. She said it might have been because she was a bit rebellious as a teenager and her father had trouble dealing with her. For those who know Cecia today, this is not difficult to imagine. She is typically the toughest person in any meeting, even in a group of seasoned immigration activists. Or it might have been because she was a star student, and her parents thought finishing high school in America would be an advantage. But either way, she wanted no part of it. "If anything, I had to downgrade my lifestyle here," she said. She still feels that her immigrant experience is different from many others because she did not come to America to escape suffering. Her struggles really began in America.

Cecia's older brother lived in Las Vegas with his white American citizen wife. Coming from a middle-class family, with a relative to visit, Cecia was able to get a tourist visa, and landed in America on August 23, 2000, right before the school year. The visa allowed her to stay only briefly, but the plan was for her to stay to finish high school and then go back to Costa Rica.

By arriving legally on a tourist visa, Cecia engaged a process that involves a few different parts of the federal bureaucracy. If you've gone on an international vacation, you may have experienced some of this through the parallel systems operated by other countries. But if you carry an American passport and traveled to, say, most any European country, Mexico, Israel, Jordan, Egypt, Thailand, or other countries on a pretty long list of popular destinations, then the experience might have been over so fast you could easily have missed it.

By default, admission of a foreign national to another country requires a visa. A visa is a pre-clearance to enter—sort of like being pre-approved for a mortgage. It doesn't really offer an ironclad guarantee that the person will be allowed to enter when she actually arrives. But it means she probably will. To get this visa, a person normally has to go to a consulate abroad and apply. For travelers to the United States, the simplest variety of this is probably the B-2 visitor visa, aka a tourist visa. These are the people coming to see Niagara Falls or to party in Las Vegas. If you are coming for short business meetings, then you should get the B-1 business visitor visa instead. But let's stipulate that this book is not going to give you comprehensive legal advice. And for most people in the world, a trip like that begins, like most legal immigration processes, with a form. It's called the DS-160. People can fill it out online. After that, they'll have to go to an interview at a U.S. consulate.

In general, there are really two big questions the U.S. consulate is going to be worried about in this process. First, is this person a security threat? Second, is this person likely to overstay or violate the terms of the visa? In other words, when you're coming as a tourist, you are supposed to spend money, have fun, and—most important—leave within (usually) 180 days. The result of this assessment is a heavy class bias, since people with steady incomes and property seem less likely to decide to become an undocumented immigrant in the United States. This is obviously a balance. If the consulate is very liberal with the tourist visas, it will probably allow in more people who end up overstaying their visas. It would be theoretically possible to be very strict—for example, giving tourist visas to millionaires only. But if U.S. consulates did that, our tourist economy would be badly hurt. Trust me, a resident of Las Vegas—we don't want that.

As an American citizen, I've never had to go through this system myself to enter the United States, but I've experienced it in two different ways. First, I used to be the director of a refugee legal aid organization in Cairo, Egypt. Sometimes when Egyptian staff members were planning vacations to the United States or to Europe and needed to apply for a tourist visa, they would ask me to sign letters verifying their employment and salary. The point of this was just to show the American or European consular officer that this Egyptian national has a decent life and a professional career back home and thus is not likely to want to give all that up to live as an undocumented immigrant. That helped them get their visas, so they could go on vacation.

Second, my kids are adopted from Ethiopia. When they were babies, when we first adopted them, our daughters had to request visas to enter the United States. They traveled on Ethiopian passports. This meant that my wife and I sat for hours with each of them on the hard seats in the visa processing wing of the American consulate in Addis Ababa, a place few American citizens go. When Americans abroad have a problem, like a lost passport, they usually go to the American Citizens Services wing. We were crowded in with dozens of Ethiopians who were asking for permission to visit the United States. Each person, when his number was called, walked up a window for a brief conversation. There wasn't a lot of privacy, and so I could hear one person after another presenting his or her travel plans, photographs of the relative they hoped to visit in America, verification of their income and living situation. In most of the cases I overheard, the consular officer said, No. We are very sorry. We are not able to grant your visa today. And the Ethiopian would politely walk away.

If you are an American and you've gone on a vacation to London or Rome, you would have experienced something quite a bit easier. You probably just made sure you had a valid passport, waited for a good deal on your flight, booked a hotel or Airbnb and thought about where to park your car at the airport. That's privilege. In more technical terms, it's a visa waiver program. The United States offers a visa waiver to nationals of thirty-nine countries. These include most European nations, a few of the wealthier countries in Asia, and Australia and New Zealand. Chileans are the only people from Central or South America who don't need a visa in advance. The only majority-Muslim country on the list is Brunei. Countries that like to encourage foreign travel usually have something like this for American citizens. For example, Mexico wants Americans to be able to fly off on a moment's notice to spend a weekend in Cabo. So the Mexican government doesn't want us to have to go through a lot of red tape. They want to make it easy, so they let us get a visa at the airport. But there is no reciprocity here. We don't make it that easy for Mexican nationals.

Visa overstays are a really big concern in American immigration policy today. Remember how Olivero and Manuela were part of a mass migration across the Mexican border? Within just a few years, it had subsided. Since 2007, visa overstays have exceeded illegal crossings in the United States, and people who overstayed make up two-thirds of the new undocumented population since 2014. The overall size of the undocumented population in the United States was falling during this time, too—just as Donald Trump was gearing up for his campaign for president. He pledged to "build a wall" to stop people from crossing the border on foot. And yet for every five new undocumented people in the United States in the year Trump defeated Hillary Clinton, three had arrived legally and just stayed too long. The wall would do nothing about this.[6]

All of this is part of why President Trump's "build the wall" slogan is so racially tinged. In 2017, the Center for Migration Studies pointed out that 500,000 undocumented Mexican immigrants had departed the United States the previous year, three times more than the number who arrived. The undocumented Mexican population in the United States was going down before President Trump took office.[7]

This data adds fuel to the argument that America's immigration wars today are more about race and changing demographics than about a genuine public policy concern. After all, isn't it odd to launch a presidential campaign with an anti-immigrant platform at a time when the undocumented immigrant population is declining on its own? Isn't it even odder to make the centerpiece of this campaign a land wall that would target a type of migrant who was no longer coming in large numbers?

In April 2019, President Trump signed a memo calling for new crackdowns on countries that have high rates of visa overstays. Keep something in mind about this, though: the actual rate of visa overstays isn't really very high. In 2016, 320,000 people overstayed a visa to the United States. That sounds like a lot. And, historically, it is. But according to the National Travel and Tourism Office, that year the United States let in 75.9 *million* visitors for pleasure. So don't flatter yourself, America. Most people who come here leave pretty fast. In fact, according to the Trump administration, there are only twenty countries from which more than 10 percent of the people arriving overstay their visas. None of them are in Latin America.[8]

When a person wants to immigrate to the United States for permanent residency, the process is partly like asking for a tourist visa, in that it will involve a trip to the U.S. consulate. But for a long-term immigrant, that will just be the finishing touch. For these visas, the first application is made in the United States, to U.S. Citizenship and Immigration Services (USCIS). That agency processes the application—whether it's for a spouse to join his wife in Cincinnati, or for a trafficking victim to bring her minor children to join her in Reno—and then once it's approved, USCIS sends the approval to the appropriate consulate. Only then does the would-be immigrant wait in the hard chairs to be called up to the window.

Here's another wrinkle: it takes a long time for USCIS to even read visa applications. Even when there is no quota, petitions take a long time to process. Have you fallen in love with a beautiful man from another country and are you thinking of asking for a fiancé visa? Well, be patient. At the USCIS California processing center, as of May 2019, the processing time for a fiancé visa was five to seven months. In immigration law, that's a fast one. Are you a U.S. citizen who is already married and you want to sponsor your foreign spouse for a green card? At the Nebraska service center, that will take twelve to sixteen months as of early December 2019. That is a slowdown. When I wrote the first draft of this chapter, in early summer 2019, the Nebraska service center's wait time for an immediate relative was ten to thirteen months. The constantly increasing delays for the government to process valid applications is part of what advocates have come to call the "invisible wall" put in place by the Trump administration. Keep in mind, these are the visas that have no quotas. They are known in the trade as "immediately available."

Back to Cecia Alvarado. If Cecia's father's plan was to improve her education, it backfired badly. She started school almost immediately after arrival, but the teachers and administrators in her new Las Vegas school did not see a sixteen-year-old star. They saw a transient who spoke no English. They put her back in ninth grade, and in an English as a Second Language (ESL) program with other new arrivals. On paper, she was supposed to be spending four periods of the day learning English. But as is often the case in schools, the plan on paper and what happened in the classroom were not the same. "They weren't teaching me English. There wasn't really instruction," she remembers. "We spent four periods. We did a few exercises. That was it."

Even worse for Cecia, she was not Mexican. Her Spanish was different. She used different words and had come to America for different reasons. The other kids in her ESL program mocked her mercilessly. She had only one friend, a girl from Guatemala. "I was rejected by the Mexican students because I wasn't Mexican. I got jumped in high school. That's one of the reasons my counselor agreed to move me to regular classes. They used to bully me, and I fought back." So in her second year Cecia was moved out of ESL.

She was saved by an English teacher, Mr. Torres, who was from Puerto Rico. "He was my only support system through high school. He checked my attendance, my grades. He knew if I was always fighting. He checked on that, too." By the time she was eighteen, she was in the National Honor Society at Desert Pines High School, in East Las Vegas, less than three miles from Sandy Miller Academy, where my kids would later go to elementary school. When she hit her eighteenth birthday, the school called her down to the office. "They told me I couldn't go to school anymore." Because of her age, they said. That was almost certainly illegal. But it was also typical of the way a newly arrived kid was treated in the public schools. Mr. Torres put up a fight for her, and she was allowed to finish. At nineteen, she graduated from high school. But academics were the least of her troubles.

If Cecia's father's plan was to give her more stability, that, too, backfired very badly. Cecia's older brother was a truck driver, and he was barely ever home. Six months after Cecia's arrival, he and his wife left the state without even telling Cecia what was going on. They just dropped her off at a woman's house and told her to live there instead. The woman was called Nuria, and she charged rent for the room. So Cecia went to work for minimum wage as a cashier at a McDonald's. She lasted there for three months, until a regular at McDonald's offered her a job at his business, a check-cashing shop. That paid more: $10 an hour. Even better, when there were no customers, Cecia could do her homework. In her senior year of high school, she moved on to waitressing at a Mexican restaurant.

There was more turmoil. Nuria worked the night shift at a casino and could tolerate no noise at home during the day, when she had to rest. After a year, Nuria kicked Cecia out. Cecia moved to a house on D Street, one of the roughest neighborhoods in Vegas. But in some ways, Cecia's life was improving. She was semi-homeless, but she was moving up in school. Her older sister had come from Costa Rica to join her for a while, although she eventually moved to Spain with her boyfriend. When Cecia was nineteen, close to graduation, she met a young man, Luis, who became her best friend.

And then her brother returned.

During his time away, Cecia's brother had dropped his first wife and picked up a new one, a seventeen-year-old girl, whom he tried to dominate and control. Cecia, who never had a stable place to live, moved in with them. But whenever her brother left the house, his new wife would take out her frustration on Cecia. "One day I came home and she was in my room. She wrote on my wall that I was a prostitute," she said. Cecia called her brother, who was out on the road. He told Cecia "it was her house and if she wanted me out, I have to leave." While she was on the phone, her new sister-in-law attacked her. In the struggle, Cecia scratched her face. Some blood trickled down, and her sister-in-law called the police. Cecia spent three days in jail, charged with battery domestic violence.

Cecia Alvarado was lucky in many ways, as we will see in later chapters. Had all this happened just a little differently, she almost certainly would have been deported. Instead she stayed in Las Vegas and eventually became a legal resident. The difference between Cecia and other undocumented immigrants illustrates much of the randomness that typifies people's experience with the immigration system. The line between who has papers and who does not often makes very little sense to a person with a normal sense of morality and fairness. But more on that later. At the moment when she was arrested, Cecia was unlawfully present in the United States, just like Fernando, Manuela, Olivero, and Adelina.

These are the kind of people who are now in the president's crosshairs.

3

The Cleaners

AT SOME POINT in early 2016, Katelyn or Alissa asked me to sub in for her at Immigration Court on a case of a young boy the Department of Homeland Security wanted to deport. By this point, Katelyn and Alissa had been defending unaccompanied children from Central America for about a year and a half. Most of these were children who had come from El Salvador, fleeing gang violence and in some cases family turmoil. They had been sent to Las Vegas because the Office of Refugee Resettlement had found a relative for them here, an adult known as a sponsor. Sometimes it was an aunt or uncle, but in some cases it was actually the child's mother or father, who had come to the United States to work years earlier. The family dynamics were hard. A young teen who had been raised by someone else was reunited with a parent who had come to America to send money home to support that child and in the process become absent from the child's life. The children's lives were hard, too. Some had seen dead bodies. Many knew about murder and rape, and that it could happen to them.

The boy I was sent to represent lived with his father, his sponsor, who worked at a fast-food restaurant and had taken the day off from work to drive his son to his deportation hearing. The dad was undocumented himself and would not go inside the court for fear of encountering ICE. He arrived in a beat-up little car and waited outside.

At that time, the Las Vegas Immigration Court was on the second floor of a strip mall. To be fair, Las Vegas is really a city of strip malls. Off the Strip, nearly every pizza shop, grocery, insurance agent, post office, bakery, and dentist is located in a row of rented bland storefronts that frame a large parking lot. There is a fairly renowned French bakery near my house, in central

Las Vegas. If it were in Brooklyn, it would probably be in a trendy area with a line out the door onto the sidewalk. But in Las Vegas, it's in a strip mall where it shares a gigantic parking lot with a beauty salon, an Office Depot, and a CVS. Depending on where you are in the city, the stores will vary. Sometimes it's a Panera or Chipotle, and sometimes it's an Ethiopian restaurant. Sometimes it's Wells Fargo, and sometimes it's check cashing. In some places you find a Smiths Food and Drug, and sometimes you see a Mariana's Supermarket. But it's always a strip mall.

There were no marble pillars at the Las Vegas Immigration Court. No inscriptions on the wall about the quality of justice. A bar on the corner sometimes had its doors open to release what must have been a very high density of cigarette smoke. Next to the court there was an immigration lawyer's office, and signs about getting photographs and medical exams for immigration applications. In the middle of the parking lot, a black glass building housed the Department of Homeland Security.

In court, I was to make an objection because the boy had not been properly served with the charging document, which technically violated the regulations. Deportation cases start with a Notice to Appear (the NTA), which needs to be given to the person the government wants to remove from the United States. With a child, the NTA should be given to the guardian, not to the child. Often DHS would fail to give the document to the right person. Katelyn and Alissa made these objections whenever they could. They never won, but defense lawyers want to preserve issues for appeal, and if you don't make an objection when you first have an opportunity, you might never be able to make it again. This means that lawyers should make objections even when they know they will lose. In a normal court, this is routine and everyone knows it's part of the system. It's part of the job of defense lawyer—whether for criminal cases or immigration—to make sure the government does its job, by the book. The judge notes the objection, denies it, and people move on. Not all immigration lawyers do this very aggressively, however, so Katelyn and Alissa and our clinic became known for making a lot of objections.

When I objected to the government's failure to give the document to the right person, I expected a quick denial. But instead the lawyer for ICE, the immigration prosecutor, threatened to have my client—who was in middle school—locked up. He complained that the clinic kept making these types of objections even though they had been denied in other cases. The immigration judge tried to help out, gently stating that we had a right to defend our client.

The ICE lawyer kept going. Well, he said, if they want the papers re-served, maybe we should take their client back into custody and give him the papers that way. I then asked if the government was threatening to take retribution on our client for having asserted a due process right. The ICE lawyer backed off. The judge moved on. This was just a master calendar hearing. All we were there to do was start the case and schedule the next hearing.

At a break, the ICE lawyer came out into the hallway. I was now worried that they really would lock the boy up because I'd made a motion in court. I told the lawyer, "You know, you said all that on the record. It's going to make a nice quote in a brief to the Court of Appeals." The attorney waved his hand. No one was going to be locked up, he said. He was acting under some kind of directive, he told me, though he didn't go into details.

"You think I went into this job to go after kids?" he said. A few weeks later, he left his job. I haven't seen him again.

I escorted my client—a boy in middle school—out to his dad, who was leaning against his banged-up car, smoking a cigarette and shaking slightly. When he saw his son walk freely out the door, he straightened up and put out his arms. He smiled. He'd thought the government might take his son that day—and I didn't tell him that the government lawyer had actually threatened to do just that. The dad was so happy his son was free, even though this was just a preliminary hearing. The dad started talking. This was the first day his son had missed school. He was doing well in school. Especially in math. Also good grades in science. English was hard. He was still learning English. This dad was proud, and relieved, and he was gushing about his son.

"He has good grades, and good attendance. That's going to count, right? That's going to help his case? It's going to count?"

Actually, no. A lot of what would matter to a normal person doesn't matter much in immigration law.

The lawyers in our office who were doing this work with children—Katelyn, Alissa, and then, after 2016, Laura Barrera—were defending children, while the ICE tried to obtain an order of removal to send them back to Central America. When I saw a child alone in Immigration Court the first time, it was chilling—a kid, maybe eleven, maybe younger, maybe a little older, with scrawny shoulders and no English, sitting alone in a courtroom at the respondent's table, with a government lawyer in a suit at the opposite table. A judge in a robe sits behind a raised desk at the front, the Department of Justice seal behind him. The judge asks the respondent—a boy—to confirm his address. The child waits for the translation, then tells the judge that's not his address anymore, because he's moved. The judge asks for the new address, and the boy gives it, with a little smile. He's answered the judge's questions well!

Does the boy even really understand why he's here? No one knows. Does he understand the notice to appear, in which the Department of Homeland Security has stated four allegations and a statutory ground of removability, citing to a provision of Title VIII of the United States Code? The government refuses to provide lawyers for people facing deportation, even for children who cannot yet read. Early in 2016, the *Washington Post* reported that a senior immigration judge had bragged during a deposition that "I've taught immigration law literally to three-year-olds and four-year-olds." Bullshit.[1]

After the election in 2016, we needed to do more. A path had already been paved for us starting back in 2014, when Katelyn and Alissa started their work in our clinic defending unaccompanied children. As I've said, I had my doubts about that in the beginning. How could a tiny law school clinic offer legal aid to a large group of people? Our job was to teach just a few students every year. But now things looked different. People needed lawyers. We were one of the few options in town.

In early 2017, as I've noted, it was possible for an immigration lawyer to think of himself as a kind of hero. On January 27, 2017, when the new president issued the first version of his ban on travel from Muslim-majority countries, American airports filled with protesters. My favorite image, from the crowd at JFK in New York, was a man with a brown cardboard sign: "First they came for the Muslims, and we said: Not today, motherfuckers!" At the front of these protests were the lawyers. Immigration lawyers with handwritten signs in English and Arabic, offering help. Immigration lawyers sitting with laptops on hard terminal floors, papers scattered around them, punching out emergency motions. The motions worked, too. The ban was enjoined. In fact, one of the first injunctions came in response to an emergency petition filed by a law school clinic not too different from the one I ran at UNLV, the Yale Immigrant Rights Advocacy Clinic.

After the election, we initially stayed focused on unaccompanied children. We knew that the Trump administration would kill the AmeriCorps program that had gotten this work off the ground. However, even before the 2016 election we had essentially determined that we couldn't go on with this formula. AmeriCorps paid poverty-level wages to our lawyers, even relative to legal aid salary levels, and imposed problematic restrictions on us. For example, if a fourteen-year-old girl came to our office with her nineteen-year-old brother, we weren't supposed to offer legal assistance to the brother. That was never going to work. Fortunately, Edward M. Bernstein & Associates, a prominent personal injury law firm in Las Vegas, made a five-year donation commitment. Every month in 2017, I was on a conference call with directors of other justice

AmeriCorps programs for unaccompanied children. The others were talking about rolling up their operations, phasing out, and closing down. Because we now had funding, we knew we could keep doing the work with kids.

Then came more bad news. At the beginning of September 2017, Attorney General Jeff Sessions announced the administration's plan to end DACA and give Dreamers just one last chance to renew their permits. They had one month to get a renewal application and a cashier's check for $495 to an office in Chicago. But when I walked into the clinic office the next morning, I found Laura Barrera, the prophet of Michigan election doom, and Arléne Amarante, a prominent immigration lawyer we had hired to keep our casework afloat for a year. Laura told me we needed to set up a DACA renewal program at the clinic. No one else had stepped forward to do renewals for free, she said, so we had to.

I worried. We'd never done anything like this. Where would we get the volunteers to do the forms? How would we supervise the cases? We'd be overloaded. This was not a good idea. But the renewal period would be over in three and a half weeks, so I said fine. Laura put out a call for volunteers and reserved a small seminar room that holds up to thirty people. Over the course of a few days we had nearly fifty people come to be trained to do DACA renewals. Mostly law students, a few faculty and staff, and some alumni. We were doing renewals within a week.

All this made it clear to me that we were capable of doing a whole lot more than we had been doing.

* * *

DACA is a big deal, but the extensive focus on it distorts public debate about undocumented immigrants living in the United States. Many politicians, especially in the Democratic Party, have learned to turn any question about immigration toward DACA and the DREAM Act. That's expedient. The Dreamers are probably the most popular subset of the undocumented population. They came as children, they speak unaccented English, and now they are vibrant young adults, going to college, buying cars and houses, starting businesses, and building careers. But they're not the only undocumented immigrants. They're not even most of them. Nearly every Dreamer I know has parents at home, the parents who raised them, the parents who brought them, parents who are usually undocumented and vulnerable. To focus exclusively on Dreamers is to ignore the full role undocumented immigrants are playing in America, and the lives they lead in our communities.

To get a broader view, I met with a committee of immigrant workers at the tiny office of ¡Arriba! Las Vegas Worker's Center, in a little strip mall on

Charleston Boulevard. The ¡Arriba! office is just a rectangle, the size of a comfortable living room in a suburban home. It shares a strip mall with a very small parking lot on Charleston with a pupusa place, a snack and ice cream shop with signs in Spanish, and a store that I think sells office furniture. (Pupusas, filled flatbreads, are Salvadoran street food.) Inside, its walls are covered with giant flipboard notes, posters from demonstrations, bulk packages of water, and papers scattered on a couple of desks. The ¡Arriba! office is furnished, mostly, with folding chairs that can be rearranged depending on the type of meeting that's happening. On this evening, I counted twenty-one people in a circle. The majority of them came from El Salvador, and a few from Honduras. There were a couple of Mexicans in the crowd, too, although this meeting was about Temporary Protected Status (TPS), and Mexicans never have TPS. There were also three teenage U.S. citizens in the group. "I'm here to support my mom," one of them told me. All of them had been in the United States for more than 10 years.

If you want an insider's guide to how the Las Vegas resorts work, this is the group to talk to. Elicia cleans hotel rooms at the MGM Grand. Ana works in housekeeping at the Flamingo. Donato cleans the floors in a kitchen at the Bellagio. Wilfredo does what he called "utility housekeeping" at the Wynn. Pablo does the same thing, with a special focus on kitchens, also at the Wynn. Tino said, "I work in all the casinos." He does demolition and remodeling. When a French steakhouse fades, Tino gets called to help tear out the interior and rebuild the space to be a new Asian fusion joint with a celebrity sushi chef. Such changes are as common as the seasons in Vegas resorts.

I was pretty curious about all the different levels of cleaning represented in this group. Donato cleans the floors in the kitchen. But so did Pablo, who described himself as having a different job. Pablo joked that if they worked in the same hotel, his job would be to clean up after Donato. What this really means is that Donato cleans while the restaurant is open. He tries to keep the mess under control during the dinner rush, like an anxious aunt trying to keep the counters clear while a large family cooks Thanksgiving dinner. The utility cleaners come in after closing. Walk through the fanciest of the resorts in Vegas and notice the gleam and glow. The lighting reflects off the glass and the floors, never a smudge in sight. It's bright and crisp, with every surface smooth and glistening and every angle sharp. Elvis sang that Vegas turns day into nighttime and nighttime into day. That takes people like Pablo and Wilfredo. And if the casinos run their operations correctly, you'll never see them during your stay. This is just part of how, in Las Vegas, immigrants are integral to everything that happens, and yet easy for many of us to ignore.

There was an obvious gender split in the group. The women worked in housekeeping, cleaning hotel rooms. They deal with the towels and bedsheets and what you might delicately call the intimate mess that some people leave after a long weekend in Vegas. If they are fortunate, they never run into the people who sleep in the rooms. The union to which most of them belong, the Culinary Workers Local 226, has been demanding that the resorts should supply housekeepers with electronic panic buttons, because some have been assaulted by guests and many more harassed. By contrast, the men in the group did industrial cleaning, typically on the lower floors of the resorts. They make the shopping and dining areas shine and keep the kitchens clean. Yet these men and women, nearly all from small countries in Central America, all seem to work in cleaning. I asked why.

Wilfredo knew the answer, which he delivered while pointing one by one at the others in the group: "Because his department and my department and her department, they're the hardest ones. And there are no tips." There are no tips because you are not supposed to see the cleanup crews who rub off the fingerprint that you might have left on a marble wall. The fact that they don't get tips is important. One of the things I learned when I moved to Vegas is that many people in the service economy here can make surprisingly good incomes. I have had female law students who used to be restaurant hosts, and men who used to be bartenders or parking valets. These students sometimes joke that they probably won't make as much in their first year as a lawyer as they did in their last year at the resort or the restaurant. But those jobs tend to go to native speakers of English. These are the people who shake hands with guests, who greet them with a smile, who pull a chair out for them. They get the tips. The Salvadoran utility cleaners are our invisible neighbors.

The Culinary Workers Union, to which most of them belong, is the largest immigrant organization in the State of Nevada, with 60,000 members, born in 178 countries and speaking 40 languages. The union goes back to 1935, four years after the state legalized casino gambling and a decade before mobster Bugsy Siegel came to Las Vegas to build the Flamingo. The casinos pay the average Culinary member—the cocktail waitresses, food servers, porters, bellhops, cooks, bartenders, kitchen workers, the laundry workers—$23 an hour in pay and benefits. Culinary also gives its members access to training (so they can change their jobs), legal defense, and assistance with down payments to buy a home. Bethany Khan, the union's spokesperson, was emphatic with me that these jobs should not be thought of as a temporary step in a person's career. These aren't the jobs held by teenagers who worked at the

Tastee-Freez for the summer in the suburb where I grew up. These are jobs meant to support a family and lead to a secure retirement. "These are career jobs," she said.[2]

The workers I met at the little office at the strip mall on Charleston were, at least at that time, in the country legally. They could work legally, which is how they could get a job with the big resort companies. There are undocumented immigrants who work inside the resorts, but they will usually work for a smaller restaurant or store that rents space from the larger resort.

The Salvadorans and Hondurans in this group had Temporary Protected Status. TPS is American immigration policy at its best, and also at its worst. It allows America, if it wants, to offer humanitarian safe haven to large groups of people who have nowhere else to go. But it also puts them in limbo, caught between the theory of law, the limits of political compromise, and the realities of life. The Secretary of Homeland Security may designate the people of any country eligible for TPS if there is an armed conflict that would threaten their personal safety if they were to return, or a natural disaster that substantially disrupts living conditions. TPS has some of the strictest selection criteria in terms of criminal background checks of any immigration status. A person with two misdemeanors cannot apply. As of 2019, there were ten countries for whom at least some people have TPS: El Salvador, Haiti, Honduras, Nepal, Nicaragua, Somalia, Sudan, South Sudan, Syria, and Yemen. The Trump administration has tried to end the protection for six of them.

People can apply for TPS only if they are already here. They can't apply for a visa to come to the United States under the TPS program. This is literally not an immigration program. It's a program that lets people stay—for eighteen months at a time. The situation of workers with TPS highlights the fact that the term "immigration law" in general is a bit of a misnomer. Merriam-Webster's says the definition of immigration is "to enter and usually become established; *especially:* to come into a country of which one is not a native for permanent residence." Yet many of the people most affected most by what we call immigration law entered the United States a long time ago. They've long ago become established and taken up permanent residence if that is defined in real-life terms, like having children, holding down a job, going to parent-teacher conferences and their kids' soccer games, and making regular trips to the supermarket. But the law does not always accept the life they are living. For that reason, immigration law is quite often not about entry or coming to the United States. It's about remaining. It's about recognition for the life people have built. Immigration law, often, is not about migrating at all. It's about staying put when the U.S. government might want you to leave.[3]

A TPS designation is intended to last for eighteen months at most, but the Secretary of Homeland Security can extend that period if the armed conflict or disaster has continued or if there are "extraordinary and temporary conditions in the foreign state that prevent aliens who are nationals of the state from returning to the state in safety." Nicaraguans and Hondurans received TPS designation in early January 1999 because of the devastation caused by Hurricane Mitch. The deadliest hurricane in Central American history, Mitch killed more than 11,000 people in October 1998. TPS status for Nicaraguans and Hondurans was extended by three different presidential administrations. To benefit, a Nicaraguan or Honduran must have been continuously present in the United States since December 30, 1998, about a week before the first TPS designation. Similarly, the 195,000 Salvadorans with Temporary Protected Status received their first TPS designation because of a series of earthquakes. Salvadorans need to have been continuously resident since February 2001. Their status had been renewed eleven times—until Trump.[4]

Few of the Central American beneficiaries were even in Central America when the hurricanes and earthquakes struck. In fact, most Salvadorans and Hondurans who have TPS had been in the country for more than twenty-two years. That means that most were in the country for more than a year before the TPS designation. Most of these people came to the United States because they were fleeing the violence of the civil wars of the 1980s and 1990s. El Salvador, for example, has a population of around 6 million people. One in five Salvadorans was displaced by the civil war. The United Nations was still on the ground monitoring the country's fragile peace accords until 1997. Or they came out of desperation, because of extreme poverty, or because many of their closest relatives were already here. The humanitarian disaster that struck their country gave an added reason why they had to remain in the United States. But it wasn't why they originally migrated, at least for most. The United States let them stay because acute disasters had struck, and making the tens of thousands of people in the United States suddenly go back would only make it worse. That was the approach until Trump.[5]

If I put myself in the role of a detached law professor, I can explain easily why TPS is a theoretical problem. The T in TPS is for *temporary*. The whole theory of this status is that it's not supposed to last forever. On this, the Trump administration has a point. But it is also very hard to say what good would come from dismantling all of these families. Today, there are 325,000 people in the United States who have TPS protection. More than 90 percent come from just three countries—El Salvador, Honduras, and Haiti. The Trump administration wants to end TPS for all three of these countries. If that effort is successful, more than 300,000 people who are now legally present and working in the United States would suddenly become undocumented, unlawfully present and vulnerable to deportation.[6]

Best estimates indicate that there are 5,700 Salvadorans in Nevada with TPS. They have 3,800 U.S. citizen children, most of whom were probably born in Las Vegas. They've lived here for an average of twenty-four years, with 30 percent of them working in the hospitality sector. Their labor generates $255.3 million for the state's GDP every year. On top of these are the Hondurans, Nicaraguans, and Haitians who live here. Numbers for those groups are harder to come by, but they are likely significant. The group that I met with at ¡Arriba! had at least eight children in the public schools, ranging from elementary to high school. By show of hands, at least seven of them owned homes; Pablo said he owned two, one of which he rents to relatives. Take away TPS, and it is not hard to imagine all of those houses going into foreclosure.[7]

The status of the thousands with TPS hangs by a thread, because in 2018 a federal judge in the Northern District of California issued an injunction against the Trump administration's plan to end TPS for Salvadorans, Hondurans, Haitians, and Sudanese. There were two main reasons for the court's ruling. First, the government changed its practices. The Trump administration looked only at whether the original justification for the protected status was still a major problem. For example, is Hurricane Mitch still the biggest issue in Honduras? No? Then Hondurans must go. But that isn't actually what the U.S. government has been doing for all these cycles of TPS renewals. Previously the government had also been looking at overall conditions and security concerns, and whether it is really in the interest of the United States to send all these people home. The Trump administration abruptly stopped doing that.

The other reason the court halted the elimination of TPS in these cases was racism: "Serious questions whether the actions taken by the Acting Secretary or Secretary was influenced by the White House and based on animus against non-white, non-European immigrants." The evidence for this was Donald Trump's general anti-immigrant statements, his claim (in June 2017) that immigrants from Haiti "all have AIDS," and his reported statement in January 2018, specifically about a proposal to protect people from El Salvador and Haiti: "Why are we having all these people from shithole countries come here?"[8]

Cleaning is emblematic of the role many immigrants play in the U.S. economy. It is hard and often unpleasant, yet needs to be done, and is unseen when done well. Consider the case of the October 1, 2017, mass shooting in Las Vegas when one man perched high in a hotel tower used a bump-stock trigger device to rain machine-gun fire down on people attending an out-door concert. He killed 58 and wounded 422. It remains, at the time I am writing this—and, I pray, still when this is published—the deadliest mass shooting committed by an individual in American history. Among those he shot at were undocumented immigrants. Many of them were at the concert because they worked for a company that supplied the portable toilets for the concert.

Their presence at the scene of this crime raises a question: should these un-documented people, the toilet cleaners, be eligible for a special type of visa for crime victims, the U visa, that would allow them to stay in the United States? Like some other types of visas, the U visa serves mainly people who are al-ready in the United States; it has a strict quota and a wait time of around a de-cade. To get this type of visa, a person must be a victim of a serious crime that is on a specified list, and must be helpful to police whenever asked. To apply, a crime victim needs a certification form signed by a law enforcement agency. It's called the I-918 Supplement B. While these concert workers gave state-ments to police, and while attempted murder is most definitely a qualifying crime, Las Vegas Metro refused for nearly a year to certify the cases. The po-lice finally relented under considerable pressure led by Nevada senator Cath-erine Cortez Masto, the Legal Aid Center of Southern Nevada, and Make the Road Nevada, a newly established community advocacy organization.

The Las Vegas Strip is hardly unique in depending on immigrants to clean up after the rest of us. Many Americans regularly welcome undocumented im-migrants into their homes to clean. People like Ines Reyes. I met her in late 2018, by which time she had been in the United States for seventeen years. She had come into the country with her daughter, Rebeca.

When Rebeca was a baby, Ines was barely able to spend time with her because she had to work so much. Every morning she had to walk thirty min-utes from their little house in Michoacán, Mexico, to her job at a furniture store, where she made $30 a day. While Ines worked, Rebeca stayed with her grandparents, whose house had a dirt floor and a tarp for a roof. When Rebeca was four, her father left for Redwood, California. He sent money back for a while, which let them improve their house a bit. They got an "old-school dish sink, with a concrete washboard for clothes," Ines said. The money coming was nice, but Ines says she wanted her husband to come home to Michoacán. He wouldn't, so she brought Rebeca to Redwood instead. But in Redwood they discovered a problem: Rebeca's dad had started another family. So Ines and Rebeca moved to Las Vegas, where Ines had a cousin. Ines began working as a babysitter. After ten days of living with her cousin, Ines managed to get a two-bedroom apartment in Spring Valley, just a few blocks from where Olivero and Manuela were living. But it wasn't very nice. "I remember there were flies everywhere," Rebeca told me. "And cockroaches."

Life in Las Vegas hasn't been easy. Ines was dragged down both by lack of money and by family issues. For a brief time, she got back together with her ex-husband, Rebeca's father, and she had another child in Las Vegas, who is now seven, but the marriage didn't last. And now that Ines cleans houses for a living, she and her children are still just getting by. However, Ines told me she appreciated that her job in America let her work and raise her own baby, which she hadn't been able to do in Michoacán when Rebeca was born. She can pick her younger child up from school and take her to the park or perhaps to Chuck E. Cheese. It's the little things.

Ines charges $100 to $120 to clean a house. Her customers are spread across the valley, in Summerlin, Henderson, and the southwestern suburbs. She says not one of her customers has ever asked her about her immigration status. "They don't care. They just want me to clean their house," she said. Her customers communicate with her by text message; Ines doesn't speak English, so she puts these text messages into a translation app on her phone, in order to understand what her customers are asking her to do. Her customers want her to show up when it's most convenient for them. Sometimes they change the schedule on short notice. Some need her to get down on her knees to clean up after their dogs, and to remove dog hair out of carpeting by hand when the vacuum fails to do it. Others want her to use only vinegar or green cleaners. But those cleaners don't work as well, Ines said, so she has to scrub harder.

Ines doesn't know if her own customers would have her deported if they knew about her status. "They need us for work," she told me. There is no anger in her voice when she talks about the anti-immigrant rhetoric abundant in America today. She just calmly explains the world as it is. "They say that we're bad people. That we're murderers. But they should know better. The heavy work is usually done by the immigrants."

When Ines and Rebeca first came to Las Vegas, Rebeca was in elementary school, and she didn't speak English. Her school initially put her in a special education class—a common story for many immigrant kids who attended schools where teachers and administrators didn't care to distinguish language differences from a learning disability. Rebeca had to repeat third grade. But Rebeca told me that when she was in fourth grade, the school started a proper program targeting kids who had to learn English as a second language. By sixth grade, Rebeca was advanced in English.

Rebeca doesn't call her mother "Mom." She calls her mother by her first name. It's a casualty, they both said, of the fact that Ines was barely home to raise her before they came to the United States. But Rebeca does admire her mother. When Rebeca was twelve, Ines occasionally brought her along to help with the house cleaning. "She would ask me to do this one thing, and I would be exhausted," Rebeca said. Back then, Rebeca told her mother: "I am going to buy you your own house." And she would eventually do just that.

Rebeca went to a magnet high school, and then on to UNLV, where she majored in political science. When she was 17, she became a beneficiary of the Deferred Action for Childhood Arrivals program—DACA. It's the same program that helped Adelina, whom we met in chapter 2.

People who met the criteria for DACA were allowed to send in an application, which was a bit like turning themselves into the government. To apply, Rebeca had to reveal to the Department of Homeland Security the address where they lived and the fact that she was in this country unlawfully. As we've seen, having DACA status means simply that action against them has been deferred. Recipients would still be deportable, and so application to the program required a leap of faith. "We didn't trust it at first," Rebeca said. She only applied after she saw a relative do it first. The employment authorization that Rebeca received let her work. She now has a job at a law office. She works as much as fifty-three hours a week sometimes, though she cuts back when she has to focus on school. The employment authorization let her get a social security number, too. The social security number let her apply for a mortgage when she was just twenty-two years old. As she had promised a decade earlier, she bought her mother a house.

There are about 800,000 people who have had DACA at some point in time. In a 2018 study, the Center for American Progress interviewed 1,050 people with DACA and asked what they did after they got their first DACA permits. Around one in seven said they bought a home. More than 60 percent bought a car. More than 50 percent said it helped them pay tuition. More than 75 percent said it raised their incomes.[9]

The house Rebeca bought is not fancy. It's square, with a small living room right off the front door. Bedrooms are down the hall to the right as you come in. The kitchen is in the back, separated from the front room by a wall. That's it. The bank would only give Rebeca a loan for $100,000. Rebeca and Ines found a local government–sponsored loan for an additional $20,000, conditioned on buying in a blighted area of Las Vegas. Rebeca doesn't see the blight, though. "This area is fine," she told me. "It's just that it's a bunch of Mexicans." The street is quiet and clean, but it's in East Las Vegas. Put the same house and the same street in parts of Los Angeles and it might cost half a million or more. That's real estate.

There was something that Ines and Rebeca hated about their new house: it had carpeting. They didn't want carpeting in the first place, and Ines's daily labor cleaning dog hair out of carpet in the suburbs doesn't help. Before they moved in, Ines and Rebeca hired a Honduran man to rip out the carpet and put in tile. He painted all the walls, too. Ines and Rebeca find it a little amusing that they, too, hire immigrants to do their most difficult jobs. Their house looks good, though. Clean and simple. They also planted six fruit trees in the backyard, lemons and guavas, visible from the kitchen window. When I saw the guava tree, I asked Rebeca and Ines if they were sure it would work. They told me it would. The tree was healthy and growing. I'd had no idea guava could grow in Las Vegas.

But not all is well. In 2017, Attorney General Jeff Sessions announced that DACA would be coming to an end because the Trump administration believed it was illegal. In September 2017, everyone with DACA was given one month to file a last renewal, and then the program was to end. It has been kept alive by another court injunction, which the Justice Department is asking the Supreme Court to reverse. That may happen in 2020. The legal theory on which DACA has been kept alive is thin. The essence of the court ruling is not that the administration can't end DACA but that it stated an inadequate reason for ending it. That's the legal thread on which the lives of people like Rebeca hang. And even with the injunction, no new DACA applicants will be accepted, only renewals. There are thousands of undocumented teenagers who finished high school in 2018 and 2019 who cannot apply.

The public debate about DACA focuses on people like Rebeca and Adelina, who are now in college. The Dreamers, by definition, were young children when they came. The common phrase is that they were brought to the country "through no fault of their own." Barack Obama used those words. The Democratic leadership in the House of Representatives used them in 2019. Even Donald Trump has used the phrase. This phrase assumes that their arrival in the United States was a bad thing, that someone must bear the fault for it, and that this someone must be their parents. Yet I have never met a person with DACA who blamed his or her parents for having come to the United States. More than that, most Dreamers I know worry intensely about their parents, who they know are more vulnerable than they are. Many of them are devoted to their parents in a way that (if I'm being honest) I've never been with my parents. It's not just that I don't call home as often as I should. I never bought my parents a house. Not in my twenties, and not in my forties. If you hurt Rebeca by taking away her DACA, you hurt Ines.[10]

Rebeca's little sister is a U.S. citizen but knows Rebeca is not. Her sister, who is just seven, says things like, "I hope Trump doesn't deport Rebeca." That's unnerving. Rebeca had a class at UNLV on national security, part of the coursework for her political science degree. In a class discussion, a white male student made a speech against DACA. "DACA recipients don't pay taxes," he said. As soon as he said it, Rebeca interjected: "Yes, I do." (I'll talk more about this in chapter 7. Briefly: Rebeca and Ines both pay taxes, the same taxes I pay. Rebeca uses her social security number for her 1040, just like everyone else. Ines has an Individual Taxpayer Identification Number (ITIN). She reports her income to the IRS.)

That was how she told her class about her immigration status. In fact, she remembers each time when she's made a public statement about her status. "Usually I try not to out myself," she said. She's done it only three times, and always in arguments like this. Another time was in a creative writing class at UNLV, when a fellow student announced that he was a Trump supporter. "There are students here who don't want me here," Rebeca says about the university where I work and where she is a student. That is unsettling, too. Still, when it happens in class, Rebeca rises to the fight. She notices something about these arguments, too. It's usually a white male student who is making the angry, anti-immigrant statement. And it is nearly always Latina women who confront him. It's something I've noticed, too. I asked Rebeca why the resistance seems to be so female-dominated. She shrugged. "No one else is doing it. So we're doing it."

To be clear, though, another part of the resistance is the lawyers. DACA would have ended in 2017 if not for litigation. That's 600,000 to 800,000 people who would have been stripped of their permits and made targets for deportation. TPS also would have ended for most of the people who have it, if not for litigation. That's more than 300,000 people. These programs have stayed alive because of temporary injunctions built on legal arguments that I, as a law professor, know are not without rebuttals. These are cases that could go either way. And they might go the other way in the end.

DACA and TPS each have their own policy foundations and legal details. But if you pull back the lens, here's the broad story: the U.S. government is targeting roughly 1 million people who today are working, going to school, living ordinary lives, and supporting families, and it wants to strip them of their papers. It wants them to leave. Once their legal status is taken away, ICE will be allowed to arrest, detain, and deport any of them. The Department of Homeland Security knows where they live, because they've been filing their forms dutifully for years. And these are the lucky ones.

PART II
THE ATTACK

4

The Unaccompanied

AMERICAN IMMIGRATION LAW does not deport people. We "remove" them. It is an interesting word choice. In regular speech, the first defini- tion of "to remove" is clinical: "to change the location, position, station, or residence of." That doesn't sound like a big deal. But there are some definitions that are more disturbing. To remove can also mean "to get rid of." Examples of how it is used in a sentence invoke diseased organs and garbage: "remove a tumor surgically," "remove the trash from my front yard."[1]

When a person is caught at the border, the government can normally put her into expedited removal proceedings, which means she can be deported within a day or two without going before a judge and usually without even having a lawyer. The government argues that immigrants don't even have a right to hire their own lawyers to defend themselves in expedited removal proceedings. The courts have yet to tell the government that this is clearly wrong.[2]

Although the United States has been turning people around at the border since the nineteenth century, expedited removal entered our law thanks to President Bill Clinton. While running for reelection in 1996, he signed the Il- legal Immigration Reform and Immigrant Responsibility Act, known in the trade as IIRIRA, or "Ira-Ira." That law made it nearly impossible for many un- documented immigrants in the United States to legalize their status, even if they have a family member who could sponsor them. The reach of expedited removal is potentially vast. While the most obvious use of the procedure is to immediately deport people caught at the border, the effect goes far beyond border towns.[3]

In 2004, the Bush administration issued a new rule allowing expedited re- moval of people caught within a 100-mile radius of a border if they entered within the previous fourteen days. Customs and Border Protection (CBP) can set up checkpoints near Tucson or San Diego, catch people, and put them into expedited removal. This is helpful for CBP, obviously. It means they don't have to catch people literally at the border. However, it dramatically expands where they can question, arrest, detain, and deport people without any oversight from a judge. If you take a look at a map of the United States, most major cities are within 100 miles of a land or sea border: New York, Los Angeles, Boston, Houston, San Diego. The entire state of Michigan.[4]

Expedited removal does not look anything like what Americans envision when they think of due process. In fact, this is what happens if you take judges, hearings, and lawyers entirely out of a process. One of the few protections that immigrants in Nevada have had, until 2019 at least, is that there are more than 200 miles between Las Vegas and the border. We are outside the border zone.

However, Bill Clinton's law—IIRIRA—goes further still. It allows immigration officers to theoretically arrest any person, anywhere, and put them in expedited removal if the person "has not affirmatively shown, to the satisfaction of an immigration officer, that the alien has been physically present in the United States continuously for the 2-year period immediately prior." This provision was not fully implemented until the Trump era. One of President Trump's first executive orders threatened to expand expedited removal throughout the rest of the country. This promised a terrifying possibility. Officers from ICE might be able to pick someone up in Spring Valley or East Las Vegas. If that person could not affirmatively show, to the satisfaction of the ICE officer, that she had been present in the United States for two years, then she could be immediately removed with no hearing, no lawyer, no charges, and no evidence presented. I've looked through my wallet. It's debatable whether any card that I carry regularly would conclusively prove that I have lived in the United States continuously for the past two years. I renewed my driver's license in 2019, so it says it was issued in 2019. A local police officer who looked my license up in the system might be able to see that I have been a Nevada resident for longer. But until 2021 I won't be carrying anything that proves on its face that I have lived here for two years. If I had a Spanish last name and a bit of an accent, this would be terrifying.[5]

For two and a half years, the expansion of expedited removal was one of the more frightening swords that had yet to drop. Then, on July 22, 2019, the administration issued the order to expand expedited removal everywhere. It went into effect the next day. It became possible for ICE officers to arrest someone anywhere they wanted and deport them within a few days, with no hearing and probably no lawyer. This has been challenged in court, and an injunction was issued against it in September 2019. But the government will fight on in the appellate courts. A policy with potentially terrifying implications was proposed, then enjoined, appealed, and left in limbo. Maybe it will be imposed, maybe it won't. But we can't stop worrying about it in the meantime. In immigration law, that has been pretty much par for the course since 2017.[6]

* * *

By the time Trump entered office, the UNLV Immigration Clinic had been representing unaccompanied children for two years. Katelyn Leese and Alissa Cooley transformed the clinic from a little boutique that took a few interesting cases for students to work on into an actual law firm serving a significant number of people. This was a new role for the law school, and not one that it originally envisioned for itself.

Because I was not highly involved at that point, I initially heard secondhand the stories that the kids had told Katelyn and Alissa. Some of the boys had grown up in middle-class families. I remember one boy—one of the few I talked to directly—who was quite angry about having been sent to America. He'd had a good life in his home country, he said, with a swimming pool in the summer. Crowding into his uncle's apartment in Vegas sucked. He was here only because the MS-13 gang had told him that if he refused to join them and went back to school in his village, they would kill him. They came to his school and pulled him out of class to tell him that. That's the kind of power they had in his village. In many other cases, the issue was *renta*. MS-13's main enterprise is the classic protection racket: pay us or we kill you. In this elegantly simple business model, it pays to be sadistic and terrifying. MS-13 does not just tell a father, Your money or your life. That's too straightforward, too polite. They send a note that says, Pay or we will drink your daughter's blood. Keep in mind, the people receiving these notes typically know people in their towns who have been murdered. A good number of the children we represent have seen dead bodies.

For the girls, there is more. It is common in our cases for a girl who might be thirteen or fourteen to tell us about how the trouble started when her body started changing. That's when MS-13 or the 18th Street Gang started noticing her. Perhaps it started with just catcalls when the girl walked out of her school. And then, after a while, they approached her. These girls flee to America because otherwise they would be raped.

Katelyn and Alissa spent two years documenting dozens of these cases. In order to do this, they needed to sit with each child and interview him or her. The lawyer in this role is like a journalist, interviewing a victim for the purpose of writing a declaration that becomes the meat of an asylum application. There are no rules about how much information should go into these declarations. For a five-year-old—and yes, we have five-year-olds fighting deportation—the declaration might be just a few lines: My name is this, my mom's name is this, and I was scared because bad men stood outside my school. For the older kids, and for adults, it's all about the details. The first challenge for an applicant for asylum is to be believed, and one way to do that is for a lawyer to elicit details, the kind of details that only a person who was really there would know. So when you interview a fourteen-year-old girl, you don't just stop when she says, They wanted me to be with them. You know what she means. You know that she doesn't want to have to say more to you. But you make her say more.

You ask: What happened next?

You ask about the five senses. In all cultures, all over the world, all people experience life through their five senses. And we remember our most terrifying experiences through them, too. A girl who has had an MS-13 member grab her breast outside her junior high school might remember what he smelled like. You get that fact for the declaration. And you get it by asking her. Details make it real. Details win these cases. Details keep kids safe. So, gently, over and over again, you make her tell you these sorts of things. You say, I am so sorry I have to ask. But can you tell me what happened next? Do you remember if he said anything? I know you don't want to repeat it. But it would really help for the judge to know. Do you remember what words he said?

He said he wanted to put his penis in my mouth.

That's the kind of detail we will need. Thank you.

If it's a boy who was beaten up, you want to ask what it felt like when his head hit the concrete. You want to ask: What did you see happen to your friend, the one they were recruiting a few weeks earlier? You'll need to ask exactly where he was when he saw his best friend's body: Where were you standing? What position was the body in?

If it is a mother who just received a promise from MS-13 that they would chop up her son into small pieces, we might ask: What did you think when you next looked your baby in his eyes? What thoughts crossed your mind?

Thank you. We will need that for the declaration. That's perfect.

I have not done many of these interviews with our Central American clients. I've trained students to do them. I've read declarations and drafts written by my colleagues. But I have only done a couple of Central American kids' cases on my own. I think that's because I spent the first two years of my legal career in a church basement in Cairo, Egypt, interviewing refugees from Sudan this exact same way. I remember interviewing a South Sudanese woman about when she was raped in a prison. I remember her describing the hard bench that was under her. I remember her telling me the insults they shouted at her. I remember her describing the bruises she had on her back from the assault, from being slammed between the rapists and that bench. I'll remember that forever, I think.

I remember a veterinarian from South Sudan, a member of the Bari ethnic group. He was a handsome man. Smooth face, thin. Always dressed well. He was clearly educated, and he spoke impeccable English, with maybe a slight British accent. He told me about how he used to listen to the BBC World Service every evening outside his house in South Sudan. That was how he relaxed. One beer, a chair, and the radio. I remember thinking that it sounded like a good way to live. His community needed a veterinarian. He had status, a routine. He knew who he was and what he needed to do.

Then Sudanese secret police came for him. They took him to a police station and beat him for a day, trying to get him to admit to working for the rebels. He told me how, after being beaten, he slowly stood up, faced his interrogators, and refused. So they escalated. They made him walk over hot coals. In front of me, he pulled off his leather shoes and socks to show me the scars on the bottoms of his feet from the burns. Even after that, he'd stood up again to the interrogators. Then they slammed him to the ground. They pointed their guns and cocked them, so he could hear that he was about to die. Then they told him to shout, "I am a Bari dog!" He tried to rise from the ground, and they hit him from behind, until he fell onto all fours. They made him crawl. Then they pointed their guns again. "Bark!" He thought they were really going to execute him. So he barked. Like a dog. Then they made him do the sounds of a pig. Then the sounds of a goat. And then back to barking like a dog. At this stage, he crumpled into a ball. He sobbed. He gave up. He was ready for them to kill him. And at that, the interrogation stopped. They had broken the man who listened to the BBC. The job was done.

When I made him tell it all back to me, he broke down again. This polished man, whose button-down shirt was perfectly pressed every time I saw him, who debated the affairs of the day, who knew anatomy, who was a leader of his village, cried at my desk in a Cairo church basement for what seemed like thirty minutes. The Sudanese soldiers had broken him first. Then I broke him again by making him tell all that to me, to help him get refugee protection.

I think I did close to two hundred interviews like that during my two years in Cairo, my first two years after law school. I don't think I can do it again. Not that many. Not like I did. However, because I did that for two years, I have some idea of what it must have been like for Katelyn, Alissa, and Laura. Except they were working with children. That had to be worse.

The purpose of getting these awful stories out of our clients and onto paper is to help them apply for some kind of relief from removal, usually either asylum or, for the children, Special Immigrant Juvenile Status. Asylum is better known by the public, but not especially well understood. When I talk to non-lawyers—and even some lawyers—about seeking asylum, the assumption most people make is that the United States gives shelter to people who are genuinely in danger. Indeed, to get asylum, to be a refugee, a person must have a "well-founded fear of being persecuted." When people are denied asylum, politicians sometimes call them fraudulent asylum-seekers, suggesting that they are abusing the system, that maybe they were lying, or at least that they weren't in real danger. The purpose of getting our clients to tell us all the awful details is to make sure they are believed, to try to make their fear evident enough to convince the immigration authorities. But that, unfortunately, is only the beginning. A well-founded fear is not enough.[7]

In January 2019, the Court of Appeals for the Eleventh Circuit, which covers the southeastern states, published an asylum decision in a case called *Perez-Zenteno v. U.S. Attorney General*. As a legal matter, the case is not especially remarkable. In fact, it's pretty routine. And that is why, if everyone in America could know just one case to understand the limits of our asylum system, I might want them to know this one. The case is about a Mexican woman, Maria Perez-Zenteno, who had fled to the United States with her children after a criminal cartel terrorized her family. I don't know her personally, but she sounds a lot like some of our clients in Las Vegas.[8]

On a spring day, Maria had taken her five-year-old daughter to the supermarket. The gang kidnapped her daughter and demanded a ransom, just short of $8,000. Desperate for her daughter's return, Maria gathered the money and followed their delivery instructions. When she showed up with the money, the gang took Maria captive, too, beat her, drove her to the outskirts of town, and raped her. They warned her to not call the police, and the terrified mother agreed. Then they returned her daughter.

A neighbor offered to keep Maria and her children safe for a fee of $50 a month. Maria began paying, only later realizing that this neighbor was actually just another part of the scheme. Now Maria went to the police. The police responded and found that Maria's neighbor had been holding a kidnapped man in her house. Then Maria received a phone call threatening her for being a snitch. At this stage, having already had her child kidnapped and having survived a beating and a rape, Maria took her children and ran north to America, where she sought asylum.

The United States government agreed that Maria was telling the truth about all of this. But the U.S. government denied her asylum claim, and that is pretty normal. The court summarized its decision this way:

> Although Perez-Zenteno was beaten and brutally raped and her daughter kidnapped, she failed to prove that she was persecuted on account of membership in a statutorily protected group. . . . Because no nexus has been shown, we hold that the petition must be denied.[9]

Let me translate the legalese. To win asylum, Maria Perez-Zenteno had to first establish that she had a "well-founded fear of persecution." She did that. Beatings, rape, having a child kidnapped—all that is persecution. She wins on that count. She was genuinely terrified. The government believed her about what had happened. And there was evidence that things like this did happen regularly where she lived in Mexico, and could happen again. She wins on that count, too. The problem, to put it as bluntly as I can, is that Maria Perez-Zenteno was not raped for the right reason. That's what the court means about failing to prove that she was persecuted "on account of membership in a statutorily protected group" and about "no nexus has been shown." To win asylum, a well-founded fear of persecution must be on account of one of five reasons: race, religion, political opinion, nationality, or membership in a particular social group.[10]

This is an area of law that came out of the horrors of Nazi Germany and the early years of the Cold War. It is not a coincidence that the more a persecutor looks like the Nazis or the Soviet Union, the easier the asylum case. So if a person is beaten for her religion, that's an easier case. If a person is locked up for being a political dissident, that's a good case, too. But that's not Maria Perez-Zenteno. She was the victim of the wrong kind of rape, and her five-year-old daughter was the victim of the wrong kind of kidnapping.

I have explained this aspect of asylum law to U.S. senators, presidential candidates, and members of Congress, and they are nearly always surprised. At the UNLV Immigration Clinic, we usually have elected officials meet with a couple of our clients from Central America, who tell their stories. The elected officials are quite often shocked to find out that the teenager they listened to is actually *losing* her asylum case and is fighting one of her last rounds of appeal. The widespread impression seems to be that if a person is so genuinely in danger, the United States would grant her asylum. That's what we do, right? The huddled masses yearning to breathe free and all that jazz. But our asylum system has never operated that way in the modern era.

The problem for many of the kids we represent is exactly the same as it was for Maria Perez-Zenteno. They've been beaten, they've been threatened, some have been raped, some have seen family members murdered. Some have been warned by their own local police that they'd better run, because the criminal gangs are so powerful where they lived. Even so, their petitions are denied, denied, denied, denied. Since criminal gangs are the main source of persecution in Central America, this lack of "nexus" is a major problem for the largest groups of people seeking asylum in the United States today. There is a center at Syracuse University that tracks this data. In 2018, overall, immigration judges granted 35 percent of all asylum claims. For Salvadorans, fewer than one in four (23.5 percent) win, and the figure is even lower for Hondurans and Guatemalans. But that doesn't mean that only one in four Salvadorans applying for asylum had a genuine fear. For a lot of them, they just didn't fear for the right reasons.[11]

There are cases that are easier, but the differences would seem pretty arbitrary to a normal person. For instance, the courts have been more accepting of persecution on account of family membership. Family can be a "particular social group," or at least a lot of courts have said so over many years. So let's say that my father reports a gang to the authorities, and then the gang threatens me out of revenge. I'm being targeted because of my family association. That claim, if the judge believes me, might succeed. I would need to go in front of the right immigration judge, to be sure. And since July 29, 2019, it's a lot harder. On that day, Attorney General William Barr issued a decision that an asylum-seeker's "immediate family" is not a particular social group, unless some evidence is introduced that it is "socially distinct." This decision, too, will be appealed and challenged, but in the short run it's sure to lead to more denials of asylum.[12]

Whether the law is on the side of the asylum-seeker or not, I can't emphasize enough how important it is to find the right judge. A study of 140,000 asylum decisions conducted during the George W. Bush administration found that for asylum-seekers of a given nationality the chance of winning asylum could be as much as nine times higher in one Immigration Court than another:

> Why is an individual fleeing persecution in China 986% more likely to win her asylum claim in one venue than in another? Why is the average national grant rate for Chinese asylum claims 571% higher than the Atlanta court's grant rate? And why are Colombian asylum seekers 232% more likely to win their claims in Orlando than they are in Atlanta?[13]

A reason this can happen is that asylum practice is subjective in many ways. Asylum-seekers do not arrive with incontrovertible documentation in their pockets. Typically, the evidence in an asylum case comes in two forms. First, there are general reports that a certain kind of human rights abuse is happening to a certain kind of person in a foreign country. Those reports come from the State Department, from Amnesty International, sometimes from the *New York Times*. Second, the applicant testifies about her own experiences. In Immigration Court, a lawyer from ICE will cross-examine her, pulling out any arguable inconsistency. Usually, if an immigration judge finds an asylum-seeker to be not credible, that kills the case. But an applicant who might be entirely believed by one judge may be entirely disbelieved by another. We had one case of a young mother who said the MS-13 gang slipped notes threatening to kill her daughter under her front door. The immigration judge in Las Vegas did not believe her, because he believed that if MS-13 wanted to threaten someone, they would do it face-to-face, not by written notes, and he believed that if someone planned to apply for asylum, she would carefully preserve the threatening notes and bring them along as evidence. I'm quite sure that this case, if presented to many other immigration judges around the country, would have won.

Our client's real mistake, objectively speaking, was to come to Las Vegas. Las Vegas has *not* been a good place to apply for asylum. Nationally, Immigration Courts granted asylum in a third of all asylum cases in 2018. The asylum grant at the Los Angeles court, just four hours down the road, was about the same as the national average: 34 percent. The grant rate in Las Vegas was nearly five times *lower*—just 7 percent. In Las Vegas, our toughest judge was Munish Sharda. He granted asylum to only fourteen people from fiscal year 2013 through 2018, out of 452 cases. He is a very nice man in person, and he ran a friendly courtroom. I like him. I like having students do their first hearings in front of him. He made favorable decisions for our clients on some procedural issues, which some judges wouldn't. It's nothing personal. It's just an empirical fact: you have nearly no chance of winning asylum with him. Judge Sharda, by the way, is not the harshest immigration judge in the United States. I have read about an immigration judge in Louisiana who had heard more than 200 asylum cases and never granted a single asylum application.[14]

One of the jobs of an immigrant defense lawyer is to explain all this to desperate people from other countries. Obviously, in court a lawyer must put his client's case forward as strongly as ethically possible. But in private, we have to tell the people we represent that we are worried the judge just won't believe them. Or we have to tell them: I know you are afraid you will be killed, but we are worried the judge won't think your fear is for the right reason. I talk to students about giving advice like this, but I'm nearly always nauseous when I have to give it myself.

It's my job to delegate most of the work, first and foremost to students. That's called "experiential legal education." I also delegate to the other attorneys in the clinic. That makes sense. I have administrative responsibilities. I have supervisory responsibilities. I have to teach classes and write legal scholarship. But, in truth, I think that ever since those first two years doing this work in that church basement in Egypt, I've avoided some of the tasks that are intrinsic to my specialty, because I am not sure I can handle them anymore. Sometimes it still falls to me to tell a man that the beating he suffered lacked something called "nexus" and the judge might not believe it even happened. On those days, when I get home, I know I'm much quicker to break into anger at my older daughter if she resists getting started on studying for her history quiz. I shouldn't be. It's not my fault, and it's definitely not my daughter's. My wife reminds me to calm down, but sometimes I don't tell her what's bothering me, either. Sometimes I don't immediately know. There's just so much bad news in my email, and in in text messages from other activists wondering if there is a lawyer available for a desperate family who just called.

While I didn't create the legal system that produces these results, I understand it, intellectually. I talk to my students about work-life balance. I know that the work we do gives people a much better chance than they would have otherwise. But at some level I feel my job is to protect people, and often I can't.

In June 2019, I had to finalize a brief to the Court of Appeals in an asylum case for a Salvadoran girl. One of our students, who had just graduated the month before, had done most of the work on the case during the previous semester. My job was to make the final revisions and to file it. The girl had told the immigration judge about how girls would get pulled out of school in El Salvador by the gangs. They would come back to class in tears, with blood running down their legs. Then they came for her. The immigration judge believed her about what happened. But the judge denied her asylum and ordered her sent back to El Salvador. MS-13 also persecutes boys, too, the judge said. They target lots of people, he said. Our client wasn't special. She had good reason to fear being raped. But the reason she was at risk for being raped wouldn't be accepted by the U.S. legal system as qualifying her for asylum.

While I was working at the kitchen table one morning, putting the finishing touches on the appellate brief in that case, my oldest daughter was sleeping upstairs. She was thirteen, a year older than this girl had been when she ran from MS-13. And I couldn't help wondering: Was this how my own daughter would be treated? Would we refuse her protection if her would-be rapist also abused other people, because that would mean she was not being singled out? I couldn't believe someone might say to her, Well, you weren't going to be raped for one of the legally relevant reasons. Sorry, kid.

It is not healthy or professional for a lawyer to think that way. It doesn't help. But it happens.

* * *

The Las Vegas Immigration Court was once in a strip mall off Pecos Road, next to a Sonic Drive-In and just down the street from a Home Depot. More recently, it moved to the fourth floor of a steel and glass building downtown, which it shares with the Internal Revenue Service. There is a parking garage attached, where I leave my Elantra. The building is across a courtyard, with a metal detector at the entrance. The guards who manage it typically let attorneys go through quickly, as they try to sort out who is there for taxes and who is there for immigration.

I've been to Immigration Courts in other cities, and they all look the same. I've been to an Immigration Court built into the middle of a private prison in the Arizona desert. It looked exactly the same as the one that is in a high office building in downtown Los Angeles, exactly the same as the old place on Pecos Road, and exactly the same as the one in the new location in downtown Las Vegas. The entire room is about the size of an elementary school classroom. I have never seen an Immigration Court with windows. In the back, there are chairs for waiting, usually about four rows. A wood fence, waist high, separates the waiting area from the court. It's painted with a clear stain, giving it a yellowish pine finish. The posts on this fence have squarish decorative knobs glued to the top. I know they are only glued down, because I once accidentally knocked one off with my bag. This little fence has a swinging little door on hinges, and behind it are the lawyers and the judge.

At the front of the courtroom sits a clerk and also an interpreter, both off to the side. In the middle, on a slightly raised light pine bench, sits the immigration judge. When he or she walks in, wearing a black robe, all rise. The judge sits below a large seal; the seal is of the United States Department of Justice. And there's the rub.

In Immigration Court, the prosecutor is Immigration and Customs Enforcement, ICE. The lawyers who sit at one of the tables up front are employed by the ICE Office of Chief Counsel. For reasons I do not know, immigration judges do not refer to those lawyers as "ICE," although that's who they are. They'll say "DHS," for Department of Homeland Security. That's not wrong.

ICE is part of DHS. Personally, I am more annoyed that immigration judges sometimes call the ICE lawyers "the government." That's not wrong, either. I get annoyed by that because the judge is from the government, too. The judge is an employee of the Department of Justice.

The other table is for the respondent, and her lawyer, if she has one. On the respondent's table, there is a bin of common forms that are likely to be necessary. A form for lawyers to fill out to make their appearance in court. That's the E-28. It's on green paper. Another form for the respondent to change his or her address with the court. That's the E-33. It's on yellow paper. We stock green and yellow paper in our photocopy room at the immigration clinic, so we can print these forms in the office. At our office there's a handwritten note next to the colored paper: "FOR IMMIGRATION ONLY." If anyone else tries to take our colored paper, we're gonna have words. Seriously. There's nothing worse than rushing around the day before making a first appearance for a new client, trying to get papers together to get out the door in time to pick up your kid at cheer practice, knowing that the court hearing is at 8:30 the next morning, and the green paper is gone. Without green paper, I have to print my E-28 on plain white paper, which means I'll have to apologize to the judge. It's not a big deal, but I don't like it. Also, any paper you file in Immigration Court should be two-hole-punched at the top, not stapled. I've gotten this one wrong more times than I'd like to admit.

All this paper makes Immigration Court a bit old-school. My friends who practice civil and criminal law use electronic dockets. They pull up the docket on their computer screen, and they can see everything happening in their client's case and get electronic notification when the court or the opposing party files something new. Immigration Court is supposed to be like this soon, they've promised. Any day now. But as of 2019, the only thing that could really be filed electronically in the Las Vegas Immigration Court was the E-28—the attorney's notice of appearance. When this new system debuted, I tried filing an electronic E-28 the day before making an appearance for a client. When I got to court, the judge didn't have the record of my appearance. It could take a few days for the filing to make it into the court record, I was told. To me, that defeats the purpose of doing things electronically. So we keep green paper in the copy room.

The lack of administrative sophistication in Immigration Court causes problems beyond office supplies. When people call our clinic asking for help, we need to be able to assess their cases quickly. We might be able to take only one new case in a given week, and we have to figure out which potential client would benefit most. In some ways it's like triage operations in combat field medicine: we have to decide which one person gets possibly life-saving treatment, who just gets a little morphine, and who gets left to die because nothing can be done. Ideally, we would like to know the basics of the case to make this assessment, but we rarely do. It would be nice to be able to look up the case electronically, for a start, to know where it stands. Our clients—the respondents—often don't understand very accurately what's going on. It's not uncommon for us to go into court planning to contest something, only to be told that our new client actually conceded the issue four months ago when he had no lawyer and was talking to the judge through an interpreter. In theory, we could find that out in advance, but we'd have to go down to the court to listen to audiotapes, which takes a lawyer or law student out of service for several hours.

In these forms—E-28, E-33—the *E* stands for Executive Office of Immigration Review, or EOIR. EOIR is a division of the Department of Justice and has its headquarters in Falls Church, Virginia. EOIR has two key parts: the Immigration Courts and the Board of Immigration Appeals. There are around sixty Immigration Courts. Most of them are in big cities, where you'd expect them to be: Las Vegas, New York, Los Angeles, Chicago, Houston, Portland, Seattle, Atlanta and so on. There are also Immigration Courts in some not-so-big places: Fishkill, New York; Eloy, Arizona; Conroe, Texas. These are the locations of ICE detention centers, and typically the Immigration Court is actually inside the detention center. It's part of the specs that private prison companies have to comply with when they get an ICE detention contact: Please include a courtroom, one that looks exactly like all the other immigration courtrooms—except in this one the judges work behind concrete and barbed wire.

When I started in Las Vegas, detained immigrants were driven over from the detention center to the court on Pecos. The shackled men in jumpsuits would fill most of the chairs in the waiting area. Once, at a kid's birthday party at an indoor bouncy house place in Henderson, I met a man whose job it was to drive the ICE detainees to and from Immigration Court. They've basically eliminated that job. Now, people in the detention center appear on a video screen, which is set up in the courtroom at the front, off to one side.

Despite the name, these courts deal with deportation, not immigration. If they were really about immigration, you could petition the court to be able to sponsor your uncle, or appeal the denial of a fiancé visa. But Immigration Courts can't hear cases like that. They have no jurisdiction. People are brought into Immigration Court because the government wants to deport them. The proceedings in Immigration Court are called "removal proceedings." If the Department of Homeland Security wins in Immigration Court, the immigration judge issues an order of removal against a person. It is true that immigrants can win in Immigration Court, in which case they might be granted legal permanent residency. That's the closest these courts come to dealing with "immigration." In our clinic, we don't fight for people to be able to immigrate, to come into the country. We fight for them to be able to stay.

Second, these are not courts in the sense that most people know. They're not part of the judiciary. The judges are not judges; they're employees. The group of federal employees who we now call "immigration judges" were once called "special inquiry officers" and were part of the old Immigration and Naturalization Service, the forerunner of today's ICE and USCIS. They worked for the prosecutor, in other words. They got the title "judge" in 1973, but they continued to be supervised by the INS. In 1983, when the attorney general created the Executive Office of Immigration Review, the judges got a little more independence, with a bit more separation between the adjudication of cases and the part of the government responsible for arresting and deporting people. But they still work for the Department of Justice. They have never been independent members of the judicial branch. According to the Southern Poverty Law Center, "Roughly three-fourths of immigration judges hired by the Trump administration have prosecutorial experience, and many previously worked for ICE as trial attorneys who represented the government in removal proceedings." (I should be clear: the judge in Louisiana who had never granted asylum is a registered Democrat and was hired during the Clinton administration.)[15]

President Trump's attorneys general have made a number of decisions to narrow the legal eligibility for asylum. His first attorney general, Jeff Sessions, also imposed performance benchmarks for case completion quotas. Immigration judges now see benchmark meters on their computers at work, which look like a gas gauge on a car, showing whether they are on track on, say, "Benchmark 3: 85% of motions adjudicated within 20 days of IJ receipt," or "Benchmark 2: 85% of non-status, non-detained cases completed within 10 days of final hearing." If their number slips below 85 percent, the indicator moves from green to yellow; if the number is even lower, the indicator goes to red. It's also worth noting that immigration judges are on probation with the Department of Justice for their first two years. We have five immigration judges in Las Vegas, and at one point in early 2019 three of them were in this probation period.[16]

A genuine court is independent from the rest of the government. In the federal system, federal judges are appointed for life, precisely so that no one can easily pressure them. We house our courts in a separate branch of government;

they're even addressed in a separate part of the Constitution, Article III. In Immigration Court, the seal behind the immigration judge looks official. It makes the room look like a court. The robe looks right. The tables look right. It's like a fake dollar bill where George Washington has been replaced with someone else but the etching is made to look similar. In Immigration Court, the judges work for the Department of Justice, which is the federal government's in-house legal department. The head of the department is the attorney general, the nation's chief prosecutor. He supervises the U.S. attorneys, who bring indictments against drug traffickers, the mafia, Michael Cohen, and people who cross the border illegally.

Before becoming attorney general, Jeff Sessions was one of the most virulently anti-immigrant members of the United States Senate. It was Sessions who, in September 2017, announced the administration's plans to end the DACA program. And in early summer 2018, Sessions announced a "zero tolerance" policy at the border. He ordered his attorneys to file criminal charges against everyone crossing the border, even if they crossed with young children. That summer the number of drug-trafficking prosecutions on the border declined because Jeff Sessions shifted so many resources to prosecuting parents for crossing the border, taking kids away in the process. When the adults were taken to jail to await rapid trials, their children were ripped from their arms and given into the custody of government agencies—which later expressed doubt they could reunite these children with their parents, because the Department of Justice imposed a "zero tolerance" policy for a misdemeanor.[17]

The Immigration Courts are part of that department.

There are two phases in a removal proceeding in Immigration Court. In the first part, ICE has to prove that the person is in fact a removable noncitizen. Much like in a criminal trial, the judge will ask the respondent to plead. In Immigration Court the plea isn't "guilty" or "innocent"; instead, you're supposed to "admit" or "deny." Most people—even with lawyers—admit the charges right off the bat. We do that, too. It's one of the first things you learn in civil procedure. Lawyers are not actually supposed to fight everything just to fight. But, much like in a criminal case, it is the government's burden to prove its case. People are not obligated to admit that they should be deported. So sometimes we deny charges. Sometimes we want to know what evidence the government has against our client. Our client has that right.

This isn't some act of legal genius. Nor is it a subversive act of resistance. It's routine lawyering, or it should be. I wouldn't hire a criminal defense lawyer who just automatically pleads guilty for his clients in every case. But denying DHS allegations is sometimes treated in Immigration Court as a transgression of sorts. I've been in the Las Vegas court when a lawyer for ICE lectured my students because they simply denied charges for a client at an initial hearing. Apparently we are supposed to roll over and admit everything. On the other hand, sometimes when we deny charges and the immigration judge asks ICE for evidence, the lawyer for ICE says, "We don't have our file, Your Honor." And then ICE asks for a continuance to find some evidence.

In the minority of cases where the respondent denies the ICE allegation, the usual course of business is for ICE to submit a form called the I-213. This is basically a police report prepared when the person encountered immigration authorities. It contains statements by DHS officers reporting how they know that this person is not a U.S. citizen and thus is legally removable. In 2019, journalists began documenting a problem that immigration lawyers have known about for a long time: the I-213s are filled with errors. But they are very difficult to challenge because government documents are presumed to be reliable and are nearly always accepted with little scrutiny by immigration judges.[18]

Once ICE has given some evidence for its allegations, or the respondent has admitted them, the case will move on to claiming "relief." If fear was any part of the reason that the client wanted to come to the United States, that would almost certainly mean applying for asylum. Once you submit the asylum application, the court schedules an individual hearing. That's the real trial in an asylum case. It typically lasts a morning, or maybe a day. However, some of our cases have gone on for several days if we have more witnesses. The attorneys for ICE often quip that "clinic cases take longer." I don't disagree.

Prepping an asylum application may not be the only thing going on, especially in the case of an unaccompanied child who crossed the border alone. For example, we would also be exploring whether a parent abused, abandoned, or neglected a child, which would make her eligible for Special Immigrant Juvenile Status. And while gang violence is definitely the main reason our clients leave El Salvador, after many interviews we sometimes find out that there was abuse in the family, too. If we find anything like this, then asylum won't be the only immigration relief we pursue.

To apply for SIJS, the child would need to be under the jurisdiction of a state family court, usually through a guardianship or custody case. The state family judge would need to find that the child had been abused, abandoned, or neglected under state law, that reunification with one or both parents is not possible, and that return to his country is not in his best interests. If the family judge agrees, then the court order can be attached to another immigration form, the I-360.

(I hope you are still following along. I know it's confusing, but this is the system, and as things stand, American law expects people of any age to be able to get through all this without an attorney. The government does not provide a lawyer to help people fight deportation.)

The I-360 gets mailed off to U.S. Citizenship and Immigration Services, where it can take up to eight months to be processed. If USCIS concludes that all the eligibility criteria for SIJS have been met, then . . . well, then we have a new set of issues to deal with. An approved I-360 is not permission to stay in the United States. It's just an approved I-360.

It's weird, I know. Why does the government send an approval that isn't an approval? Every time our clients receive an approved I-360 they call to ask us if that means the case is over. No, it's far from done. With an approved I-360, an abused child can apply to adjust his status to become a legal permanent resident. That's another form, of course. There's always another form. This one is called the I-485, and it has its own requirements. Background checks, medical checks, and so on. But that's not the biggest problem.

The biggest problem is that the immigration judge does not have authority to deal with SIJS. Even if an immigration judge can see that the child sitting in front of him is eligible for the status, he can't grant it. This means you may be eligible for a bona fide immigration status, but the institution called the Immigration Court can't help you with you that. Only U.S. Citizenship and Immigration Services can approve an I-360 or an I-485.

Congress put a quota on how many SIJ visas could be granted to nationals of specific countries. Quotas always mean waits. In July 2019, a Special Immigrant Juvenile from El Salvador, Honduras, or Guatemala could only get legal residency if her application was filed before July 1, 2016. Children who filed after that date just had to wait in limbo because of the quota.

A three-year wait, for a child found by a judge to be the victim of abuse or neglect.

During those years while the child is in limbo, the removal proceedings could legally go forward in Immigration Court. Even if eligible for protection under our law, an abused child could be ordered removed while that application is pending. Until the Trump administration, we could avoid that by asking for something called administrative closure, or "admin closure." But—in an illustration of the ways the Trump administration has changed America's immigration system—on May 17, 2018, Attorney General Sessions issued a decision that ended immigration judges' power to administratively close cases. Since then, ICE lawyers in Immigration Court now insist on forging ahead with removal even when everyone involved in the case knows that a family court judge has found that a child was a victim of abuse or neglect, deporting the child would not be in the child's best interest, and the child eventually would be eligible to stay in the United States as a legal resident.[19]

This end of administrative closure didn't get the kind of attention that the Muslim ban generated in the earliest days of the Trump administration. There were no protests in major cities demanding a return of administrative closure. It takes many words to even explain what it is. On the day Sessions's decision was announced, I read about it my email inbox. My inbox is where I have received much of the bad news of the last three years. I came home upset and worried, because I knew what the end of admin closure would mean for the kids we try to defend. When I got home, I told my wife, Cindy, that the Trump administration had made a terrible decision. She hadn't heard about it, and I started to try to explain. But then one of our kids walked into the room, the dogs barked at something, and I don't remember what happened next. I never got through the explanation. I never got it off my chest. It just takes too many words. And that, in a nutshell, is the genius of how the Trump administration has attacked immigrants, especially those who are already inside the country living in our communities.

The end of admin closure does not involve sending out truckloads of government agents to round up immigrants. It does not even lead immediately to new deportations. It's inside the machine. It removes one of the safety guards that prevented deportation orders in sympathetic cases. It lubricates the machine, allowing the gears to move faster, with the eventual outcome that much more predetermined. The effects might not immediately be felt in any concrete way. But these effects will come, because the deportation machine is running, even if it's hard to explain. It's running every day.

5

Two Arrests

FERNANDO GONZALEZ HAD been living in Las Vegas for thirteen years, and he had fixed the brake light on his truck. It is hard for me not to wonder about a racial element in the fact that he even got a ticket for that, because in March 2019, exactly a year after he got his ticket, I was pulled over because of the brake lights on my Elantra. I was driving my oldest daughter to the bus stop, two blocks from Clark High School. It was a different officer, of course, in a different place. He just helpfully warned me that I should get the lights fixed. I'm grateful for that, though I was not terribly dutiful about getting it done. It took me two months, and during that time I was not pulled over again.

Still, Fernando's life looked to be going well through the summer of 2018. Reina was here, and she was pregnant. His eight-year-old daughter was going to school and seemed happy with their expanding family. However, he did not go to court to answer the ticket that the police officer had given him in April 2018. At that particular time, he didn't have the money for the ticket. He'd spent it on actually fixing the brake light. His truck was having other problems, too. The check-engine light was on, and that meant a more expensive repair. He had to keep the truck going, because the truck was his livelihood. So he delayed on the ticket, and he also delayed on getting a smog check for the truck, which meant his registration briefly lapsed.

Not far from the old Immigration Court, there is a Home Depot on Pecos Boulevard. It looks like most other Home Depot warehouse stores. Outside in front, in the giant parking lot, there is often a small gathering of Mexican and Central American men standing around, offering their services on a day-labor basis. Home Depot customers can hire them to install whatever they just bought inside the store.

79

Early in September 2018, Fernando drove past these men on the corner and parked his truck. He went inside the Home Depot and bought a few supplies for a job. He waited in line to pay, and then walked back to his truck. As soon as he pulled out of the lot, he saw the lights: a motorcycle cop. Fernando doesn't think he violated any traffic laws pulling out of Home Depot; at the time he thought it was for the missed smog check and lapsed registration. Fernando handed over his license and insurance to the officer, thinking: "I'll accept the ticket. Fix the plates. Easy thing."

The officer checked Fernando's license, and then asked Fernando to get out of his truck. He asked Fernando to turn around. He pulled Fernando's arms behind his back and snapped cuffs on his wrists. He placed Fernando under arrest. Then he called in backup. There was a bench warrant for Fernando's arrest. It was because of the ticket from the brake light from six months earlier. The officer had evidently been scanning plates, and when he scanned Fernando's, the warrant came up.

The court docket expresses this in clinical terms. When the ticket for the non-working brake light was issued in April 2018, a court appearance date was set for July. When Fernando didn't show, the court issued a failure-to-appear warrant and suspended his license. For September 7, when police stopped him again, the docket says: "Warrant served." His original single misdemeanor charge had now become three—the original brake light problem, failure to appear, and driving without a license.

"Now many things came to my head," Fernando told me. But mostly it was shock. He'd thought things were going pretty well. "I was paying taxes and doing good."

The backup arrived. Those officers talked briefly with the motorcycle officer, and then they began talking to Fernando. "The cops were making fun of me," he told me. They pointed at the motorcycle officer. "Do you know who this is?" the new officers asked Fernando.

"No," Fernando said.

"He is ICE! He's Donald Trump! This is Trump's time. This is not the time to be messing around. You will be deported. This is ICE!"

Except it wasn't ICE. These officers were not from Immigration and Customs Enforcement. These were officers from the Las Vegas Metropolitan Police Department. They didn't work for President Trump. They answered to the sheriff of Clark County, Joseph Lombardo. They enforced traffic laws, among other things. They ran plates. They arrested people on bench warrants when tickets went unpaid. I asked to interview Sheriff Lombardo for this book. His spokesperson never got back to me.

The officers took Fernando to the Las Vegas City Jail, on the corner of Mohave and Stewart. After a few days they took him to a judge. Not in person. The judge was on a TV screen. Fernando didn't fight the charges. He pleaded guilty. He asked to fix the ticket, and the judge said he could go home the next day. But he did not go home.

At 3:30 in the morning, officers in the jail woke Fernando: "Gonzalez, roll out!" They led him down the corridor, to the exit. "At the exit, there was an officer from ICE, and two more guys," Fernando remembers. They told him, "You have a hold from ICE. You came here illegally."

* * *

After Donald Trump was elected, I knew—and so did many other people— that Las Vegas would be on the front line. As I've said, one in every thirteen people who live in the State of Nevada is undocumented, more than in any other state in the Union. And most of that undocumented population is in Las Vegas.[1]

After the 2016 election, I had ideas about how we could respond. We would build a legal defense center for immigrants. We would have a volunteer network to respond to ICE raids. I had heard Rep. Ruben Kihuen, who was elected to Congress in 2016 from a district including North Las Vegas, talk about being an undocumented immigrant as a youth, when his father told him to run and hide from the green trucks driven by la migra. From that, I envisioned seeing ICE trucks roaming the streets of Las Vegas. Maybe I would see one conducting a raid, and I would pull over and videotape it, tell the people their rights, and offer legal assistance. I downloaded guides that lawyers had developed years earlier about how to defend people during immigration raids. I got ready.

Others did the same. Activists started gathering lists of volunteers ready to respond in the event of raids. I put out a call to law students who wanted to be on a roster to respond in such a situation. More than a dozen signed up. At one point, a meeting was organized among activist groups, with a representative from out of state who was talking about a new phone app and cloud-based system that could coordinate volunteers monitoring ICE activity with legal defense centers. The idea was that if volunteers spotted ICE activity somewhere, they could summon observers, who could deter abuses by filming the scene, and lawyers, who could offer help to those swept up. It would have been possible, with some work, to organize volunteer teams to use the app. But what would we do with the information? Las Vegas only had two and a half lawyers dedicated to full-time pro bono deportation defense, plus one accredited representative at Catholic Charities who was not a licensed attorney. The two lawyers were both fellows at the UNLV Immigration Clinic, of which I was the director. I was the half, since I had to teach classes and write scholarly articles in addition to running the clinic. It would be like setting up a high-tech 911 call-in system without having an actual police or fire department: We appreciate your letting us know about the burning building. We do not have any fire trucks. Thank you for your call.

We were making a bigger strategic mistake, however. We were imagining a kind of attack on the community that never really came. We imagined ICE raids. An ICE raid is a bit like the way a pack of lions attacks a herd of zebras. Much like videos of lions hunting, you can watch videos of ICE raids on YouTube. Just search for "ICE raid" or "ICE raid factory." It's a dramatic and photogenic event. Federal agents driving SUVs and wearing nylon jackets roll up quickly on their unsuspecting targets, surrounding the people at the worksite and trapping them. Then large buses arrive. The buses seem nearly always to be white and unlabeled. The ICE agents sort the people they find inside the factory and then lead some of them onto the buses, which eventually take them away. This whole process takes a lot of time, which gives plenty of opportunity for news crews to arrive, the same way tourists on safari in Tanzania sometimes catch a lion hunt. These raids can be very large operations. A 2008 ICE raid on a kosher slaughterhouse in Postville, Iowa, involved 900 agents and netted nearly 400 arrests. At least two different documentaries have been made about the Postville raid and its aftermath—a result of its dramatic scale, and also the fact that so much TV footage is available from it.

The effects of such a spectacle ripple through a community. The BBC reported on a 2018 raid in Tennessee in which ICE arrested 97 workers at a meatpacking plant. The next day, 530 children missed school. The kids weren't detained by ICE. Their parents were just terrified. The effect on their well-being was collateral damage from ICE enforcing the law so aggressively. In Nevada, one in seven children in public school has an undocumented parent at home. So such collateral damage could happen here, too.[2]

In April 2019, ICE conducted a raid in Allen, Texas, at a business known as CVE Technology Group. According to the DHS spokesperson who held a press conference afterward, it was the largest worksite immigration raid conducted by the federal government in more than a decade. In the Allen raid, ICE arrested 280 people. You can easily find video of the raid on YouTube. Here's the thing, though: in September 2018, the month when Fernando Gonzalez was picked up for an unpaid brake light ticket and handed over to immigration, ICE initiated 300 new deportation cases in the Las Vegas

Immigration Court, including the one against Fernando. That's more than the number of people affected by the Allen raid. But there are no YouTube videos on the Las Vegas cases. They were never in the news. It was just a normal month in Las Vegas. In fact, fiscal year 2019 set a record for the most new deportation cases filed in Las Vegas, exceeding the previous record by 25 percent.[3]

A great deal of effort has been spent preparing the community for ICE raids. Many information sessions have been held informing people about their rights if ICE knocks on their door. I participated in some in the six months after the 2016 election. One was organized by a congressman, for example. I did a presentation with Arléne Amarante, a lawyer who worked with us for a year after Katelyn and Alissa left. The session I did at my daughter's elementary school was another. In June 2019, when President Trump tweeted that ICE was about to arrest "millions" of people in a nationwide sweep, there was another round of these gatherings organized by activist groups. Nevada's senior senator, Catherine Cortez Masto, distributed a know-your-rights guide online and organized information sessions for the July 4 weekend. The main advice was to not answer the door and not to answer questions. Yet while ICE raids do happen, and so does the terrifying knock at the door by ICE agents, such events are relatively rare. Today, more deportations begin the way Fernando Gonzalez's started: with a routine arrest by local police.

To understand how American immigration enforcement has evolved, it might be useful to compare Fernando with Cecia Alvarado, the Costa Rican teenager who was arrested for domestic violence years earlier when she had a fight with her brother's wife. Cecia was taken to the Las Vegas City Jail, the same jail where Fernando was taken. But she was able to leave—even though at the time she was unlawfully present in the United States. In 2018, Fernando was arrested for what seems like a more minor infraction—an unpaid ticket for a broken brake light. He ended up in ICE custody. The reason they were treated so differently relates to a new infrastructure of immigration enforcement that was built, mostly, under President Barack Obama.

Cecia Alvarado was arrested for domestic violence before this new infrastructure was in place, and that was her first real stroke of luck in an otherwise troubled adolescence. It also makes her case useful to illustrate how the criminal justice system worked before our current immigration enforcement machine was fully constructed. For three days police moved Cecia between jails, and between cells and holding rooms. She remembers that most of the other women in the jail were prostitutes and knew the routine. They'd been there before. Cecia's first thought was: "I didn't have anyone to call." This was a low point. She remembers that one of the cells where she was held had water all over the floor. Everything was wet and dark. "It felt like a dream. Like a nightmare," she told me.

Sometime in the middle of the night, the police took her from that cell. They gave her a bag with a change of clothes, a toothbrush, a menstrual pad, and a blanket. They put her in a cell crowded with bunk beds, but there was no bed for Cecia. The guards told her they didn't have any more beds. "I had to sleep on the floor," she told me. To this day, Cecia is grateful to an older African American woman who was in an upper bunk. "She asked me why I was there. She had a daughter about my age. She gave me a pillow."

During one of her transfers, police had allowed a phone call. Having been jailed for around a day at that point, Cecia decided to call the one person who might help: her friend Luis. He promised to bail her out. He worked fast: at 3 or 4 in the morning, guards told Cecia she was getting out. Cecia gave the pillow back to the African American woman, along with the bag of supplies she'd been given. The guards put her in a car and drove her to a corner in downtown Las Vegas. An officer gave her 75 cents. She walked to a pay phone on Fremont Street and called Luis. He was shocked to hear from her at that hour, telling her, "They told me they were going to let you out tomorrow."

If she had been arrested today for the same thing, with the same murky facts, she almost certainly would have been flagged by ICE. But the systems that do this were not fully in place back then. Instead, Luis came to get her.

Back then, Cecia did not think very much about her immigration situation. She remembers hearing about raids by the old Immigration and Naturalization Service at Eastern Avenue and Bonanza, a corner in East Las Vegas where there are today two large Mexican grocery stores, along with a Starbucks and a Jack in the Box. But it was background noise. It never affected Cecia. That was lucky. When Cecia was arrested for domestic violence, a booking officer told her they might notify the Costa Rican consulate. It doesn't seem they actually did. But more importantly, they did not notify the INS. And when Luis paid her bail, they let her go. Quickly, too. Today, that would not have happened.

Another bit of luck: Cecia was not convicted of domestic violence. As is common for people who have been through the American criminal justice system for a low-level offense, the process is a fog in Cecia's mind. She does not know exactly how it came about. Did she have a public defender? Did the assistant district attorney on duty the day she went to court take mercy on her? Is it because nineteen-year-old Cecia did not fit the stereotype of a domestic violence defendant? Is it because she wasn't really guilty of the crime? She doesn't know. But she was allowed to plead to just disturbing the peace, with no further time in jail. That's good, because domestic violence convictions can be a killer on immigration applications.

When she got out of jail, Cecia moved in with Luis's family for about two weeks, but then she went back out on her own. "I just lived wherever people had a room where I could stay. I had all my stuff in one bag." She and Luis had been only friends, but they started dating in February 2004. Around the same time, she started taking a few classes at a local community college, the College of Southern Nevada. In December 2004, she and Luis married. Cecia got pregnant almost immediately. In 2005, she gave birth to a daughter, who is now a teenager. Luis was a U.S. citizen, too. Another stroke of luck.

Cecia had one more thing going for her. She had originally come to the United States on a tourist visa. Once she overstayed her visa, Cecia Alvarado had become an undocumented immigrant. Just like Fernando, the handyman from Guatemala. Just like Olivero, who traveled across the desert carrying a Snickers bar. Just like his wife, Manuela, and their little daughter, Adelina, who followed to join him. Just like Ines, the housecleaner, and her daughter, Rebeca. Except that all of them crossed the border on foot, entering without inspection, rather than overstaying a visa. The reason for this difference mostly had to do with social class. Cecia came from a middle-class family in Costa Rica that had sufficient means to convince an American consular officer to give her a tourist visa.

In a matter of months, Cecia Alvarado went from being an undocumented visa overstayer who easily could have been deported to a legal resident and the mother of a U.S. citizen. Cecia filled out the application for permanent residency herself, mailed it off to U.S. Citizenship and Immigration Services, which was then a relatively new agency in the new Department of Homeland Security, and obtained her green card.

About four years later, in March 2008, the Department of Homeland Security launched a program called Secure Communities. Secure Communities is very simple. When a person is arrested by a local police department, her fingerprints are taken. That's a routine part of the booking process. The Las Vegas police want to check if the person they just arrested for DUI near Caesar's Palace on a Friday night is also wanted for armed robbery in Missouri. To do that, Las Vegas Metro sends the prints to the FBI, to run them against national databases.[4]

Secure Communities added a wrinkle to this system. Under Secure Communities, when local police send booking information and fingerprints to the

FBI, the FBI forwards the info to the Department of Homeland Security, which includes ICE. The federal government calls this "interoperability." This means that every time someone is booked into a jail, he is also being simultaneously reported to immigration. At first, this "interoperability" was supposedly voluntary. Local police would be asked to sign an agreement if they wanted booking information to be processed through immigration. This offered a sense of local control—and it seems very appealing. If police arrest someone for a serious crime, why not also check if he is in the country unlawfully? If a person is a repeated danger to public safety, why not have her deported once her criminal sentence is done? This kind of deportation is quite popular, and probably is one thing in immigration policy that can find broad consensus in both political parties.[5]

The trouble is that lots of people who get booked into jails are not serious criminals. As University of Denver law professor César Cuauhtémoc García Hernández explains, by combining routine criminal history checks with immigration enforcement, "an ordinary traffic stop or other minor police encounter could lead to an inquiry into a person's criminal and immigration history." Small mistakes can mean that you get booked and released, or even that you spend a night in jail—especially if you are poor. Poor people have trouble paying tickets. Poor people get cited for doing business without a license or trespassing if they try to sell things on the street. Also, some people commit minor crimes but are not grave threats to society. Petty theft, vandalism, driving under the influence—I wouldn't try to justify such behaviors, but I think most people believe they should be dealt with proportionately. Secure Communities was sold as a way to identify and remove dangerous threats to public safety. But in 2010, only 15 percent of the people identified through the program had been accused of a violent crime or major drug offense. The others were people arrested for more minor crimes.[6]

When Fernando was stopped by the officer on the motorcycle, he was about to get married to Reina, who was herself about to give birth to their child. Reina was a legal resident. But Fernando was EWI. He had crossed into the country illegally. And so—despite his lack of a serious criminal record, his eight-year-old U.S. citizen daughter, and another U.S. citizen child on the way—he could not get papers easily. He was not lucky.

The difference in experience with the immigration system between Fernando and Cecia begins with the systems that were put in place in 2008 to integrate routine local policing with federal immigration enforcement. As UCLA law professor Jennifer Chacón has written, at the turn of the twenty-first century the "assumption was that state and local governments not only had no role in the regulation of immigration, but also had very little to do with the enforcement of federal immigration law." This meant that a routine local arrest would not necessarily lead to deportation. No more. Today, as Prof. García Hernández commented, it is "difficult to identify where criminal law ends and immigration law begins." There has been such a thorough blurring of the roles of local police and federal immigration agents that a new word has even been coined: *crimmigration*.[7]

By the time Fernando was arrested, a minor arrest by local police in Las Vegas could flag a person for federal immigration enforcement. Those systems were built during the George W. Bush and Obama administrations. But that's not really the whole story. Had Hillary Clinton won the election in 2016, Fernando would almost certainly not be facing deportation today. Having a system to flag someone for ICE is one thing. But the second step is that ICE has to decide whether to actually try to deport a person who is flagged.

Immigrant advocates often called President Obama the "deporter-in-chief" because of the large number of deportations that occurred under his watch. Trump, for all his anti-immigrant bluster, has yet to match Obama's deportation numbers. But this fact masks considerable complexity, in two big ways. First, Obama pursued very different policies at the border than in the interior of the country. Thanks largely to massive investments in Customs and Border Protection, apprehension rates rose dramatically for people trying to cross into the country. At the peak of the Mexican undocumented migration, when Olivero came with his Snickers bar, the federal government estimated that it caught only a minority of the people who tried to cross the border. But by the end of the Obama era, the apprehension rate was up to 70 percent.[8]

Inside the country, in places like East Las Vegas and Spring Valley, a different set of policies would determine the fate of someone like Fernando. The basic goal of the Obama administration in the interior was to prioritize deportation of undocumented immigrants with criminal records, which President Obama eventually called his "felons, not families" policy. It took a long time for this policy to evolve, and from beginning to end it had detractors on both right and left.[9]

Late in the George W. Bush administration, ICE had launched a series of large workplace raids across the country that rounded up thousands of undocumented immigrants. In 2006, an ICE raid on a meatpacking plant in Greeley, Colorado, resulted in 300 arrests. In May 2008, ICE directly arrested 1,755 people on its own, mostly through raids on places where immigrants were known to work. Such crackdowns have some appeal to people who perceive the problem of undocumented immigration to be mostly about illicit employment. But they result in a number of problems. First, they penalize the workers more than the employers. Second, the mass roundups often lead to constitutional violations, which results in some of the potential deportations being blocked in court. That's because in the United States, federal agents are not supposed to be able to just confine people to their workplace for interrogation without cause, but that's basically what happens in a workplace raid. Federal agents may secure a warrant to search a business believed to employ immigrants illegally. It does not mean they have probable cause to detain every person they find on-site.[10]

But that just masks a broader concern. An ICE raid is shocking. The deployment of massive numbers of agents and vehicles might seem appropriate to take down a drug cartel's compound. But brought to bear against a business where, at worst, there are people working without the right papers, this kind of show of government force intervening in daily life smacks of totalitarianism. And then there are the people who are rounded up in a workplace raid, the workers. They are people trying to earn money to support families. They have long-standing ties to the community. They have friends. They have kids who need to be picked up at school that afternoon.

It's not clear to me how aggressively ICE, and its predecessor the INS, actually operated on the streets of Las Vegas during the pre-Obama era. In conversations with Latino colleagues who grew up in Las Vegas, I have heard stories about *la migra* standing outside a Mexican grocery and demanding papers in the 1990s. I've heard from several longtime Las Vegas residents about ICE supposedly setting up a checkpoint at Bonanza and Eastern, in the heart of East Las Vegas. I've heard about a supermarket hiding people in its freezers while immigration agents checked papers outside the front door. I don't know which parts of these accounts are reliable. But I have also seen, from recent experience in 2019, how fears and stories like this spread, often with little basis. I've seen how the idea that a community is being hunted by the government becomes lodged in people's minds, especially in the minds of children.

ICE arrests did not immediately stop when Obama took office in 2009, but the Obama administration did slowly turn immigration enforcement in a different direction. Instead of a showy emphasis on raids and arrests in which ICE would directly nab people on its own, the focus shifted toward increasingly efficient linkages with local police. The Obama administration coupled this with a new focus on using discretion and priorities to target only certain undocumented immigrants. This took a while to be implemented, and in some ways it only really took hold in Obama's second term. In 2014, the Secretary of Homeland Security, Jeh Johnson, imposed a three-tiered set of enforcement priorities to guide ICE enforcement and to implement President Obama's "felons, not families" policy. The top priority included people caught at the border, but for people inside the country the top priority was limited to suspected terrorists, convicted gang members, and convicted felons.[11]

The lower priorities included anyone convicted of three or more non-traffic-related misdemeanors, or "aliens convicted of a 'significant misdemeanor,'" a new category that including driving while intoxicated and domestic violence. This meant that Obama's "felons, not families" was false advertising. Three trespass citations would make a person a priority. An old DUI could still break up a family. Moreover, the word "felon" tends to make people think of a violent criminal, but low-level drug possession is also often a felony. Still, for most undocumented immigrants, the benefits were real. Traffic tickets would not make a person a target for ICE. A broken brake light would not, either. Also, most of these priorities depended on convictions, not mere arrest. Cecia Alvarado had been arrested for domestic violence—a significant misdemeanor under the Obama policy—but she had not been convicted. She would not have been a priority, either. Most important, people like Olivero and Manuela, and people like Rebeca Reyes, who had not even an unpaid traffic ticket against them, were deprioritized entirely. They were not targets. One study estimated that 87 percent of the undocumented population in the United States benefited from the 2014 enforcement priorities. They still didn't have papers and legal status. But they were left alone.[12]

On January 25, 2017, one of President Trump's first executive orders retracted the 2014 enforcement priorities. Ostensibly, the Trump administration replaced these with a new list of priorities, but the most important line in the new policy was this: "ICE will not exempt classes or categories of removable aliens from potential enforcement. All of those present in violation of the immigration laws may be subject to immigration arrest, detention, and if found removable by final order, removal from the United States." That describes every undocumented immigrant in the United States. It describes Fernando, Manuela, Ines, and Olivero. It also would target people with DACA if the administration succeeds in ending that program, making Adelina and Rebeca targets. The same goes for people with TPS, which means all the people I met at ¡Arriba!. Thomas Homan, who served as ICE director early in the Trump administration, said at a press conference: "If you're in the country illegally, we're looking for you." Journalists have reported sharp upticks in ICE arrests of people without criminal records.[13]

There is some interpretive debate about what the Trump priorities really mean. The more critical view is that they basically eliminate the concept of enforcement priorities by making everyone a priority. There are government officials who defend the new approach, arguing that ICE still emphasizes certain immigrants (such as those with more serious criminal records) over others, while being willing to arrest anyone. ICE now often talks about "collateral arrests," meaning that ICE officers may go out looking for a person who has a criminal record, but if they find some other undocumented immigrants, they may take them, too.[14]

The phrase "criminal record" is evocative and also quite ambiguous. It can capture everything from a person who committed multiple assaults with a deadly weapon to a person who once took a leak on the sidewalk. In 2017, the most common criminal conviction for people arrested by ICE was intoxicated driving, followed by drug crimes. The next two on the list for the first year of the Trump administration were non-DUI traffic offenses and immigration offenses. In other words, in 62,517 deportation cases in 2017, the criminal offense was itself an immigration offense—usually crossing the border illegally.[15]

What is clear is that ICE is now much more indiscriminate. In fiscal year 2018, ICE made 44 percent more arrests than in fiscal year 2016. The Pew Research Center reported that "while ICE arrests overall rose from 2016 to 2017, arrests for those without prior convictions drove the increase." The number of deportations of people whose worst crime was a traffic offense increased by 42 percent between the last year of the Obama administration and the first year of the Trump administration. Meanwhile, from 2017 to 2019, the number of people detained by ICE who had a serious felony conviction actually dropped, as ICE went after more people with no criminal record or only a misdemeanor.[16]

In March 2019, *USA Today* reported that ICE had set a record for arrests of undocumented immigrants with no criminal record. The number of people detained by ICE nationally rose from 38,310 at the end of September 2018 to 47,486 at the end of 2018. But according to an analysis by Syracuse University, the number of people detained by ICE who had a record of serious crime actually *declined* 17 percent over the same period. ICE was now detaining 39 percent more people with no criminal convictions.[17]

People often claim that Obama violated the law by not targeting many undocumented immigrants. But policies like this had been blessed by the Supreme Court in 2012:

> Discretion in the enforcement of immigration law embraces immediate
> human concerns. Unauthorized workers trying to support their families,
> for example, likely pose less danger than alien smugglers or aliens who

commit a serious crime. The equities of an individual case may turn on many factors, including whether the alien has children born in the United States, long ties to the community, or a record of distinguished military service.[18]

In other words, the harsh immigration laws that allow the potential deportation of millions of people are merely tools. They are not mandates. It is up to the president and those he appoints to use these tools with discretion—to embrace immediate human concerns, as the Supreme Court said. Had Fernando Gonzalez been arrested under the policies in force in 2015 or 2016, he probably would have been flagged for ICE when he was booked into the Las Vegas City Jail, but ICE most likely would have left him alone. He would have gone home to Reina. He would have been there when Reina gave birth.

6

Psychological Warfare

A COUPLE OF ILLEGALS should come to your house and kill that ugly bitch of yours. Now that would be PC." I received that as a direct message on Facebook at 9:37 p.m. on a Wednesday night in January 2019, after I'd been in the news being quoted about immigrants. Facebook listed the author of the message as being located in Mesquite, Nevada, which is a town on the Arizona border along I-15, seventy minutes from our house. The fact that the person who'd written that message was not far away from my family was probably what unnerved me most.

This wasn't the first time my views about immigration had provoked a response. At the end of January 2017, just after Trump's inauguration, I had shared on Twitter an article about refugees being detained at airports under the Muslim ban. I got a reply from someone who used a profile picture of a white man in a black hoodie, with big dark sunglasses. He wrote: "No jewboy . . . this is called nationalism. I know this makes the jew turn into a demon. but we are winning." On another occasion, when I testified to the Nevada legislature, a man held a sign behind me that said, "Stop the illegal invasion." I wasn't aware of it while I was testifying, but several of my friends from immigrant rights organizations noticed. The concept that the United States is being "invaded" is now used fairly regularly by anti-immigrant politicians, including President Trump. The shooter who killed twenty-two people in El Paso in August 2019 said in his online manifesto that "this attack is a response to the Hispanic invasion of Texas."

The hate messages I've received are nothing, in terms of quantity and intensity, compared to what's been said to other activists and politicians who are outspoken on immigration and race issues—especially those who are female, immigrants, or people of color. I know a female legislator who has been followed to her car.

There is a man in Nevada who has a YouTube channel and likes to stage confrontations on video with pro-immigrant activists and politicians. In one of his videos in 2019, he featured Mayra Salinas-Menjivar, one of the key lawyers in our clinic. Mayra is a Salvadoran American who came to the United States alone when she was seven years old and finally became a U.S. citizen in 2018, *after* she had passed the Nevada bar exam. She'd become a key advisor on pro-immigrant legislation in the Nevada legislature. The YouTuber posted a picture of her with the caption "One of the most dangerous people in Nevada! Formerly an illegal (Mayra Salinas) became a Citizen is now assisting illegals at UNLV Immigration Clinic." Mayra called him and his friends "our fans." That's putting a brave face on anxiety. On one of his videos, he included a screenshot of one of our students, an African American man who was testifying before a state legislative committee, with a caption: "Another paid young shill at the UNLV Immigration Clinic. The job market sucks for them and find ways to pump the wealthy Soros agenda." In one video, he included a picture of me testifying to the legislature, seated next to Mayra, with the caption "Remember this guy plays the race card. He compared the deportation and jails to the Nazi Regime since is a Jew."

In March 2019, this YouTuber intruded on a student meeting about immigrant rights at the UNLV student union and said, "Michael Kagan, we will hold you accountable. . . . You are not going to destroy Western civilization." He posted a video of that online. On the same day that happened, paper signs were taped by the door to our clinic that said, "Stop aiding illegal aliens, call ICE. UNLV favors illegal aliens over citizens; We will report to DHS." The signs were taken down quickly. Our dean, Dan Hamilton, sent a strong note to the law school community. We received care packages from other student groups on campus. This was touching, and it helped. But many anxious emails followed, especially from students. The concern wasn't really about the signs. It was about whether something worse might happen in the future.

I have seen a tally of more than a dozen expressions of racial hate on the UNLV campus in the 2018–19 school year. Some were arguably isolated, and anonymous: "Kill the Blacks" written on notes in the library, the N-word scratched onto the door of an African American student's dorm room, and a swastika scratched onto the door of a Jewish student. And some were very public: in May, a bomb threat was posted at the entrance to the UNLV Center for Social Justice. That kind of thing.

These incidents take a toll. They worm their way into your mind. They generate emails and meetings about security procedures. For those in positions of responsibility, there's a need to provide reassurance. They feed into a general atmosphere of growing dread, as well as persistent distraction. It has the effect of psychological warfare on a battlefield. I don't think a local, bigoted YouTuber was cooperating with the White House, but in terms of the effect on the community, he might as well have been.

Freedom of Information Act requests have found internal ICE documents planning arrests in which immigrant children were referred to as "juvenile criminal aliens." Internal communications from ICE officers from 2017 show an unnerving enthusiasm. "Happy hunting and target building," said one email. According to the *Daily Beast*:

> "I'm guessing you'd prefer to be on the arrest team?" a supervisory deportation and detention officer at the Austin field office asked a volunteer.
> "YOU KNOW IT!!!!!!" the agent responded.[1]

A Facebook group for Customs and Border Protection employees, which was secret until it was revealed by ProPublica in July 2019, included jokes about throwing burritos at Latina members of Congress ("burrito at these bitches"), fantasies involving President Donald Trump sexually assaulting Rep. Alexandria Ocasio-Cortez, and comments like "oh well" and "if he dies, he dies" in response to the death of a Guatemalan teenager in Border Patrol custody. CBP had around 20,000 agents. The secret group had 9,500 members. It turned out that the chief of the border patrol, Carla Provost, was a member of the group. She told a House committee that she hadn't seen the offensive posts and that she joined in order to keep tabs on how she was "representing [her] workforce."[2]

The constant apprehensiveness that something bad might happen was new to me, but it is part of life for many other people, and for some the anxiety never fully goes away. Rigoberto Torres is a living example. I asked to meet him because I had heard about his reaction in June 2019 to the widely disseminated photograph of Oscar Alberto Martínez and his twenty-three-month-old daughter, Angie, who had been found facedown and dead in the Rio Grande. The image, broadcast and reprinted throughout the country, showed Oscar's dark T-shirt wrapped around his daughter's small body above her soggy red pants, her little shoes still on her feet. I had heard that Rigoberto thought that Oscar and Angie's fate could have very easily have been his own.

Oscar and Angie died because of U.S. government policy. According to the law, people can, entirely legally, present themselves at a legal port of entry on the U.S. border to begin the asylum process. This does not mean they will win asylum. The law merely allows them to apply. The Trump administration thwarted this through a practice called "metering," which basically means only giving a small number of people per day the chance to start this process legally. The rest are told to wait. That's what happened to Oscar and Angie. They had been waiting in Matamoros, Mexico, for the chance to apply for asylum in the United States. CNN reported that at that port of entry, U.S. border guards would take only three appointments per week for asylum-seekers. A waiting list of more than 2,000 people had built up in Matamoros. Desperate, Oscar tempted fate in the river to try to reach Brownsville, Texas. Had a legal procedure actually been open, he and Angie would probably still be alive.[3]

Oscar and Angie were from El Salvador, like Rigoberto Torres. When Rigoberto saw the image, he knew he'd crossed the same river not far away. He knew he'd been luckier. The river, he explained to me, is sometimes calm, and that's how it was for him. Other times, it kills.

Rigoberto arrived at the riverbank in 1989. He was sixteen at the time, and traveling alone. He had fled the end stages of the Salvadoran civil war. He remembered seeing awful things as a young teen. "People gutted," he said. "People without heads." I mentioned to him that if he had arrived the same way today, he might have ended up as a client of our clinic, although Rigoberto managed quite well without an attorney. He first went to Southern California, but he moved to Vegas soon afterward, starting as a kitchen worker in a Chinese restaurant and later getting trained in electronics and computer repair. He would have lived his life undocumented, most likely, except for the TPS program. In August 1993, he met Tillie, a master's student at UNLV. Long story short: by Labor Day Weekend, she was pregnant. They got married and raised three children in the neighborhood along Charleston Boulevard, on the west side of town. Because of the marriage, Rigoberto was able to adjust his status, and eventually became a citizen. He still carries his social security card with him because he's worried about his status being challenged. He explained to his daughter that he carries it "just in case." He told me, "It's a habit."

Once Rigoberto was driving his van near a friend's house in East Las Vegas when a police officer pulled him over. The officer claimed that his taillight was broken, but Rigoberto says that wasn't true, and he challenged the officer.

"If you don't like it, go back to where you came from," the police officer told him. Today, that language evokes Donald Trump and the "send her back" chant from his 2019 Greenville rally. But this happened to Rigoberto in 2011 or 2012. That's the kind of experience that gives Rigoberto the nagging worry that he will never be really accepted in the United States, no matter his legal status as a full-fledged citizen.

On June 17, 2019, the president sent a tweet declaring that the following weekend, DHS "will begin the process of removing the millions of illegal aliens who have illicitly found their way into the United States. They will be removed as fast as they can." Congressional offices and immigrant rights groups mobilized know-your-rights information sessions for immigrants. Meanwhile, the UNLV Immigration Clinic had no attorney present for the first time since 2013. Laura Barrera had left in the spring, and Mayra had left shortly thereafter. I understood their reasons for leaving: the clinic paid better than we had in the AmeriCorps days, but we still offered no career path even for the most dynamic immigrant rights lawyers in the state. It was a setback. If we were to build an immigrant defense program in Las Vegas, we had to be able keep lawyers like Laura and Mayra, and we couldn't.

Their departures came at a bad time for me personally. My younger daughter, Tesi, had been having strange struggles in school. In the fall of 2018, when she was in third grade, my wife, Cindy, convinced me we had to pay attention. We scheduled a neuropsych assessment, but the waiting period was substantial, and meanwhile Tesi was falling apart. She wouldn't do her schoolwork. She fought with us and her sister. She stopped smiling. I missed work taking her to specialist appointments. Finally we were told that our daughter had dyslexia and anxiety, among other issues. I had a responsibility to learn about her needs and to be her advocate, the way I did for clients in court. More than that, I had to learn how to be patient and to take time to help her when, honestly, I was mentally somewhere else. In my head, I was in immigration court. Always. I advise my students against letting this happen to them. Self-care and all that. But I suck at it.

We finally replaced Laura with Martha Menendez, who led the state chapter of the American Immigration Lawyers Association. But she was not set to start her job until July 1, and even that start date was in doubt because of HR paperwork. After much urging from my wife, we had arranged a two-week trip to Seattle, where Cindy's family is from. I would let the clinic go, with no lawyer on staff, no matter who called us. That was right around the time the president tweeted about the upcoming raids.

As soon as Trump sent his tweet threatening raids that would deport "millions," my phone began buzzing with messages. It was mostly group chats of activists planning responses. Community information sessions were arranged.

There was talk about setting up a hotline. I knew, as did many experts on the immigration enforcement system, that the president was blowing smoke. ICE does not have the capacity to round up and deport "millions" so quickly. There were press reports citing DHS officials that the real number would be more like 2,000. This was still scary, because they were talking about targeting families with children, and it was even being called the "family op." Still, 2,000 arrests spread across the country would barely be noticed in ICE statistical reports, if not for the president generating a media storm.[4]

I soon saw that local advocates were canceling meetings regarding long-term strategic priorities and instead setting up community information sessions to respond to the fear of mass raids. That seemed to me to be a mistake. After all, psychological warfare is designed to shift people's focus away from the real attack. But the community's panic was genuine. So, even though I was sure that the announced raids were a mirage, I felt guilty for leaving the clinic—one of the few places that might defend a detained immigrant—with no attorney, and spending time with my family. For me, a white American who was not a target, the stressful emotion was guilt. If I were an immigrant myself, it would have been fear.

I asked my wife about cancelling our trip to Seattle. She nixed that, and we went, for which I'm grateful. But that doesn't mean I wasn't distracted while I was there or that I could focus on my kids like I should. While we were in Seattle, Maya, who was thirteen, told me frantically that her social media was blowing up, kids talking about rumors of ICE checkpoints at various street corners in Las Vegas. I tried to explain to her that it wasn't real, which led my teenage daughter to get agitated with me. This wasn't helping me to get separation from work.

On June 22, the president announced he was delaying the raids for two weeks. On July 7, Ken Cuccinelli, who had been tapped by the president to run U.S. Citizenship and Immigration Services, went on two Sunday talk shows to say that ICE was once again planning to deport "a million" people. This made no more logistical sense than it had two weeks earlier. Plus, Cuccinelli didn't even lead the agency that would carry out the supposed operation. He led USCIS, which processes applications for visas and asylum. USCIS doesn't deport anyone. Regardless, we heard that there were still supposedly 2,000 targets, including families with kids. A few activists set up a hotline—a cell phone number, really—staffed by a single lawyer and just one or two community leaders. A week passed. On July 23, the *New York Times* ran a headline: "More than 2,000 Migrants Were Targeted in Raids. 35 Were Arrested."[5]

That's thirty-five arrests across the whole country. The raids had turned out to be fiction, just as I'd thought. At the same time, the climate of racial taunting, the threats from the president, the "send her back" chants, the TV stories about children locked up behind chain-link fencing, the babies taken from mothers—all of it sent a message: This can get worse. There are no guardrails. There is no safety net. In late August 2019, immigration lawyers reported that the government was now insisting on deporting children with cancer, HIV, and epilepsy who had previously been allowed to stay to get medical treatment. Before 2017, I didn't even know there was a political constituency that wanted to deport sick children. We were falling, and there seemed to be no bottom.[6]

Even when the raids don't come, the toll is very real. Even if they know what is really going on, community groups and leaders who pride themselves on serving the concerns of real people cannot ignore community panic. Since I'm not bilingual and not Latino, I get only a taste of this. I know that when the fear is reaching my own kids' social network, it is spreading wide. I know the stress that some of my friends and colleagues felt when they got frantic calls on the phone. On one of the days I wasn't supposed to be working, I did meet a Latina activist at a café near my house after someone called the newly created hotline to report that he had seen a group of immigrant workers being loaded onto a truck outside the café. It sounded specific. It sounded like a raid. But the owner of the café said nothing at all had happened. And the lists of supposed ICE checkpoints in Las Vegas that my daughter had seen her friends spreading on social media, though mostly fiction so far as I could tell, were still getting shares and likes.

On June 24, 2019, the *Journal of the American Medical Association* (*JAMA*) published a study from California that had focused on 397 U.S.-born teenagers who had at least one Mexican immigrant parent. The teenagers had been studied in 2016, before the election, and again in 2017, a year after the election. In 2017, nearly half had worries about deportation and family separation, and they had clinically observable symptoms of anxiety and poor sleep. The next month, *JAMA* published an analysis of national birth data that found that "the 2016 US presidential election appears to have been associated with an increase in preterm births among US Latina women."[7]

Psychological warfare can wear its targets down. It will lead to burnout among community leaders. It may desensitize warning systems, so that if real raids ever come, people's defenses will be lowered, although there is a countertheory that the fear of raids has actually helped spread knowledge of civil rights among the immigrant population.

Psychological warfare also distracts. Perhaps the most accurate statement President Trump made about ICE's operations was during a White House event on July 15. "Many, many were taken out on Sunday, you just didn't know about it," he said. "You didn't see a lot of it." That is sort of true. ICE is always arresting people and always deporting people. There were 4,167 deportation cases pending against Las Vegas residents in the local Immigration Court at the end of February 2019.[8]

The image of an ICE raid, of ICE agents swarming a neighborhood and seizing a father in front of his children, is so potent, so viscerally unsettling, that it is difficult to get people to think about how ICE usually works. For ICE to directly arrest a person in the middle of an American city requires a great deal of work on the part of ICE officers. Instead, what they usually do is just persuade local police departments to hand local residents over to be deported, quietly, behind closed doors, and often in the dead of night. This is what happened to Fernando Gonzalez after he didn't pay a ticket for a non-working brake light.[9]

A national study found that

> in the last part of the Obama administration and the first part of the Trump administration, most arrests were conducted through [programs that link local arrests to immigration enforcement]. However, the proportion of arrests that resulted from the collaboration of local incarceration authorities experienced a noticeable spike under the Trump administration.[10]

The main engine for this, the Criminal Alien Program (CAP), accounted for 41 percent of ICE arrests in the first year of the Trump administration—up from 34 percent in the last year under Obama.[11]

The role of local police in ICE arrests is even more pronounced in Las Vegas than nationally. In fiscal year 2018, in Clark County, there were only 167 at-large arrests in the community by ICE. That means ICE officers made direct arrests on their own, in the field—what people normally think of when they think of an immigration raid—only a dozen or so times a month. In the same year, CAP, which operates at the Las Vegas City Jail and which likely doomed Fernando, accounted for 457 "arrests" by ICE.[12]

An even bigger number of ICE "arrests" came from the Clark County Detention Center, which is run by Clark County sheriff Joe Lombardo. That system operated under a different name—the 287(g) Program. Under this program, Las Vegas Metro police officers in the jail were deputized to work as federal ICE officers. They even wear ICE uniforms. They interview detainees and start their deportation paperwork. With the 287(g) Program, the local jail does more than just follow a request from ICE to hold a person. The local police officers actually make and process the requests themselves, in the name of ICE. They do ICE's work for them. In Clark County, the 287(g) Program accounted for 676 ICE "arrests" in 2018.[13]

Together, CAP and the 287(g) Program accounted for 83 percent of all of the "arrests" that ICE made for the year in the county. That's in line with national patterns. According to a 2019 study, four out of five deportations from the interior of the United States resulted from the person being transferred directly to ICE from another law enforcement agency. Basically, everyone who has been focused on ICE knocking on people's doors in their homes has been looking in the wrong direction. ICE was taking people out of view, just like the President said.[14]

In 2014, my former co-director at the UNLV Immigration Clinic, Fatma Marouf, began threatening to sue the Clark County sheriff—at the time, Doug Gillespie—for illegally detaining people to hand them over to ICE. She worked with the National Immigration Law Center (NILC), which is based in California. They sent letters threatening a lawsuit. They found a law firm to handle the case. They were ready to go. Then, in July 2014, Sheriff Gillespie announced that his department would no longer hold people based on ICE detainers. That didn't address the city jail, but it was a big deal. We thought we had blocked part of the deportation pipeline before Donald Trump even announced he was running for president.

It takes a great deal of work to get to the point of threatening a lawsuit against a police department like Las Vegas Metro. A small clinic like ours would struggle to handle a complex lawsuit in federal court. Instead, we try to partner with a larger organization, like the American Civil Liberties Union or NILC. But that's not enough. In the United States, an advocacy group typically cannot just sue over any policy that it opposes. A lawsuit will require a plaintiff, a person personally affected. Often, before threatening a lawsuit, months of work will have been done to screen for the best plaintiffs, and draft papers ready to file in court. All that work gets shelved when the target of the lawsuit retreats, as Sheriff Gillespie did.

Joe Lombardo took over as sheriff in January 2015, and for two years—the last two years of the Obama administration—he did nothing publicly to change the policy. In 2017, however, he fully renewed his jail's partnership with ICE, even as ICE increasingly began hunting immigrants who did not have serious criminal records. Less than a week after President Trump's inauguration, the mayor of Las Vegas, Carolyn Goodman, issued a defensive statement saying that "the City of Las Vegas . . . [is] in compliance with ICE regulations, and continue to work with federal authorities." In May 2017, the Las Vegas City Jail began using a policy calling for any foreign-born person to be reported to ICE.[15]

This process was a fog for Fernando Gonzalez when he went through it. As we've seen, the night after he pleaded guilty for not paying his brake light ticket, he was roused from bed in his cell at the Las Vegas City Jail in the early morning hours. Thinking he was going home to Reina, his pregnant fiancée who was about to give birth, and his eight-year-old daughter, he folded his sheets and got himself ready to get out of jail. But that hope ended when he saw ICE waiting for him with chains and shackles. He said to them, "Why? I was supposed to be released today."

They replied: "Were you born here?"

He answered honestly. "No."

"That's the problem," they said.

The ICE officers put Fernando in handcuffs and put chains around his waist and feet. They put him in the back of a van "with two Mexican guys" and took him to the federal building, across the street from the federal courthouse. It was still dark out when they arrived and started the paperwork. The ICE officers offered him immediate deportation. Fernando said he wanted to stay and fight his case. He tried to plead with one ICE officer that his second child was about to be born, but the officer told him he should have said that to the police who had originally arrested him for the unpaid brake light ticket.

While they waited at the downtown office, ICE gave him an old sandwich on multigrain bread and apple juice. Fernando has a very good memory for the food he was given in jail, and he is emphatic that ICE fed him better than the Las Vegas City Jail. He said that one of the meals at the city jail seemed like "dog food." Once the paperwork was done at the ICE office, he was taken to a detention center on Water Street in Henderson, a suburb of Las Vegas and the place where I first lived when I got my job at UNLV. Water Street is in the old part of Henderson, near where the Basic Magnesium factory supplied the U.S. war effort in World War II. The detention center is run by the city, allowing Henderson to subsidize its municipal budget by detaining people for ICE. People like Fernando.

Fernando estimated that he arrived at Henderson around 10:30 a.m., because he remembers it was before lunch in the jail there, which is served between 11 and 11:30. He told me that all the meals in Henderson are early. Breakfast is around 5:30 a.m., lunch at 11, and dinner around 4:30. Main meals are different every day, with a rotating weekly menu. Macaroni and cheese, chips, and a hamburger—that's one day. Vegetables, chicken, and fruit puree—that's another. A meat patty, mashed potato, and a pineapple slice—another meal. The meals are served by inmates to each other, which Fernando said improves the attitude.

Fernando does have one negative food report from Henderson, which involves a fellow detainee he calls "Jesus," because he was tall and thin with long hair and looked like paintings of Jesus. Jesus normally ate everything and was always hungry. He used to ask other people if they wanted to finish their food, and then he would eat their leftovers. One day in Henderson, "the mayonnaise was rotten." The meal that day was hamburgers, and the detainees had assembled their meat patty sandwiches before they discovered the problem. "It was like oil. It was not white. It had a bad smell," he told me. No one wanted to eat it, but the guards were rushing them and threating them that they would go without food. Then Jesus, who normally ate everything, stood up and shouted that he would not eat. He threw the food on the floor. Six officers immediately surrounded Jesus and took him away. But the guards then gave everyone else new mayonnaise. "He became a hero," Fernando said.

Fernando shared a cell with a Mexican man who was about fifty years old. Fernando tried to help him by translating the letters and papers he had gotten from the judge. The man was married to an American citizen but had no lawyer. Meanwhile, Fernando said, "I was thinking about my family. We hadn't paid the bills. I wasn't making money in jail." Reina wasn't working. They had a credit card bill. They had to pay around $1,000 a month in rent. Fortunately, his mom had bought nursery furniture for their coming baby. But that was all they had.

Reina went into labor while Fernando was detained in Henderson, and the stress of not being there for the birth was hard on him. Reina had had a difficult pregnancy. She had been sick with the flu, and a doctor had put her on a special diet. They had spent time in the hospital, and for a couple of days doctors talked to them about possibly delivering the baby by C-section at around eight months because they thought Reina had tuberculosis. She turned out not to have that illness, but while he waited, sleepless, to hear news about Reina and the baby, Fernando kept having images flash in his mind of babies being taken away from their mothers to intensive care. "You have the feeling you don't know what's going on," he said. Eventually his mother called to tell him that Reina had given birth to a daughter, whom they called Diamond. Both mother and child were healthy.

After being detained for a little under three weeks—he knows how long it was because they served ice cream once a week in Henderson, he said, and he had ice cream twice and was about to have it a third time—Fernando was released on bond, the result of a petition made by his lawyer. By law, the minimum bond that an immigration judge can set is $1,500. For Fernando, whose most serious criminal offense is an unpaid traffic ticket, the judge set bond at $2,500. Immigration bonds have to be paid in cash, too.

While he was locked up, Fernando's eight-year-old daughter didn't know where he was. "Reina lied to her. She said I was working far away. That's why I wasn't at home," Fernando told me. "She was so, so sad. She wrote me a letter. 'You know how much I miss you and I love you.' She made me cry with that letter."

He is still fighting his deportation. "We go to church. We feel very faithful, that something good will come of all this nightmare," he said. "I don't want to worry in front of my wife. But inside, I'm devastated. I can't count on my future." He worried every day. He says that Reina tells him to keep his faith up. When I talked to him, Fernando seemed to be more practical: "It's up to the judge."

Occasionally when I talked to him I saw a flash of anger, just the slightest bit. Usually when this would happen he would say, "I'm not a criminal," and talk about how he had tried on several occasions to say this to ICE officers. None of them seemed to care.

* * *

The idea of sanctuary was originally religious. In ancient Greece, temples could offer sanctuary to criminals, and the early Christian church continued this practice in medieval Europe. In essence, sanctuary offered a kind of immunity from law, but instead of immunity given to a person (like diplomatic immunity), it was immunity for anyone at a particular location. Today, the closest we have to this might be diplomatic institutions. Think of how Julian Assange, the founder of WikiLeaks, found shelter for years at the Ecuadorian embassy in London, making it impossible for the British police to arrest him.[16]

Sanctuary entered American immigration politics in the 1980s. When Central American refugees who had fled civil wars—in which the United States was a major player—came to the States, they were often denied asylum. Many churches and some synagogues offered shelter to them from the old INS, which wanted to deport them. This was civil disobedience on the part of church or synagogue members, since there was, and is, no formal legal protection for someone who stays inside a church. ICE has a "sensitive locations" policy that is supposed to restrict arrests at schools, hospitals, and places of worship, but it is just an internal policy and can be overridden by a higher official. When a church shelters someone who is wanted by the federal government, it is literally daring federal agents to storm the sanctuary. The church is protecting the person through its moral authority, not the law.[17]

In 1989, San Francisco became known as the first "sanctuary city." When applied to a city or state, the term "sanctuary" has quite a different meaning than when it is applied to a religious institution. Actually, the word does not even appear in the San Francisco Administrative Code, Sections 12H–12I, which is the set of rules that people call the "sanctuary ordinance." The ordinance says: "It is hereby affirmed that the City and County of San Francisco is a City and County of Refuge." In truth, this ordinance, and the many others that have followed it in other cities and states, offers neither sanctuary nor refuge. Unlike a Greek temple, an American city cannot legally shield anyone from federal authority. And unlike a private church, a municipality cannot engage in civil disobedience.[18]

The San Francisco use of the word "sanctuary" is a mistake, in my view, because it confuses everyone, and in the end this confusion hurts the people such efforts intend to help. I freely acknowledge that shortly after the 2016 election I added my signature to a letter calling for my university, UNLV, to become a "sanctuary campus." I signed the letter because I liked many of the policies that it called for, such as offering guidance and support to undocumented students on campus. I don't think campus police should be turning students over to immigration (and so far as I know, they aren't). At the same time, I remember a planning meeting before the letter was written where a professor from another department said, "Okay, we know we want to be a sanctuary campus. Now what do we mean?" That is my point. The "sanctuary" label is symbolic. Especially after the election of an anti-immigrant president, a sanctuary declaration is in part a way of shifting public debate. But it also raises expectations for people on all sides of the immigration debate. I have lost count of how many times I have been asked things like, "If UNLV becomes a sanctuary campus, will ICE not be able to come here?" Answer: The campus is open to the public, which means ICE can come on campus even if the president of the university hangs a sanctuary flag from her window.[19]

There is barely any legal definition of a "sanctuary city." Regardless, in his first week in office, President Trump issued an order that declared: "Sanctuary jurisdictions across the United States willfully violate Federal law in an attempt to shield aliens from removal from the United States." The only definition contained in that order referred to Section 1373 of the Immigration and Nationality Act, which says that a local or state government "may not prohibit, or in any way restrict, any government entity or official from sending to, or receiving from, the [Department of Homeland Security] information regarding the citizenship or immigration status, lawful or unlawful, of any individual." Usually this is relevant when someone is booked into a local jail. But while local governments cannot prohibit information about a detainee's immigration status from being sent to ICE, they are not required to go out of their way to tell ICE about the people in their jails. They should answer questions on citizenship and immigration, if asked, and if they have the information. But they do not need to hold detainees for extra time for ICE, and they do not need to tell ICE when someone is scheduled to be released. When local police and jails help ICE, they are doing it on their own account, and entirely voluntarily.[20]

Broadly speaking, there are two kinds of policies that get talked about as forms of "sanctuary." The first is when a local government offers services to immigrants. The San Francisco ordinance, for example, prohibits city agencies from asking about immigration status when determining eligibility for any benefits and services. That means that an undocumented immigrant gets treated the same as anyone else when applying for a program run by the city. Another version of this would be to actually offer proactive services aimed specifically at helping immigrants. Yet there is no need to use the "sanctuary" label to do that. For instance, the University of Nevada, Reno, and UNLV have hired resource coordinators to assist undocumented immigrants in finding services to help them get through college. In 2018, our clinic began a pilot project, led by Mayra Salinas-Menjivar, to offer immigration legal aid to students, staff, and their families. In 2019, we expanded that project to the College of Southern Nevada. But none of these educational institutions call themselves "sanctuary" campuses.[21]

The second meaning often attributed to "sanctuary" policies has to do with cooperation with ICE, and this is what the Trump administration cares most about. The original San Francisco ordinance prohibited local government and police from assisting in immigration enforcement. It is very important to be clear both about what this means and about what it *does not* mean. It does not mean that ICE cannot arrest people in San Francisco. It does mean that local police and government do not help them in all cases. It means that when people are arrested on a minor offense in San Francisco, they shouldn't be turned over to ICE. However, that does not mean local police cannot cooperate with ICE when doing so makes sense for local priorities. Despite its reputation as the quintessential sanctuary city, the San Francisco ordinance allows police to cooperate with ICE if they arrest a person who has a history of violent or serious felonies.[22]

We actually have some data showing that in cities and states that do not cooperate with ICE, ICE has to do more of its own work and this slows down the pace of deportations. For example, consider New York County, New York—aka Manhattan. In fiscal year 2018, ICE made 887 at-large arrests there, compared to only 167 in Clark County, Nevada. But ICE actually arrested fewer people overall in Manhattan than in Clark County: 1,373 in Clark County compared to 1,113 in Manhattan. The reason for this seems to be that the local police don't hand people over so easily in New York. ICE took only 89 people through the Criminal Alien Program operating in conjunction with local jails in Manhattan, for example. The same pattern occurs in Cook County, Illinois, where there were 1,334 ICE arrests in total in 2018—roughly the same as in the Las Vegas area, despite having a population more than twice as large. In Cook County, ICE makes about half of its arrests at large. When ICE has to do more of its own work, fewer people get deported.[23]

By contrast, the City of Las Vegas has a policy of active cooperation with ICE, for minor offenses as well as for major crimes. That is why Fernando was in detention when his second daughter was born, and why he is now facing the very real prospect of deportation. The Las Vegas Department of Public Safety runs the jail where Fernando was held after being arrested for not paying his traffic ticket. The department's policy states:

> When a person identified as being foreign born has been arrested and booked, the Law Enforcement Support Technician (LEST) will fax information regarding the inmate to an Immigration and Customs Enforcement and Removal Operations (ICE/ERO) agent.[24]

That is a breathtaking policy, especially in a city that has whole neighborhoods in which more than a third of the population is foreign-born. Remember two things here. First, not every foreign-born person is an undocumented immigrant. Not even most of them. Most are citizens or legal residents. My own daughters are foreign-born. Second, no federal law requires a city to actively report anyone to ICE. At most, federal law requires disclosing immigration information about a person if the city has the information and ICE asks for it. That's what Section 1373 says. But the City of Las Vegas policy says that whenever a foreign-born person is arrested, the jail will report that individual directly to an ICE agent. That's what would happen to my daughters if they are ever arrested, even for the most minor infraction. And that appears to be what happened to Fernando when he was in the city jail.

The facts about so-called sanctuary policies rarely seem to matter. I once had an argument with a mom who was waiting with me while my daughter took an extracurricular class. She said, "Las Vegas is a sanctuary city, so ICE isn't allowed to operate here." That isn't even remotely true, but that didn't stop her from being outraged about it. I told her that ICE can and does operate in Las Vegas, and that by no one's definition was Las Vegas a sanctuary city. She told me I didn't know what I was talking about. I replied that I teach immigration law at UNLV. Her rejoinder: "I am really surprised they let you do that because you seem to know so little about what's really happening." And so it goes.

The policies of the City of Las Vegas went beyond reporting people to ICE. When ICE found out about Fernando, they issued something called a detainer to the Las Vegas City Jail. A detainer is just a request to the jail to hold a person up to forty-eight hours extra and to notify ICE about release times so that ICE can take the person upon release. That is most likely how ICE knew to show up in the early morning hours on the day when Fernando thought he was going home. This is how ICE arrests so many people in Las Vegas even though its agents rarely make an arrest on their own in the field. The reason Fernando is facing deportation is that the City of Las Vegas handed him over. By choice.

PART III
THE DEFENSE

7

How to Talk to Your Neighbors About Immigration

I HAD TO TAKE my Elantra in for repairs. This meant that I needed to summon an Uber to drive me to work. This was during the spring of 2019. The driver was a middle-aged white man, probably older than me. He knew I was headed to the university, and he asked me if I'm a professor. I said yes. Then he asked me what I teach. I said I teach in the law school. And then he asked me what kind of law.

This is always a moment of decision for me. If I am tired, or if I just want to look at my phone, I can say, "I teach administrative law." That's honest. Administrative law is a class I teach. If I go that route, the conversation is over. No one wants to talk to me about administrative law. But this day, I did the brave thing.

"I teach immigration law," I said.

"Well, if you ask me," the driver said, "I only have problems with the ones who do it illegal."

Okay, here we go. This is what I asked for. I knew it was coming, and I thought this would be a good way to spend my twenty minutes in the car. Maybe, one white man talking to another white man, I could get him to open his eyes a little to what I saw in the community where we both lived. And maybe I would understand a little more the feelings of people who, in my mind, were making life so hard for so many.

"Yeah, okay," I said. "But you know, it's not easy to come legally. A lot of people don't realize—"

The driver cut me off. "Sure, but we all have to follow the law, right? You're a law professor, right? Don't you want people to follow the law?" And he wasn't done. "Don't get me wrong! I'm married to a Mexican. I love Mexicans. Beautiful. I love the women, obviously!"

Oh my. At this point, I tried to recalculate. As a progressive white man, should I keep engaging on immigration, should I push back on the objectification of women, or should I find some way to capture the intersectionality of the moment in a single pithy remark, like Alexandria Ocasio-Cortez probably would? Should I demand that he stop the car and let me out on the side of the highway so that I could walk to work in a fit of outrage, or should I just say I don't want to talk anymore and stare at my iPhone?

I tried to keep my courage. "You know," I said, "most of the undocumented immigrants in Las Vegas have been here for ten years or more. If someone came illegally, and then they raise a family, paid taxes—"

The driver interrupted again. "Okay, but the border now. All these people, should we take everyone?"

"The people fleeing violence?" I asked.

"Should we just save all South America?"

The influx of women and children at the border was, for the most part, not from South America. The people were mostly from three countries: Guatemala, Honduras, and El Salvador. All three are in Central America. But I know that's not the point. A challenge in these conversations is to not quibble over the minor facts. I have no reason to think that this man's opinions would be any different if the United States were in fact experiencing an influx from Peru or Ecuador.

"You know, it's legal to seek asylum," I said. If my driver were true to his initial objection only to immigrants who "do it illegal," then my factual statement about asylum law should have settled the matter. But of course, the law is not really the point, either.

"We shouldn't take everyone," he said. "We can't save the whole world."

Since the 2016 election, there's been a lot of journalistic effort spent trying to understand people like my Uber driver. In the quintessential article, a journalist from New York City goes to a diner in Indiana, talks to some people, and writes an article about what we should have known before November 2016. It's not that they're racist, these articles seem to say. They're just frustrated. It's unemployment. It's a hometown in decline. It's opioids.

Thomas B. Edsall, a *New York Times* columnist, has highlighted research indicating that white Americans don't really oppose a large immigrant population, at least not in those terms. The places where anti-immigrant sentiment is most intense are places where the immigrant community remains relatively small but has increased most rapidly. The strongest pro-immigrant sentiment is in big cities, where the immigrant populations are the largest. When Americans live among many immigrants, they typically end up liking immigrants. In other words, it's not as if there is really such a thing as too many immigrants in a community. However, when white Americans in places where they are used to mostly seeing other white Americans suddenly see a few people who are different . . . well, some people are apprehensive about it.[1]

USA Today has calculated something called the Diversity Index, a number from 0 to 100 that rates the chances that if two people in a particular zip code are chosen at random, they will be from different races. The higher the number, the greater the diversity in that area. Clark County, Nevada, which includes Las Vegas, has an index of 72, exactly the same as Cook County, Illinois, which includes Chicago. Los Angeles is 78. The Bronx, 81. Basically, what USA Today is asking is this: "What is the chance that the next person I meet will be different from me?" In Las Vegas, and in most of these big cities, the chance that a random person next to me will be racially different from me is high.[2]

Edsall points out that places like Erie County, Pennsylvania, have a Diversity Index much lower than the big cities—just 29 for Erie. The United States as a whole is almost twice as diverse as Erie County. But Erie County is changing rapidly. The chances that a white person will randomly meet a non-white person rose from 19 to 29 percent in twenty years. Meanwhile, Erie County—which used to vote for Democrats, including Barack Obama—swung to Trump in 2016. Anti-immigrant sentiment is especially strong there, even though the county still doesn't really have a large immigrant population.[3]

I've read lots of material like this, and it has not necessarily helped me be more effective in talking to people like my Uber driver. For a while after the ride, I wondered if there was some different talking point I should have tried. Later, I came up with other things that I wish I had said to my Uber driver. For instance: If you discovered that the contractor who built your subdivision had hired undocumented workers to install the drywall—as is likely the case if you live in Las Vegas or Phoenix and your house was built in the last quarter century—would you then rip the drywall from the studs and tell your neighbors to do the same? Why not? Was it not built in violation of the law? Are you not living between illegal walls built by people who came here illegally? If you think this sounds absurd, well, then why would you rip apart the family of the man who built it for you? Why do we target only the people, and not the products of their work that make our lives more comfortable?

I wish I had said that. But I didn't. Instead, I tried to persuade him. I tried to be less confrontational. We were just two white men talking in an Uber—and

I imagine that's why he talked to me at all. I have a law degree and high status, and I am comfortable with immigration and diversity. He was older than me, driving an Uber for a living, and he was harsh on immigration. He doesn't want asylum-seekers from "South America" to be allowed in. And I didn't know what I could say to change any of that. After twenty-five minutes in the car, I arrived at work. We had failed to bridge the canyon dividing the United States. I felt dirty for having participated in the conversation. And, of course, his side of the argument was running the country.

I am often asked by people who are sympathetic to immigrants for advice on what to say when talking to someone much more resistant. The truth is, I don't always know. Part of the problem is that the way people react to immigrants and immigration—whether they are for or against—is often visceral. I am especially alarmed by public opinion research showing that anti-immigrant sentiment often can't easily be reasoned with. For example, Democracy Corps and the Roosevelt Institute conducted focus groups in Macomb County, Michigan, after the 2016 election. Macomb had voted twice for Obama, and then voted in 2016 for Trump. The focus groups included people expressing anger about hearing Spanish spoken in grocery store checkout lines. I don't get this. I really don't. I fail to grasp how someone speaking another language to another person affects me, unless I'm trying to eavesdrop on their conversation, which is creepy.[4]

The Macomb County focus groups also elicited a statement from a woman who said she hoped that President Trump will "fix our healthcare situation, but that comes back to the immigrants." She said:

> I went and finally signed up for Medicaid, and I'm standing in the damn welfare office, and I'm looking around at all of these people that can't even say hello to me in English. But they're all there with appointments for their workers, which means they have the healthcare, they have the food stamps . . . If you can come from somewhere else, why can't we all get it?

You could try to respond to this as a serious point about healthcare policy. There is no real reason to think that immigrants caused any important problem in the American healthcare system. If anything, young immigrant workers will be necessary to both staff and pay for the services to cover the health needs of America's otherwise aging population. There is more going on, obviously. The woman who said this in a focus group was describing a low point in her life: *I'm standing in the damn welfare office.* To be there was humiliation. At this moment, she saw other people—probably immigrants, but all she knew was that they didn't speak in English. They didn't say hello to her. To be clear, white, English-speaking Americans do not always say hello to each other, either. But it got under her skin. By implication, this woman probably did not get the help she wanted from the office. She assumed that these other people speaking in another language must be causing some unspecified problem, her unspecified problem. And she seemed to think that *they* were implicitly taking something that should have gone to her. *They have the healthcare, they have the food stamps.*

We can empathize with the woman who is saying this. We can, and we should, try to address whatever it is that led her to finally walk into that welfare office that day. But we can't let her off the hook, either. Whatever was happening to her, she projected it onto a group of strangers. We cannot run from the fact that at moments of vulnerability, some Americans are prone to blame people who are different from them, mainly because they are different and in the wrong place at the wrong time. The tragedy is made worse by the fact that the people this woman resented so intensely were different only in certain ways. If she had taken a moment to think about it, it should have been clear that they were probably also not experiencing the best of times. They, too, were in the damn welfare office.

We're caught in a trap.

Nevertheless, the report that includes these focus group interviews is actually optimistic, looking at all of the data. It concludes: "Many [voters] are put out of reach by their racist sentiment, Islamophobia, and disdain for multiculturalism. . . . But a great many are not. Most support legal immigration, many are open to a multicultural America." The report emphasizes that a significant number of the people interviewed went to great lengths to say they supported legal immigration. They may be open to conversation.

So here is a little guide, the best that I can offer, on how to answer some common statements people make in good faith about immigration.

Why don't they come legally?

The answer to this question begins with understanding that for nearly all undocumented immigrants there was no legal pathway to the United States. The people in this book illustrate this—Adelina and her parents, Manuela and Olivero; Ines and Rebeca; Fernando; even Cecia, who entered legally but quickly overstayed her visa. There was no other way any of them could have done it.

The lack of a legal pathway is really only a partial answer, but it is an important issue for many people. Politicians and much of the media focus on a binary line—legal immigrants and illegal immigrants. I continue to believe that this is important for many Americans for a very good reason: we believe in the rule of law. We like rules to be followed—mostly, anyway. However, the expectation that we should follow the law, more or less, assumes several things that may not be true in immigration law. We assume that our law at its core is fair, that it does not discriminate, that it is proportionate—imposing large consequences for big transgressions and small consequences for smaller mistakes. Most of all, we assume that the law can be followed. If immigration law fit this description, I would join other Americans in being skeptical of people who choose an unlawful path. But I can't judge someone for failing to follow the law if following the law is impossible.

While undocumented immigrants typically don't have an option to immigrate legally, the law does give them an option: don't come. President Trump has said as much. He reportedly once yelled at his Secretary of Homeland Security, "We're closed!" But it is interesting that even Trump usually only says things this harsh in private. It is one thing to say, in the abstract, that immigrants should come by following the law. But it is quite another to look someone like Fernando or Adelina or Cecia in the eye and say: "We don't want people like you." To most people, this sounds hateful, because it is. But that's actually what the law says. Sometimes people who say they only object to "illegal immigration" are masking the reality that they're really against immigrants, at least those not from Europe. But I still draw a little hope from the evident desire to mask this sentiment. People feel there is shame in saying such things. I also believe that many Americans are genuinely willing to accept immigrants but want the system to be governed by logical rules and are confused about why it seems so chaotic and lawless.[5]

I asked Nevada senator Catherine Cortez Masto—a senator who has become increasingly outspoken in defense of immigrants—how she responds when people object that immigrants are breaking the law. She confirmed that she gets variations of that question at town halls around Nevada. She did not answer with anything technical about how immigration law works in the real world. "It starts with knowing members in your community," she said. "The more you get educated about the real life of people in your community. These are our neighbors, who you may know or not. And if you don't know them you should get to know them."

Think about someone like Fernando, the Guatemalan handyman with the broken brake light. He came to Las Vegas to be with his mother, because she wanted him to come. He has two children and is a loving spouse. He and his wife were brought together in America, after the poverty and turmoil of their village in Guatemala sent their families in different directions. He makes his living working in other people's houses. Americans, at an individual level, trust him. They hire him and they bring him into their homes to do his work. But immigration law offers him nothing. No path. If the law is applied strictly—which is what ICE is trying to do—he will be taken from his daughters, his wife, and his home because thirteen years ago he came to the United States illegally.

Maybe the problem is with the law, not with the man.

Don't we still have to enforce the rules? They broke the rules

No one would really want the government to strictly and rigidly enforce every single law in every single case. Everyone who has ever had a traffic cop let them go with a warning knows this. As a general rule in our system, the government has wide discretion to enforce rules to avoid harsh, cruel, and disproportionate consequences. We do it all the time.

For white-collar crime, it is explicitly part of Department of Justice policy to not enforce every law with maximum force when doing so would do more harm than good. Before prosecuting a corporation for wrongdoing, federal prosecutors are required to consider "collateral consequences, including whether there is disproportionate harm to shareholders, pension holders, employees, and others not proven personally culpable." To some extent, all immigrants are asking for is the same consideration that the federal government gives to corporations. The law may allow ICE to detain and deport undocumented immigrants. But is it too much to ask that ICE consider the impact that doing this would have on their children, on schools, on churches, on the communities in which they live?[6]

A colleague of mine, Mark Kuczewski, teaches medical ethics at the Loyola University School of Medicine in Chicago, where he started a program to admit DACA beneficiaries to medical school. When he talks about immigration, he asks people to imagine a scenario: You failed to come to a complete stop at a stop sign on your way to a job interview. You got the job as a result of that interview, and since then you've been promoted twice. You met your spouse at work, and now you have children together. Now imagine that ten years later a police officer comes to your door. The authorities have discovered your failure to stop at that stop sign, way back then. There is a warrant for your arrest. You offer to pay a fine, but the officer says that won't be enough. You also will lose your job and be taken from your spouse and your children. In fact, everything you've built in your life after failing to stop at that stop sign is now illegitimate and must be taken away. That is immigration law when it is enforced rigidly, with no sense of proportion or discretion.

They don't pay taxes and the government gives them benefits

These two issues really boil down a suspicion that undocumented immigrants are cheating the system somehow. This suspicion makes sense if a person also is under the impression that undocumented immigrants could have come to the country legally if they wanted to. Thus there must be some reason why they chose to come the illegal way, as if being undocumented is the equivalent of having an offshore bank account to evade taxes and regulations.

Here are the facts: Immigrants pay lots of taxes, and they get fewer benefits than citizens (undocumented immigrants in particular). I often find that people are surprised when I tell them that undocumented immigrants pay taxes, and I am surprised they are surprised. Property taxes and sales taxes are the most straightforward. There are seven states that have no income tax at all, including Nevada, Washington, Florida, and Texas, which all have particularly large undocumented immigrant populations. In these states, sales and property taxes are basically the whole ballgame. When you buy a television set or a car, you pay a lot of sales tax, and the cashier does not ask you for your immigration papers. Same with property taxes. You pay directly if you own a house, or indirectly in your rent if you don't. The tax collector doesn't care about your immigration papers. The government just wants your money.

The Institute on Taxation and Economic Policy calculated the numbers for each state in 2017. (To look up how much tax revenue your state collects from undocumented immigrants, check the ITEP website: https://itep.org /immigration.) Nationally, the roughly 11 million undocumented immigrants in the United States pay $11.7 billion in state and local taxes every year. California alone collects $3.2 billion from undocumented immigrants. Texas gets $1.6 billion. And this is just state and local taxes.

Income and payroll taxes are bit more complicated, but only a bit. Most of us pay our income taxes (federal or state) and social security/Medicare taxes through withholding on our paychecks. I imagine that this is where people may be confused about undocumented immigrants and taxes. Undocumented immigrants usually aren't authorized to be employed in the first place. If they do get a normal wage-earning job, they likely used a fake social security number. Employers are not required to verify social security numbers, but they will still withhold the regular taxes from paychecks. The result is that the Internal Revenue Service collects billions of dollars every year in social security taxes every year from mismatched social security numbers. (One of my col-leagues at UNLV Law, Francine Lipman, is a national authority on this. In one of her articles, she reported that the IRS collected $9 billion in mismatched social security and Medicare taxes in 2005.)

Having a social security number is only a very rough indicator of someone's immigration status. An immigrant needs employment authorization to get a social security number. But once you have a number, you keep it, so even if an immigrant's legal status expires, she keeps her valid social security number. Even if an immigrant is not eligible for a social security number, she can apply to the IRS for an Individual Taxpayer Identification Number (ITIN) to file a tax return.

The murkiest part of undocumented immigrant taxpaying is probably self-employment, which is obviously important for a population not legally em-ployable in a job with a normal payroll. Many people pay taxes by using ITINs, but it is difficult to find a good estimate of how much. According to the Bipar-tisan Policy Center, in 2010 the IRS received more than 3 million returns filed with ITINs. Many people using an ITIN could probably make their money outside the official system if they wanted to, so this is a positive sign about in-come tax compliance generally. Still, do some undocumented immigrants who work independently cleaning houses or installing drywall fail to report their income to the IRS? For sure, yes, just as citizens don't always report their income to the IRS. How much money does the federal treasury lose, though? It's important to remember that people at the lower end of the income scale don't pay much in income taxes anyway. The standard deduction for a married couple in 2018 was $24,000, and the lowest tax bracket is just 10 percent. That means that a married couple living on $30,000 in income will owe only about $600 in federal income taxes. An undocumented immigrant family at that in-come level doesn't have much tax burden to evade even if they wanted to.[7]

Now, let's talk about federal benefits. Federal law generally groups non-citizens into two groups: "qualified immigrants" and "not qualified." Quali-fied immigrants are basically legal permanent residents, refugees, and victims of human trafficking. Undocumented immigrants are "not qualified." So are many people who are legally in the country but who are here temporarily, like students and tourists. The Department of Health and Human Services has published a list of thirty-one federal programs for which not-qualified immi-grants are not eligible. These include Medicare and Medicaid, the Children's Health Insurance Program (CHIP), and Temporary Assistance to Needy Families (TANF, also known as "welfare"). Undocumented immigrants can-not get health insurance subsidies under the Affordable Care Act (ACA). In fact, they are not even allowed to buy private insurance with their own money on the state exchanges that the ACA set up.

There are exceptions, of course—especially for emergency medical care and immunizations. Some states have decided to offer health insurance to un-documented immigrants, independent of the federal government, in the same way that some states have raised their minimum wage above the federal mini-mum. California has done this with health insurance, for example. Most states have not. Remember, also, that undocumented immigrants pay more than $3 billion in state and local taxes in California.

They're taking our jobs

Let me start by saying I'm not an economist. Here's what I understand: As a long-term investment, being open to immigrants is a great deal for the United States. In the short term, immigrant labor is beneficial, too—but the picture might be more complicated, in that immigrants probably do compete with citizens for low-skilled jobs, at least sometimes. But that does not mean that immigrants actually lower incomes for citizens. Nor does it mean that kicking immigrants out would improve the economy for everyone else. In fact, a large influx of immigrant workers is probably a sign of an economic boom. That's very much the story of Las Vegas, where the immigrant population exploded over the last thirty years as the overall population—and the overall economy—exploded, too.

Before I dive into data, I think it's important to acknowledge that individual people don't experience the economy the way economists analyze the economy. As individuals, we apply for jobs, one at a time. We've probably all been frustrated at least once when we didn't get a job we really wanted, a job we thought was a really good fit. If you actually see the person who got the job instead, it's hard not to feel bitter about it. It's hard not to think: They liked her more than me. And if that person is different in race or gender, well, it's easy to see how racial or gender-based resentments might deepen. I confess that, as a white man, I've been in many conversations with friends, family, or colleagues where someone claimed not to have gotten a job because "they really wanted a [woman/person of color]." I haven't always objected. In fact, I rarely have. I'm not proud of that. I haven't said, Well, there are reasons the employer may have thought that other person was more qualified than you. That feels rude to say, especially to a family member or friend. We all sometimes need to be able to make excuses, even lame ones, to keep our self-confidence up so we can go on to apply for the next job. But when the excuse targets a minority group, things can get dangerous for a diverse society like ours.

When we compete for a single job, "the economy" feels like the Hunger Games. It's a battle for a single, scarce resource. But one job application is not the economy. When someone gets a job at, say, UNLV, she also ends up shopping at nearby stores, she gets her hair cut, she takes her kids out to eat, she hires a babysitter every so often, she pays a person to clean her house, and so on. From one job at one institution, you have money circulating among a bunch of other people, some of whom save up to buy their own houses, some of whom get married and have kids who will eventually need to go to college, and over the long run there are more and more jobs available at UNLV. Here's how the Hoover Institution, a conservative think tank, explains it:

> Simplistic appeals to economic logic, gilded with nativist assumptions, hint that the arrival of millions of immigrant workers cannot help but compete for a finite number of American-based jobs. When labor supply rises, Econ 101 says that wages fall, right? Wrong. The problem with this kind of approach is that it ignores the dynamic nature of the US economy.[8]

When an influx of immigrant workers arrives in an area, it may look like there is more overall competition for jobs. In economist-speak, the labor supply is rising. But that's only part of the picture. The number of jobs available is likely to be rising as well, which is probably why immigrants and other workers are coming to that area to begin with. That is why, overall, higher levels of immigration correlate with overall wage growth, even though it looks like individual immigrants are competing for individual jobs with citizens. Basically, you want to be in a job market that immigrants want to come to.[9]

Here is a deeply troubling fact, which may explain some of the intense division about immigration in the United States today: the Great Recession seems to have hurt native-born workers more than foreign-born workers. More specifically, immigrants recovered in terms of employment and wages faster after the recession ended. According to the Pew Hispanic Trust, "In the year following the official end of the Great Recession in June 2009, foreign-born workers gained 656,000 jobs while native-born workers lost 1.2 million." This is a racial divide that is hard to ignore, especially in view of the anti-immigrant campaign that we now know Donald Trump would launch just a few years later. During that first year after the recession, foreign-born Hispanics gained 435,000 jobs. Non-Hispanic whites *lost* nearly 1 million jobs over the same period.[10]

Why would foreign-born workers appear to be recovering from the recession when native-born workers were still basically in recession? Pew attributed it to something pretty obvious: immigrants are willing to migrate. As a Pew researcher put it:

> One factor might be greater flexibility on the part of immigrants. Research by others suggests that immigrants are more mobile than native-born workers, moving more fluidly across regions, industries and occupations.[11]

The immigration process, whether legal or illegal, draws people who are extremely adaptable, and obviously it attracts people who are willing to relocate. It is hardly surprising that a person who has already moved from Mexico to Los Angeles will be willing to move to Las Vegas on a moment's notice if word comes that a job is available. At a time of rapid economic change, this flexibility is a tremendous advantage. However, it's not that immigrants are directly taking jobs from native-born American citizens. Rather, they're reacting faster to new jobs being created in new places. A construction worker in Phoenix is not in direct competition with a factory worker in Wisconsin. It's also important to keep in mind that in 2010, the year after the recession was officially declared over, the unemployment rate for immigrant workers was still roughly twice as high as it was native-born workers. To blame low-wage immigrants for the hardships of low-wage native-born citizens is to pit the weak against the weak, with a dangerous dose of racism.[12]

A better approach, in the first place, would probably be to protect workers, period. Rather than worry that immigrant competition will marginally reduce the lowest wages from $11 an hour to $10.35 (or whatever the supposed effect might be), raise the minimum wage for everyone to $15. More to the point: If we're worried at all about immigrants undercutting citizens in the workplace, the best thing to do is make sure no one is working in the shadow economy. Undocumented immigrants are the easiest workers to exploit, which also means they are the worst kind of competition for citizens.

We have a recent experiment on what would happen if the government suddenly gave a large group of undocumented immigrants access to legal employment. After President Obama initiated the DACA program in 2012, the Center for American Progress studied the impact that obtaining employment authorization had for the young adults who benefited. According to a 2017 survey, "the average hourly wage of respondents increased by 69 percent since receiving DACA, rising from $10.29 per hour to $17.46 per hour." That's a lot. A very large percentage—56 percent—said they had changed jobs to improve their working conditions, which is extremely important if we are concerned that exploited immigrants will undercut other workers. Just as important, DACA recipients engaged in the kind of activity that economists like best—the kind that generates income and jobs for other people. One in twenty people who received DACA had started a business, significantly higher than the national entrepreneurship rate (which is 3.1 percent). Sixty-five percent bought their first car. That's obviously good for the auto industry, but it also means a lot of sales tax revenue for states and cities. Sixteen percent bought a house—think of Rebeca, who promised her mother that she would buy her a house, and did. They bought in an area where the local government specifically wanted to encourage home ownership and renovation. That raises property values for everyone—and property taxes that support local schools.[13]

We have to get rid of criminals

If you want to find consensus on immigration between Democrats and Republicans, call for the deportation of immigrants who have violent criminal records. Sen. Cortez Masto told me that when she was state attorney general (during the Bush and Obama administrations), she worked to integrate immigration enforcement more with community policing for exactly this purpose. That's not something that would generate enthusiasm among pro-immigrant activists. But she told me: "That was working." She stressed that the cooperation was "based on priorities." Screening people who are arrested by police for possible deportation makes sense, in isolation, if you want immigration enforcement to focus on people who have a criminal record. But prioritization is key, because police don't only arrest people for violent felonies. They also arrest people who not paying speeding tickets.

To be clear, there is debate about whether linking law enforcement with immigration enforcement is a good idea. Even some police groups—including the Major Cities Chiefs [Police] Association and International Association of Chiefs of Police—have expressed doubts about the increasing entanglement of local law enforcement and immigration because it is likely to undermine trust in the police among immigrant communities. Moreover, if I or a member of my family were a victim of serious crime, I don't think I would care about the offender's immigration status any more than I would care whether he filed his taxes on time. To me and many others, immigration status is a peripheral matter. But that's not how it plays out in politics.[14]

For example, in January 2019, Wilber Ernesto Martinez-Guzman, an undocumented Salvadoran immigrant, was charged with four murders in the northern Nevada town of Gardnerville. The murders are difficult to comprehend. He killed a couple in their eighties, a seventy-four-year-old woman, and another woman in her fifties. He later apparently tried to pawn jewelry belonging to the victims. His only previous record, apparently, was a speeding ticket. President Trump tweeted about the murders, claiming they showed the need for his border wall: "Four people in Nevada viciously robbed and killed by an illegal immigrant who should not have been in our Country." The *Las Vegas Review-Journal* headline was this: "Suspected Undocumented Immigrant Pawned Jewelry after Northern Nevada Killings, Police Say." Yet the police did not really quite say that. "His status with immigration is not a major contributing factor here," Carson City sheriff Ken Furlong said, according to the same *Review-Journal* article.[15]

Murders like this are rare, but they are so gruesome and terrifying that they can shape public debate. Our brains are wired to remember stories better than abstract facts. We also want to find explanations for incomprehensible tragedies. But there are many facts that could be learned about people accused of violent crimes. Do they have credit card debt? Do they eat fresh vegetables, or only fast food? How often do they talk to their parents? Did they struggle in school, and did the schools address their difficulties? Why fixate on the immigration question?

If there is any non-xenophobic logic here, it's probably the theory that a person who breaks one law—the Immigration and Nationality Act—may be more likely to break other laws. But this doesn't really hold up to a moment's thought. If I told you that I claim business expenses on my taxes that I really shouldn't, or that I never come to a full stop at a stop sign, does that tell you anything about my propensity to commit armed robbery? Of course not. In fact, if anything, being an immigrant makes a person statistically *less* likely to commit crimes of all types. A Cato Institute study of Texas crime data found that

> in 2017, illegal immigrants were 47 percent less likely to be convicted
> of a crime than native-born Americans and legal immigrants were about
> 65 percent less likely to be convicted of a crime than native-born
> Americans. . . . This result holds in just about every case, including
> homicide, sex crimes, larceny, and most other crimes.[16]

Another study has found that communities with larger undocumented immigrant populations tend to have lower crime rates.[17]

Immigration status just doesn't have much to do with common crime, and there's no real reason to think that it should. Might someone cross the border illegally because he is engaged in drug smuggling? Maybe, but that's not a terribly smart way to smuggle drugs, because Customs and Border Protection will be hunting you with aircraft and infrared cameras. Might someone crossing the border illegally be desperate to escape violence or find a way to support an impoverished family? Much more likely. The good news is that, according to a Pew poll in 2018, 65 percent of Americans do not think that undocumented immigrants are more likely than other people to commit serious crimes.[18]

The trouble is that the isolated but vivid, awful stories will keep coming. There are close to 11 million undocumented immigrants in the country. If even a tiny fraction of them commit serious crimes, there will be enough stories for every demagogic politician who needs to make a speech.

The good news in politics—as far as I can tell—is that while Americans want security and order on the border, most don't think immigrants are bad for their communities. In a CNN poll in June 2019, only 15 percent said that "deporting all people living in the U.S. illegally" should be a top priority. Eight in ten said that "developing a plan to allow some people living in the United States illegally to become legal residents" should be the top priority. Eight in ten.[19]

They should speak English

When asked in a 2017 poll if they agree with the statement that they are "not bothered by people who don't speak English," 56 percent of Americans say no. Apparently, Americans are bothered by this.[20]

I can't really think of any situation where it is appropriate to object to other people speaking in a different language to each other. My great-grandparents spoke Yiddish and, I would imagine, some Polish and Russian. Now my whole family speaks only English, and I kind of regret we forgot Yiddish. Not surprisingly, the longer immigrants are in the United States, the more they speak English. And not surprisingly, recently arrived immigrants are less likely to speak English. A study of immigrants in California found that about half of immigrants who arrived in the last ten years do not speak English well, and about a fifth don't speak English at all. But in the second generation—people with a foreign-born parent—only 4 percent don't speak English well.[21]

Still, this is a concern about immigrants that just will never go away, whether people are upset about Yiddish and Italian in 1920, or Spanish and Chinese today. Perhaps for some people this is a genuine, if somewhat paternalistic, concern. It is good for immigrants to learn English, and I would be happy to have some of my tax dollars pay for English classes. Since I only speak English myself, I love it when some of the clients we represent in our clinic gradually learn English and eventually end up talking to me without an interpreter. But I know learning foreign languages is hard. I have failed at it myself. I don't think immigrants in the United States need anyone to tell them that it is important to learn English. In one survey, 96 percent of foreign-born Latinos think that teaching English to children of immigrants is important.[22]

Too often, the objection isn't really that immigrants don't speak English, but rather that they don't speak only English. Immigrant families often speak other languages at home. I see this when I pick up my daughters at friends' houses. Often their moms talk to the kids in Spanish (or, in the case of one friend, French). The reason for this varies. Sometimes it is because the mom isn't comfortable in English. More often it is because the foreign language is the language of intimacy and family. What is consistent is that the kids sass back in English. As a dad, I am somewhat comforted to know that the sound of a frustrated parent trying to get a preteen to do something is the same in all languages.

In 2018, the Equal Employment Opportunities Commission sued the Albertsons supermarket chain. According to the complaint, at one of its branches near San Diego, managers prohibited employees from speaking Spanish to each other. This seems to be about repressing people's identity and suppressing an asset they often have that people like me don't: being bilingual. Maybe it's about people in the majority put in the unfamiliar position of feeling left out, of not understanding something in their own country.[23]

So here's the best answer: Stop listening to other people's conversations, and go about your business.

We should bring immigrants based on merit

It is very common for Americans to think that we should try to engineer migration to bring in the best people. In one poll, 79 percent agreed that immigration priorities "should be based on a person's ability to contribute to America," compared to only 21 percent who chose "having relatives in the U.S." The Trump administration has promoted the idea of "merit-based immigration," which loosely means taking people who have special educational backgrounds and skills that are needed in the United States.[24]

Calls for merit-based immigration are insidious. In the hands of President Trump, "merit" often just seems to mean more immigrants from Norway, fewer from Haiti and El Salvador. In August 2019, the Trump administration published a new rule to prohibit immigration by people who are likely to become a "public charge," even if they have never received government benefits in the past. In the morning on August 13, 2019, Acting Director of Citizenship and Immigration Services Ken Cuccinelli told NPR that he supported the idea of "Give me your tired and your poor who can stand on their own two feet, and who will not become a public charge." Then, when asked later in the day on CNN about his rewriting of the famous Emma Lazarus poem inscribed on the base of the Statue of Liberty, Cuccinelli said: "Well, of course that poem was referring back to people coming from Europe where they had class-based societies."[25]

Even without this overt favoritism for European immigrants, "merit" is a problematic concept. It smacks of social engineering and a government master-planning the economy, Soviet-style. Normally, we assume that if the economy needs more computer scientists, over time more people will choose to pursue that profession. Merit-based immigration positions a federal agency as the arbiter, decreeing that we need this kind of person and in what number. We already have aspects of this in our employment-based immigration system, and it is expensive and inefficient. Immigrant lives often involve many changes of career as people adapt to the economy in which they are living. We would probably not want to expand a system in which such choices require permission of a federal agency. It certainly would not be in keeping with the normal American approach to the economy.

"Merit" immigration seems to suggest that only people who have graduate degrees and who work in white-collar professions have value. It's an insult to everyone else. It is the peak of arrogance. I much prefer what I heard from Geoconda Argüello-Kline, the secretary-treasurer of Culinary Worker's Union Local 226: "You work, then you buy homes, you buy clothes, you buy gas, you educate your kids," she said. "You need people to clean the hotels. They need the same type of dignity as the person who went to school to learn about computers."

Why should we take so many people with so many problems?

President Trump has a strange way of talking about how immigrants end up coming to the United States. In his 2015 campaign announcement speech, right before he said that Mexican immigrants are prone to be rapists, he said this:

> The U.S. has become a dumping ground for everybody else's problems. . . .
> They're sending people that have lots of problems, and they're bringing
> those problems with us.

The president often talks as if foreign countries choose the immigrants to send. It's as if he thinks there is a migration team waiting somewhere, with a head migration coach who tells an individual, at just the right moment, "You go in now."

In some ways, this is just one of the president's many strange verbal tics. But it serves a purpose. Normal immigration stories emphasize traits that Americans value, because these are stories about people wanting to be American and choosing to come here. Think, for example, of Olivero trying to navigate the border. Discipline, hard work, lots of sacrifice, hope for the future, dedication to family and children, a dream of freedom and opportunity. Reasonable people will have reasonable concerns about the fact that Olivero entered illegally and paid a smuggler to take him. They should. That's not good for rule of law or security. But most Americans can still find a lot to admire in Olivero as a man. Plus, immigrants are voting with their feet. They are voting for *us*.

It's much easier to be staunchly anti-immigrant if we instead think of a clever foreign adversary plotting to dump that country's worst people on us in a kind of unarmed invasion of the undesirables. If immigration normally happened that way, it would make sense that the immigrants who are "sent" would be less admirable people. This all-powerful, plotting foreign leader would surely want to keep the best at home and export the troublemakers.

America's most sympathetic vision of immigration understands that people who come to the United States are often running from something, and that if given liberty and opportunity they will do amazing things—the huddled masses yearning to breathe free. Trump is not the first person to invert this, to take the fact that immigrants flee poverty and violence and use it against them, to say that if people flee terror they must themselves be terrible. If Mexico has poverty, then Mexican migrants must be bringing poverty. If El Salvador has a high murder rate, then Salvadorans must be bringing murder. This is nuts. It would be like assuming that my ancestors brought anti-Semitism to America because anti-Semitism was a big problem in the Russian Empire and in Poland.

Trump's basic idea is that immigrants are sent and that they bring the problems that they flee. Logical or not, this isn't new. An old cartoon published in the *Brooklyn Daily Eagle* shows a giant European general in an old-fashioned military hat wielding a shovel that he uses to hurl little people across the Atlantic Ocean to America. In the drawing, the little immigrants are so tiny that we can't see their faces, but labels tell us they are "paupers," illiterate and poor. They're bringing problems. My great-grandparents might have seen that cartoon. It was published in May 1921. We're still caught in that same trap.

8

The Strip Mall Resistance

CECIA ALVARADO, the Costa Rican teenager, had been lucky, but only up to a point. Her time in America had been marked by moving from house to house while trying to finish high school, until finally she was arrested for domestic violence when her sister-in-law threw her out. If that episode had happened today, she almost surely would have been handed over to ICE and deported. But instead, she returned to moving between friends' houses. She graduated from Desert Pines High School in 2003, at age nineteen. In the spring of 2004, a friend who worked at the College of Southern Nevada helped her take a couple of free classes. Yet her new marriage and pregnancy stalled her college plans. She became a stay-at-home mom to her daughter, Elisa, for about five years, which had not been her plan.

Still, on paper, Cecia's life had turned a corner. Luis, her husband, who had been the only person she knew to call when she was in jail, sponsored her for immigration papers, and she became a legal permanent resident. Before the romance with Luis, she had been a semi-homeless undocumented immigrant looking for a place to lie down in the Las Vegas City Jail. Now she was a legal resident and a mom with a home. And that's about where her luck ended.

Luis had what seemed to be a steady job with a cellular company, and he and Cecia bought a house right before the Great Recession. They took a balloon mortgage, which meant that their payments, easy at first, were set to go up $2,000 a month at a specified time—which was also around the same time Luis found out that his job in Las Vegas was going to be cut. He was still more fortunate than some, because he was offered a new position in Albuquerque. So Luis, Cecia, and Elisa moved to New Mexico. This lasted only a few stormy months.

"We never had a very stable marriage," Cecia told me. Luis filed for divorce. He had already gone to a lawyer in Albuquerque, demanded that she leave the house, and given her papers to sign. She refused, and took Elisa. She went to look for a lawyer of her own in Albuquerque, but they demanded a $5,000 retainer. Cecia had nothing. She was now alone with a five-year-old daughter in a new city where she knew no one, and where her ex-husband had served her with divorce papers.

"I remember I stayed up all night reading about family law in New Mexico," she said. And then Cecia Alvarado, who not long before had been a student in English as a Second Language classes, and whose plans for college had stalled out after a couple of free courses, wrote and filed a motion to dismiss in an Albuquerque court. She could not be divorced in New Mexico, she argued, because she and Luis had not lived there long enough for the state to have jurisdiction over them. She was going back to Vegas.

Luis's lawyer was not happy. He called her and told her that it would be kidnapping if she took Elisa out of New Mexico, and threatened to call the police. Cecia did not stop. She rented a U-Haul, packed her and Elisa's things, and then reported to a New Mexico sheriff's station. She told the desk officer who she was and about her plans to drive west to Nevada. The sheriff's department wasn't interested, so she set off with her daughter through the deserts of New Mexico and Arizona.

This was Cecia's second arrival in Las Vegas. The first time, when she was sixteen, she had not wanted to be there and had ended up lost. This time it was different. Her house was in foreclosure, her marriage was ending, and there was a lawyer threatening her with arrest. But Cecia now had a plan. When she and her daughter arrived in Las Vegas, she pulled up again to a police station. "I told them I'm not missing," she said. Then she went back to the house they had lived in, took the tires from a car Luis had left behind, sold them for cash, and used the money to hire her own lawyer and file her own divorce papers against Luis, in Nevada. Meanwhile, the judge in New Mexico ruled on her motion to dismiss. She won.

Cecia Alvarado is the kind of person a community needs in difficult times.

For the next few years, Cecia raised her daughter, worked part-time, and took classes when she could. She centered her life at a church, La Luz del Mundo (The Light of the World). Daughter, work, church, and a little school. She was living the most stable life she had had since leaving Costa Rica. But then, on June 16, 2015, Donald Trump announced his campaign for president, and this changed her plans.

"I remember watching that," she said. "All I could think was, 'Oh my God.' It scared me. Before that I never heard an attack so direct to the community." She meant Trump's attack on immigrants. *When Mexico sends its people... they're bringing drugs. They're bringing crime. They're rapists.*

Cecia's reaction is notable in one sense, since she is not Mexican. Moreover, she'd spent much of her time in high school in Las Vegas being bullied by Mexican kids. Rivalry between Mexican and Central American youths is a common story that I have heard from friends, colleagues, and clients who have grown up in low-income, heavily Latino neighborhoods in the United States. But that was no longer relevant for Cecia.

"When he says Mexicans, he means all of us," she told me. She asked herself: "How are we going to prepare for this?"

As before in Cecia's life, on paper she had very little to offer. While she did have a green card, she still had no college degree. She says that her difficulties writing in English had slowed her down. Plus, she was working and supporting a child in elementary school. When she tells this story, she emphasizes her church, which stresses citizenship and public service. Her motto is "My profession in service of my community," a mission that she says comes from the church. But the trouble was that in 2015, Cecia didn't really have a profession. So the first thing Donald Trump's candidacy really led her to do was to go back to the College of Southern Nevada and enroll full-time. Then, one day during the 2016 campaign, Cecia walked out of the Department of Motor Vehicles and was approached by canvassers who were registering people to vote. They asked her if she was eligible to vote. Cecia said no, she wasn't, because she wasn't an American citizen.

"But I can volunteer," she said. And she did. "Full-time, almost."

For the rest of the 2016 election campaign, she knocked on hundreds of doors in East Las Vegas. She called and texted voters. On many days she would get up at 7 a.m. to start "knocking, texting, knocking, texting"—finding voters. She was still knocking and texting at 6:15 p.m. on election day. Still finding more people who could vote, and getting them to a polling station.

In a very plausible alternative history, Cecia and the other volunteers she worked with could have changed the course of American history right at that moment, as the sun set on the end of the 2016 campaign. The last day of early voting in Nevada was November 4, 2016. A photo widely shared on social media at the time showed a long line of people under street lights in the dark wrapping around the outside of Cardenas, a large Mexican grocery store on Bonanza Road in East Las Vegas, in the heart of the Latino community.

Another photo showed the inside of the store still packed with people waiting to vote at 9:05 p.m. "Democracy at Cardenas," someone wrote on Twitter.[1]

On the morning of November 8, 2016, election day, the Trump campaign and the state Republican Party sued the Clark County registrar for having extended voting at Cardenas. The Nevada Republican Party chair, Michael McDonald, said that voting hours had been extended to rig the election, "so a certain group could vote." That claim was racially charged, and also baseless. The polls closed at 8 p.m., but the rules in Clark County require polling stations to stay open until every person in line by the closing time has voted. A polling site in Henderson, a whiter area of town, also stayed open past 10. Still, for a few hours on November 8 it was possible to imagine that the throngs of people at Cardenas—many of whom got a door knock or a text from Cecia—might turn the election. Nevada is small, but it is a swing state, and its elections are typically close. In a close presidential election it is not difficult to produce electoral college scenarios where Nevada decides the result. And, in a narrow sense, Cecia won. Hillary Clinton carried Nevada by 2 percent. On the same day, Nevada elected Catherine Cortez Masto by roughly the same margin. She became the first Latina to serve in the United States Senate. But of course, by even narrower margins, Florida, Pennsylvania, Michigan, and Wisconsin had something else in mind.[2]

Also in an alternate history, Fernando Gonzales would not have been detained by ICE or put into the deportation pipeline, even though Trump won the 2016 election. When we look at the deportation pipeline, the scary thing for immigrants is that most of it was under the command of a stridently anti-immigrant Administration in Washington. But the primary entry point to the pipeline was actually not controlled by Donald Trump. Immigrants in Nevada seemed to have some potential salvation in the fact that Trump did not win this state, and the state Democratic party had increasingly staked its future on voter mobilization in the immigrant community. In theory, state-level power could be used to make it harder for a newly hostile federal government to put large numbers of people into the deportation pipeline. The primary entry point to the deportation pipeline was local policing. That is where ICE found most of the people that it arrested, and that is where the people of Las Vegas could establish a first line of defense. The sheriff of Clark County and the Las Vegas City Jail had to comply with Nevada laws, laws that Donald Trump couldn't control. So, to me at least, it seemed obvious what we needed to do in Nevada. We needed to cut the local police out of the pipeline, and if we did that, we could save many families that would otherwise be broken up.

In February 2017, during the Nevada legislature's biennial session, a newly appointed state senator, Yvanna Cancela, introduced a bill that would have prohibited local police and jails from investigating immigration status or responding to detainers and notification requests from ICE unless there was a judicial finding of probable cause. It was initially co-sponsored by much of the Democratic leadership in the Nevada senate. And yet the bill never got a hearing.[3]

First, law enforcement was strongly opposed, led by Las Vegas Metro, Sheriff Joe Lombardo's department. The bill would have ended the 287(g) Program the department had with ICE—the agreement by which local police officers were delegated to serve as federal immigration officers inside the largest jail in Las Vegas. They were not just handing people over to ICE but actually doing the work for ICE in identifying immigrants to deport. But it was more than that.

The bill Sen. Cancela proposed, known as SB223, barely had a plain-language name. In most other states, it would have been known as the Trust Act, because the idea was to encourage trust in local police for a diverse community by keeping the police separate from federal immigration. Yet we had almost no organized campaign behind it. I remember being at one brainstorming meeting before the legislative session in 2017, trying to come up with ideas for bills, including this one, but I remember nearly no coordination to back this bill. That one's on me, because I didn't try to coordinate with anyone else, either. I had purchased tickets on Southwest to fly up to Carson City to testify and advocate for SB223, but I didn't even know if anyone else from Las Vegas was going. Looking back, I'm embarrassed at my own naivete about what this would take.

Immediately after SB223 was formally introduced, the Republican minority leader in the State Senate, Michael Roberson, released a statement:

> This "Sanctuary State" bill is, without question, the most recklessly irresponsible piece of legislation that I have witnessed during my six plus years in the Nevada Legislature. This Democrat bill will undoubtedly result in violent criminals, who have no business being in our state, to be released back into our communities to wreak more havoc on Nevadans.[4]

They had their messaging down, simple and clear. This bill would make Nevada a "sanctuary state." They gave it a label, and they appealed to emotion: fear the violent criminals. Roberson knew what he was doing. In blunt political terms, "sanctuary cities" and "sanctuary states" are not popular, especially with swing voters in the suburbs. In an early 2017 Harvard-Harris Poll, 80 percent of respondents said that local authorities "that arrest illegal immigrants for crimes" should be required to turn them over to immigration authorities."[5]

I have never been fully satisfied by the public polling about so-called sanctuary policies. In other polls, 80 percent of Americans support a path to legalization for undocumented immigrants in the country and are overwhelmingly against their mass deportation. If Americans are so against deporting most undocumented immigrants, why would they be in favor of having their own local police hand people over?[6]

I have a couple of theories, though I confess that I cannot prove them. One has to do with the label. "Sanctuary" implies immunity from law. There is a context for this, as we've seen. From sheltering people from the Fugitive Slave Act before the Civil War to churches sheltering Nicaraguan refugees in the 1980s, there is a noble American tradition of shielding people from unjust laws. But as I said earlier, this is civil disobedience. It's not something a city or state can be asked to do. What the so-called sanctuary laws typically do is not a defiance of law. Instead, they use the autonomy of local governments, which is built into our system of federalism. A local government can say, "We welcome immigrants, even when the federal government does not." If the federal government tries to deport people who don't have a serious criminal record, a local government can say, "We are not going to be part of that." But not being part of it does not mean they can obstruct federal law enforcement. It just says, "Hey, federal agents, you're on your own with this one." I fear, however, that when people hear "sanctuary," they think it's a defiance of rule of law. That's not going to be popular.

Another problem is that the integration of local policing with ICE is complicated and confusing. That Harvard-Harris Poll asked a single question about local police "that arrest illegal immigrants for crimes." If there is any near-consensus in American politics on immigration enforcement, it's for deporting immigrants who have been convicted of serious violent crimes. I find, when speaking to community groups, that I have to remind and explain to people that you can be arrested for very minor offenses—especially in a state that treats traffic tickets as a criminal offense. When people think of someone who's been arrested and booked for a "crime," I suspect people imagine someone arrested for a serious offense. I don't think people envision a broken brake light. I'd really like to see a poll or focus group on whether most Americans think someone should be turned over to ICE if their worst deed in the United States is not paying a traffic ticket. This is why, although the main change from Obama to Trump has been increased enforcement against people without serious criminal records, the main talking point from the Trump administration has been about immigrants as criminals, featuring a simple phrase: *criminal aliens.* Who would support sanctuary for criminal aliens? That sounds like a scary group.

In the face of accusations that they were trying to make Nevada a "sanctuary state," Nevada Democrats in early 2017 caved, and fast. The hearing was canceled. SB223 was dead. Sen. Roberson tried to press his advantage. He wanted to put a state constitutional amendment on the 2018 ballot that would ban sanctuary legislation in Nevada forevermore. That was blocked in the courts. Then Roberson ran for lieutenant governor in 2018. He lost, pretty badly. That was small consolation, though it was an indication that his brand of anti-immigrant demagoguery had limits. Meanwhile, just a few months after the death of SB223 in Carson City, the governor of Illinois, a Republican, signed the Illinois Trust Act, which was nearly identical to Sen. Cancela's bill. But in Illinois it had a name and, more important, a coordinated campaign behind it. That was a sign of how weak we were in Nevada.

Instead, in Nevada, when Fernando Gonzalez was pulled over for an un-paid traffic ticket in 2018, he was handed right over to ICE. Had we been stronger in 2017, he might have gone home to Reina and his daughter. But we were disorganized, and I was naive. Our failures had consequences for people like Fernando. It eats at me.

* * *

The most famous undocumented immigrant in Las Vegas is probably Astrid Silva. As her story was told by President Barack Obama in 2014, she came to the United States at age four, and at the time, "her only possessions were a cross, her doll, and the frilly dress she had on." Her rise to prominence began in 2009 when she slipped a note telling her story to Sen. Harry Reid, then the Senate majority leader, who was beginning a difficult reelection campaign in Nevada. Astrid spoke at the Democratic National Convention in 2016 and de-livered the Democratic Party's Spanish-language response to President Trump's first State of the Union address in 2017. It is nearly certain that who-ever wins the Democratic nomination for president in 2020 will have had his or her photo taken with Astrid Silva, maybe more than once.[7]

Astrid is a leading example of the generation of Dreamer activists who rose up in the early years of the Obama presidency. They pushed for passage of comprehensive immigration reform, or, as an alternative, the DREAM Act. Their central public tactic was to tell their own stories, and by doing that to take the shame out of being undocumented in America. A prominent slogan was "Undocumented and unafraid." They shifted immigration politics, at least in the Democratic Party, by challenging the line between legal and illegal immigration as the default demarcation between good and bad immigrants. If bright young people who crossed the border as young children were "illegal" in the only country they had ever known, then maybe the problem was with the law, not with the people.

Sen. Reid's 2010 reelection was a pivotal moment in Nevada politics, and probably in the long-term political trajectory of the Sun Belt. Reid was not originally favored to win in the year of the Tea Party revolt. A big part of Reid's political survival was his mobilization of Latino voters. Harry Reid's roots are very much in Old Nevada. He was born on the eve of World War II, the son of a miner from the town of Searchlight. His mother did laundry for brothels, and Reid apparently once tried to strangle a man who attempted to give him a bribe. Yet this man from Old Nevada was especially adaptable to a rapidly changing state and understood the political value of organization. In recent election cycles, national political correspondents have written features about Nevada as a model for mobilization of Latino and Asian voters, which offers great hope to Democrats in states like Arizona and Texas.[8]

Yet the Obama years showed the painful limitations of immigrant rights campaigning that is focused on a few well-known Dreamers meeting with candidates and of voter mobilization aimed first and foremost at electing Democrats to office. Sen. Reid was reelected in 2010, and so was President Barack Obama in 2012. But the DREAM Act never passed. Nor did comprehensive immigration reform. The primary tactic of immigrants telling their stories and meeting politicians had a real impact in terms of changing how many people thought about immigration law. It normalized a population that had been shamed and suppressed. But it's a thin strategy that basically depends on achieving an ambitious plan A: pass major immigration legislation in Congress. That requires winning a presidential election, the majority of the House of Representatives, sixty votes in the Senate (enough to overcome a filibuster), and not having Democrats push immigration reform aside because they need to focus on other priorities like the economy or healthcare. When everything depends on passing legislation, plan A is a dream, and there's no plan B.

The riddle in Las Vegas was how to translate the Democratic Party's interest in getting immigrants to vote into policies that would actually protect immigrant families. In 2018, Nevada Democrats, relying in no small part on immigrant voters, won a U.S. Senate seat, the governor's mansion, and both houses of the state legislature (including a supermajority in the Assembly)— and yet the police department and city jail in the state's largest city cooperated actively with ICE. How could this be?

Leo Murrieta, an old hand in political organizing in the Latino community in Nevada, told me that the stepped-up engagement of the Democratic Party with the Latino community was key, but it has been focused nearly entirely on elections. That's hardly surprising; running and winning elections is what a political party does. "What happens after the elections?" he said.

A political party wants votes, and it has an incentive to get its voters to the polls. But it doesn't really have any incentive to encourage political organizing that might demand politically difficult choices be made once a party member is in office. For a Democratic candidate for office, it is great to have people to pose with for photos, as a way of signaling general support for the immigrant community, and to have a mobilization system that operates in November of even-numbered years, but only then. "Democrats like to come to take pictures. They want gold stars just for showing up," Leo told me. "We just didn't believe that system works."

Leo runs the Nevada branch of Make the Road, an activist organization originally established in New York City. It is located, like so many things in Las Vegas, in a strip mall. Leo is executive director, but he has little private meeting space, so he often holds court at the Cardenas cafeteria nearby. Make the Road's office space in East Las Vegas is pretty similar to the ¡Arriba! storefront office on Charleston, where I talked to the circle of TPS beneficiaries (chapter 3). Mi Familia Vota, a key voter mobilization group, has its office in a little strip mall, too, also in East Las Vegas, next to a storefront church. From these little spaces, they have built up membership-based organizations, respond to emergency cases, send teams out to knock on doors, organize community meetings, and, when necessary, hold press conferences. But neither Make the Road Nevada nor ¡Arriba! existed at the beginning of 2017.

The benefit of politicians coming for photo ops with prominent immigrant activists is that they leave their phone numbers. Once they get into office, the activists who helped them in the campaign will probably have access to officials in key places in the administration. This access doesn't fix structural problems, but often a phone call to the right official can stop an inhumane deportation. A lot of individual immigration cases were solved that way during the Obama years. But when Trump replaced Obama, the VIPs who posed for pictures no longer had access to anyone with real power. If the only organizing on the ground is centered on elections and elections only, then the only answer will be to elect a different person next time. That leaves an entire community defenseless for at least four years.

Leo was explaining to me something that I didn't quite understand when I was trying to become more engaged in immigrant rights work immediately after the 2016 election. In Nevada there had been a massive show of organizational strength on election day, which had narrowly swung the state away from Trump. And yet in early 2017 during the state legislative session when we tried to push through a bill that might protect immigrants, this organizational power was nowhere to be found.

Even if there had been more organization behind the 2017 effort, the battle would have been difficult. Leo pointed out that partnerships between local police and ICE are part of much larger problems with the way police interact with people of color generally. "I think Democrats fear police," Leo said. He was referring to the reluctance of Democratic leaders to appear to be soft on crime. "This is a conflict for white progressives." For a moderate politician in a swing district, it would be far more convenient to believe that the police are usually a positive force in the community, that law enforcement has a sense of proportionality, and that they would never needlessly break up a family over a traffic ticket. But it is easier for some people to accept this than others. Case in point: Rigoberto Torres, a U.S. citizen, was pulled over—allegedly for a brake light that was out—and told to go back to where he came from. Fernando Gonzalez was pulled over for a brake light and ended up locked up, missing the birth of his daughter, and facing deportation. By contrast, I was pulled over by the police for the same issue in 2019, and I was just given a friendly warning. If your experiences are more like mine and less like Rigoberto and Fernando's, the idea of getting into a political conflict with the police seems to be politically reckless. It doesn't play well with suburban swing voters. This means that any effort to change how the police operate will always be a gigantic political fight. But back in 2017, we weren't ready to have even a small fight.

* * *

As a lawyer, I've often represented other people in court. I have myself been a party to a civil action only twice. The first time was when I was a law student and I sued our ex-landlord in small claims court for failing to return our security deposit. The second time was against Wilbur Ross, the United States Secretary of Commerce. It was about the United States census.

My time living in the Middle East taught me what happens when a census is politicized. My first year out of law school, when I was working in Cairo, Egypt, I represented a Sudanese statistician who had been hired to produce a count of displaced persons in Omdurman, outside of the Sudanese capital, Khartoum. The government of Sudan did not like the numbers his census produced, and he was arrested by state security. They tortured him for more than a week to try to get him to repudiate the census he had conducted. Later I lived in Beirut, a city in which nearly every building more than fifteen years old bore bullet marks from the Lebanese civil war. That war had been one of the dominant items in the news throughout my childhood. One of its causes was a failed power-sharing arrangement between religious sects, especially Maronite Christians, Shi'ite Muslims, and Sunni Muslims. The division of power was based on the relative population of each group—in the 1930s. A big problem was that no census had been taken in Lebanon since 1932. The country had evolved, but no one had the political courage to recount. Refusing to count was a way to avoid grappling with a country that had changed. A census is usually merely boring, but sometimes people will kill just to prevent a census from happening, or to manipulate its numbers.

The United States census embodies two revolutionary principles. First, our government must be founded on facts about who we really are as a country—an "actual enumeration," not a fiction adopted for political convenience. Second, a government that aspires to democracy must obsess about making sure every person is counted. In the late eighteenth century, we agonized about how to count African Americans; the result was the notorious three-fifths clause, in which enslaved persons were not considered to count as much as free persons. Today, we agonize over how to count immigrants.[9]

The earliest record that I have of my family in the United States is a handwritten ledger from the 1930 census, which lists the Brooklyn household headed by Sam Bernstein, my maternal great-grandfather, and Lilly Bernstein, my great-grandmother, along with Millie, my grandmother, who was then four years old, along with her older sister, Beatrice. The ledger that bears their names has a slender column under "Citizenship." For Sam, who had come to America first, it says "Yes." For my great-grandma Lilly, the census taker scribbled "Al": alien.

The question about citizenship was last asked on the full census in 1950, the year my father was born. It was removed because it wasn't seen as important enough to include in future tallies. That does not mean that the census stopped caring about citizenship and immigration. It is not as if we don't know how many citizens and non-citizens there are in our country. We do know. In 2017, there were 22,337,765 non-citizens living in the United States, or 6.96 percent of our population. We know that because the Census Bureau tells us. In fact, throughout this book I've quoted data about the citizenship and immigration status of the population of Las Vegas. That data comes from the Census Bureau, but not from the "actual enumeration" that is conducted every decade. Instead, it comes from the American Community Survey, in which the census collects extremely detailed information from a sample of the population and then uses statistical modeling to create data for the whole population. This sampling method is considered the most accurate in social science, in part because it adjusts the sampling if certain people don't return their questionnaires.[10]

Despite the usefulness of modern social science methods, many of the official uses of the census require not sampling but "actual enumeration"—the full census in which every household has to respond. For this, it is essential that the Census Bureau gets people to cooperate by answering the questions, which first and foremost requires that the census form be as short as possible and ask only what is absolutely required. That's a big reason the citizenship question was moved out of the full census after 1950.

Since then there has been periodic consideration of putting the citizenship question back onto the census form, but the idea has usually been nixed. Before the 1990 census, the director of the Census Bureau said that asking people about their citizenship and immigration status would make the census seem like "an enforcement agency," and as a result, immigrants—both those in the United States legally and those who were not—would be very likely to "misunderstand or mistrust the census and fail or refuse to respond." In 2019, experts in the Census Bureau estimated that if citizenship was included in the census, 8 percent of households with at least one non-citizen would simply not participate. In other words, people would not be counted. The numbers on which our democracy depends would be wrong.[11]

An undercount on the census would mean that certain parts of the country might end up with less representation in Congress and state legislatures—especially cities with large immigrant populations. It would mean that less money would flow from the federal government to these areas. Dozens of federal programs use the census to allocate funds. More specifically, it would mean that certain schools would see their funding cut, because the census would report that they served a community with fewer people than actually lived there. Schools like Sandy Miller Academy, where my children went. Schools like the one where my wife taught fifth grade in central Las Vegas.

In March 2018, Commerce Secretary Ross announced that he would put a question about citizenship on the 2020 census. About a week later, New York State led a group of eighteen states, ten cities, and four counties in filing a lawsuit to stop the citizenship question. But Nevada was not among them. Nevada's attorney general at the time, Adam Laxalt, had aligned himself with conservatives on immigration even before Trump had the Republican nomination. (Laxalt was the Republican nominee for Nevada governor in 2018. He lost.) Nevada had the highest per-capita undocumented population of any state in the country. If fear in the immigrant community would lead any state to suffer an undercount, it would be us. But Nevada was not fighting.[12]

Around this time, emails circulated looking for individuals who might be interested in suing the Commerce Department. A second lawsuit was planned in Maryland, with private citizens as plaintiffs, rather than state and local governments. There were twenty-two plaintiffs in the lawsuit, *Kravitz v. United States Department of Commerce*, led by Robyn Kravitz from Prince George's County, Maryland. I am very proud to have been one of them. In the complaint filed in court, I show up in paragraph 20. It states that I live in Las Vegas, I vote, I use the roads, and my daughter attended a public school that received Title I funding. That's it. I thought it was important, if only symbolically, that Las Vegas and Nevada be in this fight.[13]

Several more lawsuits were filed around the country, and some got merged with others. By the end, there were two main cases—the one based in New York, led by the State of New York and the American Civil Liberties Union, and ours proceeding in Maryland. The New York case went to the Supreme Court. The issue at the Supreme Court was narrow and technical. Did Secretary Ross give a good enough reason for his decision to ask about citizenship, despite the well-documented dangers of doing so? The Commerce Department said it needed this information to help the Justice Department enforce the Voting Rights Act, but that argument never made a great deal of sense.

Our side had an additional, more explosive argument—that the citizenship question was added deliberately to discriminate against Latino and other minority residents, and thus had an unconstitutional intent. We initially lost this argument. The district court initially decided we didn't have enough evidence for that claim. Then luck intervened.

In August 2018, a Republican political consultant called Thomas Hofeller died. There had been testimony that he was one of the first people to urge the Commerce Department to add the citizenship question. Files found in his estate showed that he had specifically recommended adding the citizenship question because it would be "advantageous to Republicans *and non-Hispanic Whites.*" This was the kind of evidence that the district court had initially thought was lacking on our discrimination claims. It showed that the census question was really about racial discrimination. A lower court decided to reopen our case in Maryland—which meant the Hofeller files were likely to go before a judge.[14]

On June 27, 2019, the Supreme Court ruled. Five justices—Chief Justice Roberts, plus the four liberal justices—found that the reason Secretary Ross had given for adding citizenship to the census was essentially phony. Writing with polite restraint, Chief Justice Roberts said that there was "a significant mismatch" between the reasons the Commerce Department gave and its actual behavior. The government thus did not yet have a green light to ask about citizenship on the census. They had to come up with a new explanation for the citizenship question—an explanation that would be both genuine and not illegal. That new explanation would be reviewed again by the judge in New York. Meanwhile, there would be a separate challenge under the Constitution's equal-protection clause in our case in Maryland, claiming that the whole enterprise was an act of intentional racial discrimination to bias the government in favor of non-Hispanic whites.[15]

Against all that, the government had a deadline. The Supreme Court issued its decision on a Thursday. The Census Bureau was supposed to start printing census forms on the following Monday.

On Monday, President Trump told reporters, "I think it is very important to find out if somebody is a citizen as opposed to an illegal. It is a big difference to me between being a citizen of the United States and being an illegal." There was talk of an executive order, though it was never completely clear how that would change the legal posture of the case. It was a legal circus for a few days, but a week and a half later President Trump conceded that there would, in fact, be no citizenship question on the 2020 census. On July 16, the federal courts in New York and Maryland entered permanent injunctions prohibiting the government from including a question about citizenship in 2020. We won.[16]

The census cases provide one of the more successful examples of high-profile litigation in federal court stopping a Trump administration measure directed at immigrants. Objectively, though, few of these cases have produced decisive victories. The first cases challenged the Muslim ban, the prohibition on immigration from several majority Muslim countries. They ultimately failed.

Some readers will object to my use of the term "Muslim ban" because it presumes an Islamophobic intent. "Travel ban" is more neutral. I use that label sometimes as well. I agree with the rationale that Prof. Shoba Sivaprasad Wadhia gives on this in her book *Banned: Immigration Enforcement in the Time of Trump,* where she writes: "The bans signed by the president do not merely restrict travel (e.g. a long weekend to Disneyworld) but in fact prevent people from entering the United States, period." Much as with other immigration questions, entire lives and families are at stake, and with that, the question of who belongs in this country—not just who can travel. More to the point: the ban applies mostly to Muslim people, albeit only from certain countries. The man who signed the orders, Donald Trump, has made it abundantly clear in public statements before and after he became president that he does not like Muslim people being in the United States. That's the point.

President Trump issued the first version of the ban one week after his inauguration. That one left legal residents of the United States, as well as refugees and other would-be immigrants, stranded all over the world. It's also the one that produced the iconic image of immigration lawyers as airport heroes. It was rapidly blocked by multiple federal courts. That was at the end of January 2017. But afterward, the government issued a revised version of the ban. In June 2018, the Supreme Court, by a vote of 5–4, allowed the ban to stand.

Heroic legal efforts had modified the original policy and slowed it down. However, Trump eventually won. The initial legal victories—the emergency injunctions—bought time, but for all the bravado of ACLU press releases, most major challenged to Trump immigration policies at the national level have ultimately failed. Given time, the administration has usually gotten its way. The census cases resulted in a clear victory only because the government was fighting a clock as well as the courts.

To be clear, high-profile court fights have made a dramatic difference in people's lives. District court injunctions kept Temporary Protected Status in place and kept the DACA program alive, at least for the lucky people who had permits to renew. Those cases are working their way to the Supreme Court. The DACA case will be decided in early 2020, while this book is in press. Between DACA and TPS, nearly a million people are in the crosshairs, in danger of being subject to ICE and deportation. The protection they have now may be running out, barring another miracle in court—or a new president.

The best explanation I have heard for why the lawyers and courts have proven inadequate on their own to protect immigration came from Bliss Reqúa-Trautz. She is a community organizer with the National Day Laborers Organizing Network (NDLON, pronounced "En-Da-Lon"), which has been a national engine of grassroots organizing for immigrant rights. NDLON sent Bliss to Las Vegas in late 2017, and her arrival was part of a new influx of community organizing among immigrants in Las Vegas, aimed at changing the political dynamic that had left so many people so vulnerable. She started ¡Arriba! Las Vegas Worker's Center, where I had met the cleaners from the resorts on the Strip.

"We're on a highway," Bliss said, beginning a critique of the way immigrant rights activism had evolved during the Obama administration. "There are three lanes on this highway," the three different branches of the federal government: the presidency, the Congress, and the courts. "The executive lane is where we mostly lived under Obama," she said. What she means is that tremendous efforts were devoted to electing a candidate who would be sympathetic to immigrants. Then, even though immigrant communities often suffered under the Obama administration, individual cases could often be solved by tapping into relationships with members of the administration. But Obama is gone. In her book, Prof. Shoba Sivaprasad Wadhia quotes an immigrant activist talking about how things are worse under Trump than under Obama: "There's really no one to talk to. No one has access to the White House. No one has access to people at DHS because everyone who was either an ally or friend and even career people that we knew have left these agencies."[17]

"Right now, the executive is the origin of all the attacks on the community. So that lane is closed for construction," Bliss told me. "Next to that is the legislative lane." That's Congress, in other words, which in theory could pass immigration reform legislation. "You've got a fifteen-car pileup in that lane."

"Our success has all been defensive. It's all been in the judicial lane," she said. But the truth is, most of that success has been to stall or mute policies that would hurt people. It's kept DACA and TPS alive longer than I might have thought possible. But going to court is not enough. Bliss's point is that the immigrant rights movement needs to be able to move quickly between lanes. It's a mistake to become too comfortable with just one mode of operating, because that can suddenly be taken away.

* * *

¡Arriba! had not even been in existence for a full year when, in late March 2018, the family of Cecilia Gomez came to ask for help. Cecilia was a Mexican mother of three boys and a resident of Las Vegas since the 1990s. She went to the U.S. Citizenship and Immigration Services office in Las Vegas believing she would be getting legal permanent residency. Her oldest son, Yonathan, a student at Wesleyan University, had flown back to Las Vegas to accompany her to the interview. When Cecilia was taken back into the office for her appointment, ICE agents were waiting for her. Instead of giving her legal residency, they arrested her.[18]

ICE thought it had a removal order against Cecilia that had been issued in 1998. An order to appear in Immigration Court supposedly had been issued to Cecilia back then, but because she'd never shown up, the removal order was issued in absentia. Cecilia had a good reason for not showing up to court, however: the notice had been sent to a donut shop in Los Angeles, not to her. Nevertheless, ICE had a removal order and sent her off for deportation without further hearing. This was the kind of case that, during the Obama years, might have been solved discreetly with a well-placed phone call to a sympathetic official. But those days were over. With ICE holding a removal order, and with the weakness in immigrant advocacy in Las Vegas we had seen a year earlier during the Nevada legislative session, Cecilia looked doomed.[19]

Bliss recruited Laura Barrera, the young lawyer at the UNLV Immigration Clinic. Procedurally, there are only a few things a lawyer can do in a situation like this, where ICE has a final removal order against a person. First, a motion to reopen the case was filed in Immigration Court. But there was no timetable for when an immigration judge might rule on it, and Cecilia might be deported to Mexico in the meantime. It would also be possible to file an emergency motion for habeas corpus in the federal district court, a tactic that has increasingly been used in cases like this around the country. But again, there was no telling whether a judge would even read the motion before a bus delivered Cecilia to the border. Instead, ¡Arriba! made noise. Cecilia's sons, Bliss, and Laura organized an online campaign targeting ICE and spoke at press conferences staged outside the USCIS office and outside ICE. The case was covered by nearly every major newspaper and local TV station in southern Nevada. All of this made me very nervous. Law is a small "c" conservative profession. We are trained to advocate for clients in court filings and formal hearings, not at press conferences. I wondered if I'd face any blowback for allowing the clinic to be part of this effort. But, on the other hand, what else should lawyers do when the government tried to take a mother away because she didn't answer a letter that was sent to a donut shop?

ICE brought Cecilia all the way to the border. It seemed like we were on the verge of another defeat. Anxiety set in. And then, with ¡Arriba! generating near daily media events back in Vegas, it brought her back. The Immigration Court reopened her case. USCIS—the agency that initially had called ICE and had her arrested—eventually awarded her legal residency.

Cecilia Gomez still lives in Las Vegas today, saved by a community organization that did not even exist in Las Vegas a year before her arrest, by people willing to come out to protest on her behalf, by her children's willingness to fight for their mother, and by a young lawyer who had about a year and a half of experience since passing the bar exam. There were motions filed in court. There were press conferences, online campaigns, phone calls to the ICE office, and a great deal of media coverage. These were not tactics that I'd learned in law school, nor were they skills I'd previously taught as a law professor. It was still obvious to anyone paying attention that good people were under very serious threat. Indeed, two years earlier, ICE probably would have ignored Cecilia Gomez. But her case showed something else, too: This community was not helpless. This would be a long and difficult struggle. But the people of Las Vegas were learning to put up a fight.

9

Dirty Immigration Lawyers

IN THE FIRST YEAR of the Trump administration, Attorney General Jeff Sessions gave a speech to the division of the Justice Department that runs the immigration courts. He complained that the asylum system was being abused. Then he told them: "We also have dirty immigration lawyers who are encouraging their otherwise unlawfully present clients to make false claims of asylum providing them with the magic words needed to trigger the credible fear process." Immigration lawyers know this as the "dirty immigration lawyers" speech. It was an insult to what we do, of course. But it's also a label we can wear with pride. My obsession since 2016, basically, has been to find as many dirty immigration lawyers for Las Vegas as we possibly can. We don't have enough.[1]

Nationally, only 37 percent of immigrants in deportation cases have lawyers, because the government does not provide a lawyer as it does in criminal cases. Immigrants in detention—who have had their physical liberty taken, and who are at most immediate risk of deportation—get a lawyer even less often. Immigrants who manage to get a lawyer get out of detention four times more often—44 percent of the time, compared to 11 percent of the time with no lawyer. Those detained without lawyers typically don't even put up a fight in Immigration Court. Only 3 percent of detained and unrepresented immigrants even ask the court for any relief from deportation.[2]

We've not been successful in finding enough lawyers. At the end of 2019, the UNLV Immigration Clinic and Catholic Charities remained the only legal assistance programs in Las Vegas with a primary focus on deportation defense. Catholic Charities did not employ a licensed attorney, relying on a nonlawyer who had an alternative certification from the Department of

Justice and who thus could not practice in regular federal courts. The UNLV Immigration Clinic is the only program with a significant focus on people in ICE detention. We expanded with two attorneys for children in 2014 and made that program sustainable with the Bernstein & Associates donation. In 2018, the New York–based Immigrant Justice Corps called me, offering to send us a fellow for two years—a recent law graduate, on a model loosely reminiscent of Teach for America. As a result, in fall 2019 one of our former students, Paloma Guerrero, would become the first lawyer in Las Vegas dedicated to defending detained immigrants pro bono, full-time. We were building, slowly. And yet: between Catholic Charities and the Immigration Clinic there were three lawyers, one faculty member who is really only involved in legal work half-time (that's me), and one DOJ accredited representative who is not an attorney. For immigrants who can't pay a private attorney, that's it. Remember: by this time, ICE was starting 300 to 400 new deportation cases in Las Vegas *every month*.

I'd really thought we would have been further along by this point. I'd thought we would have a bona fine deportation defense center. Instead, we'd added one unstable position at a time, creating an awkward structure in a law school clinic. It was better than nothing. But it was definitely not what I'd planned. It felt, some days, like a failure.

In June 2019, I went to Immigration Court in Las Vegas with one of my students on a new case. Our client was a teenager from El Salvador. My student Patrick Tarzi had interviewed him for the first time the day before, having volunteered to do this for no credit over the summer and taking time off from his summer job. The boy we were representing had crossed the border into the United States alone. After initially being held by the Border Patrol, the federal government put him in a group home on the East Coast until they found his aunt and uncle in Las Vegas.

Most of this boy's family had been murdered in El Salvador. I didn't know why yet. That's not unusual when we have just started on a case. I didn't know yet if they'd been murdered for a reason that would fit the technicalities of asylum law. I knew that this boy had good reason to be terrified, that he would be applying for asylum, and that he had come to Las Vegas, which meant—given the track record of our judges—he would probably eventually lose. Such is the reward for coming to live with family.

While we waited for the judge to be ready, I looked around the courtroom from the table at the front. The benches were filled with other children, some accompanied by parents and some on their own. Mostly the kids looked like they were in middle school or early high school, but some were younger. There were no other attorneys in the room, other than the lawyer at the other table, who represented ICE. She was looking at her phone. Then Jasmine Coca from Catholic Charities came in. Thirty-five people who had to face the court that day, some of them children entirely on their own, and only two of them had a legal representative.

This was a first master calendar hearing, and the thirty-three people who did not already have representation would be offered a delay to find a lawyer. But if they came back to the next hearing, roughly six weeks away, still without an attorney, they would have to go forward alone, representing themselves. At this particular moment, our clinic had no lawyers in the office, and it was summer, when things are especially slow at a university.

I was stressed by the scene. Should I offer them all representation? I knew I couldn't do that. Because our clinic is one of the few places people could call—and one of the few phone numbers the court would give these new respondents—there would be pressure on us. This is one of the first inequalities of human rights work. The person who steps up to do a little will be put under immense pressure to do everything. Meanwhile, the people who do nothing will not be bothered. That's really what made me angry in court that day. If lawyers are devoted to justice and law and all that, then where were they? The answer is obvious, of course. These folks can't pay. Lawyers have to keep the lights on.

At work, we had staffing problems. At the end of February 2019, Laura Barrera, who deserved to be promoted to a more senior position, moved on to the Florence Immigrant and Refugee Rights Project in Tucson. They're one of the immigrant rights organizations that I admire most, and I was happy for her and for them. But her departure was a defeat.

These were not good times. At home, my own kids were struggling. I was taking my youngest daughter to specialists, trying to diagnose a learning disability. My oldest daughter was a defiant teenager. I didn't stay on top of her schoolwork the way I needed to—the way she needed me to. At work, I had failed to find the resources to build the legal defense program that I had hoped for. The police were handing people over to ICE every day. I couldn't stop that, either. In May 2019, ICE filed 407 new deportation cases in Las Vegas, the most ever in a single month. I was enraged by my own limitations, as a lawyer and also as a father.[3]

One night in spring 2019 I went out to the Smiths supermarket on Rancho. I think my wife had run out of Diet Dr Pepper, which she's addicted to like I am to coffee. And then I felt pain in my chest, something I had never experienced before. Maybe it was heartburn. Probably. I ended up looking up the symptoms of a heart attack on my iPhone. I remember being just a touch out of breath. I remember I was in the bread aisle. But the pain went away. I got the soda, and some extra toilet paper that we needed. I felt shaky, and more than a little scared. I went home and never told anyone, not even my wife. A normal late-night run to the store.

* * *

By 2018—the first midterm congressional election under President Trump— Cecia Alvarado had become the Nevada state director of Mi Familia Vota. By the end of the year, she was leading a team that registered 10,712 new voters for the midterm elections, made 11,792 phone calls, and sent more than 108,924 text messages to get people to the polls.

In the 2018 elections, Democrats in Nevada won a supermajority in the state Assembly, flipped a U.S. Senate seat from the Republicans, and rejected Adam Laxalt, the Republican candidate for governor, who as the state's attorney general had backed several anti-immigrant initiatives of the Trump administration, including his attempts to intimidate sanctuary cities. The margin was less than 50,000 votes statewide in both the gubernatorial and Senate races. Cecia's team had knocked on 93,641 doors.

During the 2019 Nevada legislative session, we tried, again, to stop police from turning people over to ICE without restraint. But it played out a little differently this time than in 2017, when the bill that Sen. Yvanna Cancela had proposed was killed as soon as Republicans issued a press release about it.

In 2019, the main bill was sponsored by the middle child of Rigoberto Torres, the Salvadoran man who had crossed the Rio Grande in 1989 and who still nervously carried his social security card "just in case." In 2018, his daughter, Selena Torres, had been elected to the state assembly. A high school English teacher by profession, she was just twenty-three years old when she was sworn in. She had grown up in the same neighborhood she now represented, the area along Charleston Boulevard on the west side of town. She told me, "I had a family friend who was scared to go to my swearing-in because they were worried that they could be processed by immigration." She wanted to do something about that fear.

Torres's bill didn't restrict police from doing anything, but it required them to publish statistics about the actual criminal background of anyone they handed over to ICE. I liked this approach because I was tired of the sheriff saying that he worked with ICE to get rid of the "worst of the worst," and then getting phone calls from people whose criminal record consisted of an unpaid traffic ticket. I thought forcing the City of Las Vegas and the sheriff to publish data might get them to limit cooperation with ICE to cases with more serious criminal records. Sunlight is the best disinfectant, as the saying goes. Torres sold it as an effort to build trust in police by disclosing to a scared public that their cooperation with ICE was in fact limited.[4]

The transparency measure didn't pass. In terms of the bottom line, it seemed depressingly like 2017 all over again. We still could not get legislators to pass a bill keeping people from being turned over to ICE in darkness, without any regulation whatsoever. Yet there were objective signs of progress, even if that progress was slow. First, unlike in 2017, Torres's bill got hearings. They were tense hearings, at which people in MAGA hats lined up to talk about the murders that had been committed by an undocumented immigrant in Gardnerville, Nevada, but hearings were held. And not only hearings. Torres's transparency bill got votes. It passed the Nevada Assembly. Then, in the Nevada Senate Judiciary Committee, Assemblywoman Torres had a particularly tense exchange with State Senator Ira Hansen, a Republican, who accused her of violating her oath of office by not enforcing immigration laws. She told him that she didn't know of any law that required local police to deport people, and that if he had such a law, "I suggest that you get that statute and email it to me." It was sarcastic, and fierce. Definitely different from 2017.

It wasn't clear if the Senate Judiciary Committee would even vote on the bill. But activists from Mi Familia Vota, Make the Road, and Progressive Leadership Alliance of Nevada organized a phone banking and social media campaign to pressure the Senate majority leader, Nicole Cannizzaro. People were sending text messages and made phone calls, and #AB376 was briefly trending on Twitter. Some of the organizational strength that had produced lines of voters on election day was now being used to promote pro-immigrant legislation. That hadn't happened just two years earlier. Cannizzaro let the bill have a vote in the committee, and it passed—for the moment. The bill was gutted later, whittled down to a single provision requiring that police inform a detainee about the purpose of an interrogation before questioning about immigration. That isn't much, but it was still the first explicit restriction on police cooperation with immigration that Nevada had ever enacted. So while this was a defeat, it showed that some of the muscle that had mobilized immigrant voters in elections could also be turned toward promoting policy change to protect immigrants. It was not enough, but it was an improvement from 2017.[5]

In the course of this debate in the legislature, Sheriff Lombardo appeared at a public breakfast at a downtown Mexican restaurant to address the controversies about his partnership with ICE. Speaking with cameras rolling, he promised to stop turning people over to ICE if they had only been arrested on a misdemeanor, including traffic offenses, except for intoxicated driving and domestic violence. This promise still had not been clearly implemented in policy by the end of September 2019, and it was frustrating to be lied to. But it was clear that the Sheriff was on the defensive. In 2017, we were ambitious but entirely unprepared, and we were simply trounced on the political battlefield. It 2019, it felt more like we'd fought to a draw, and that we might be able to do more next time. I thought: If only the Nevada legislature met more often. We were getting closer.

Meanwhile, there were real, substantial victories on other issues. Most important, Nevada passed one of the most sweeping pro-immigrant occupational licensing bills in the country, making immigration status irrelevant for nearly all professional licenses in the state. Selena Torres sponsored the occupational licensing bill, too. It was not a simple law, and I remember in the early spring Mayra Salinas-Menjivar telling me that it was not ready for 2019. Maybe this would just start the wheels turning and we'd be able to try again in 2021, she told me. But Mayra worked nightly on the legislative language, and the governor signed it in May—the work of two Salvadoran American young women, one the daughter of a man who had waded across a deadly river to reach America, the other a former unaccompanied child who earned her law degree before being allowed to sit for the citizenship exam. Best of all, it's a law that will increase earning power and improve livelihoods. It would let people like Fernando Gonzales get a contractor's license.[6]

That's an important lesson that I've learned from the individuals who work more closely than I do with the people most directly affected by anti-immigrant policies. I tend to fixate on the deportation pipeline, on the role of the 287(g) Program, and on the looming threat of expedited removal. They are real, grave threats to very good people. But for a community to build the political capacity to defend itself requires a broader view than I tend to have. Leo Murrieta told me that when Make the Road hired him to set up the organization's office in Las Vegas, he thought that the focus would be on racial justice, policing, and ICE. Those things are parts of his organization's work today, but when they began knocking on doors he found people asking for things he hadn't expected. Earned paid sick days ended up becoming a high priority—and the Nevada legislature passed a bill to partially address it. An increase in the minimum wage. Tenant protection. None of those bills would be thought of as immigrant-specific. But they help immigrants, because immigrant families are working families, like everyone else.

Assemblywoman Torres told me something very similar: "We have to understand that the needs of immigrants are not just to be here in this country, but also to live well in this country, to have access to gainful employment, to have access to healthcare, to have access to a quality education system. The needs of immigrants in this community, and the politics of it, have to change because we need to meet those day-to-day needs." When I look at a case like that of Fernando Gonzalez, I see a man who was handed over to ICE by a local jail for an unpaid ticket for a brake light that didn't work. I want to stop that. But it is also important to remember why he didn't pay the ticket. It's because he was short of money. One of the reasons Fernando struggled with money was that he could not get licensed as a contractor, which meant he had to work on the margins of the building trades and charge lower rates. It's not unreasonable to imagine that if Torres's occupational licensing bill had been in place and Fernando had been able to become a licensed contractor rather than an unlicensed handyman, he would have been able to pay that ticket, and he would never have been arrested at all.

* * *

During the difficult summer of 2019, when the president of the United States was threatening massive raids in American cities, ICE arrested a woman in Las Vegas named Adriana Arellana Cruz. Adriana had been in the United States for twenty-four years. She had worked, legally, as a housekeeper at Caesar's Palace, struggling to raise three children as a single mom. She had been issued a removal order during the Obama administration after getting a traffic ticket—a victim of Las Vegas Metro's partnership with ICE. ICE was now coming to carry out the deportation.

ICE arrested Adriana on a Thursday. The desperate call from her kids came into a hotline that was manned by Cecia Alvarado, the Costa Rican teenager turned political organizer. When panic spread because of the president's threats, Cecia had set up the hotline with Erika Castro, an organizer with the Progressive Leadership Alliance of Nevada. In theory, a project like that should have trained volunteers to receive the calls, developed a method of screening legal claims, and ensured that teams of lawyers were available. It wasn't quite that. It was really just Cecia answering the phone and a lawyer, Hardeep Sull, who's known mostly as Dee—"my user-friendly name," she calls it. Dee told Cecia: "I'll provide the attorneys, but you guys have to staff the phone lines."

Dee Sull grew up on a farm in Langley, British Columbia, the daughter of a truck driver and a janitor. Hers was one of only two Indian families there, she told me. She's been in Vegas since 2003, although she came originally intending to work on international business transactions, not immigration law. She got an early internship with a retired immigration judge who had moved into private practice, and she had practiced immigration law ever since.

Most immigration lawyers in Las Vegas work in small firms, often just one or two lawyers. One of the problems in getting pro bono legal defense for people in removal proceedings is that these cases are so time-intensive. Dee estimated that a fair price for the hours it takes an attorney to prepare a strong asylum claim in Immigration Court might be $30,000 or $40,000. She knows that some lawyers do it for much less, though she worries that to run a law practice with more affordable fees might lead attorneys to cut corners on the work. I tend to share her concern. "It is a lot of money. But how do you nickel-and-dime your life?" she said. "I love my job. I want to be able to sit there and give back into the community—and pay my staff." Whatever the fees, most people who are not detained do manage to find an attorney, but people like Adriana, who was locked up, usually don't. Dee took on Adriana's case for free.

Given my own problems making enough time and mental space for my children, I sometimes think it's not healthy to talk to Dee for very long because I always leave with the feeling that I'm not working nearly as hard as she is. "Each day, I feel like I'm going into the battlefield," she said. "I look at it as, today it's immigration. But tomorrow what will it be? Immigration is the easy target." Dee preaches the value of being there and continuing the fight. She said her kids tell her, "You love your clients more than us," though she thinks there's value in her displaying a work ethic for them. She brought up her Sikh faith, which she said emphasizes service, and which was also established to protect an oppressed minority.

Given the difficulties of the Las Vegas Immigration Court, Dee tells her clients the same thing I tell my students: Our chances of winning at first are very low. We're going to prepare for the appeal. She told me about a client who panicked after losing in court. Dee doesn't speak very much Spanish, though she notes that "you don't have to speak the language to see the pain." But when Dee told her this was only the beginning—"We'll come back next week. We'll be there for the appeal"—the woman smiled and began crying in relief.

Adriana was arrested on a Thursday. Dee got the call on Friday. She is very clear what would have happened if Adriana's kids hadn't found a lawyer for her. "Adriana would have been on that plane that Tuesday," she said. Over the weekend, the ICE detention center wouldn't let her children have a contact visit to say goodbye. They couldn't hug. They couldn't look directly at each other. They had to talk through a video screen. Dee points out what this means: "That's family separation. It's here in Vegas. It has been for a long time.

Adriana's family—that's mainstream Vegas. Do you want your neighbors' kids' mom being dragged off?"

Dee's firm worked all weekend and filed an emergency appeal at 4 a.m. Monday. Meanwhile, Mi Familia Vota and Make the Road organized phone banks. Their members called the ICE office so often that ICE shut their phones down. They got the story into the press. Adriana's youngest child (twelve), the middle one (sixteen), and the oldest (twenty-one) were all on camera repeatedly. Children pleading for their parents on the news has become a common sight in the Trump administration. It is not without some controversy. There is concern that their suffering is being exploited to produce drama, and that forcing a child to tell her story over and over again will only compound the trauma. In the legal community, there are many traditional lawyers who never use the media and frown on those who do. Maybe lawyers should limit themselves to the court filings. But, as we've seen, in immigration matters the "court" is an employee of the prosecutor. If a lawyer doesn't think about trying to get outside of that system, she might not be doing her job.

Dee won a stay of removal—an order prohibiting deportation—from the Ninth Circuit Court of Appeals. That court also ordered the immigration court to reopen Adriana's case. But the phone banking and the media campaign continued. I was not involved in the case as a lawyer. Seeing the efforts from the outside, I thought the main issue was that Adriana remained detained even after the stay of removal. But Dee told me later that there was more going on. She was afraid that ICE would go forward with the deportation despite the court order. She said that had happened to another of her clients earlier in the year. That's why she wanted to keep the public protests going for Adriana. "I've got to shame these people to follow an order," she told me. That reminded me of my sobbing fifth-grade daughter in November 2016 telling me, "It's just a piece of paper." The fact that lawyers, of all people, do not have automatic confidence that the federal government will adhere to court orders is a disturbing marker of our times. "It's going to be the community at large that will shame ICE," Dee told me. Lawyers can't do it alone.

On Tuesday, the day she might have been deported, Adriana Arellana Cruz came home. Dee had gone back to the Immigration Court and, with Cecia and other volunteers there watching, got bond set: $5,000 in cash. Somehow the family had to find $5,000. At that point in time, the kids couldn't even pay rent. They had been evicted just after their mom was arrested—part of the compounding trauma that often follows taking a parent out of a home. But they got lucky: ¡Arriba! had recently set up a bond fund. This is a strategy that has increasingly been deployed in cities around the country. It's just a bank account—in this case, part of a non-profit organization, and managed by a board of immigrant community members who have all been affected personally by ICE detention. The fund hadn't really been made public yet, but they had quietly raised some money, and the immigrants on the board authorized the $5,000 for Adriana.

When I look back at Adriana's case, I see a process that was anything but smooth. The hotline that her children called didn't have a sustainable infrastructure behind it. It was really just Cecia. She could only manage that for about two weeks. "When the phone is ringing, you know that there is someone in trouble on the other end of the line. I slept with the phone next to me because I didn't want to miss a call," she said. Cecia wanted to be there for people. But she also knew that their needs usually couldn't be addressed because the resources simply weren't available. There needed to be trained volunteers in shifts, a screening tool, social workers for both volunteers and callers, and pro bono lawyers ready to take referrals. None of that was in place when Adriana's desperate kids made that phone call. Still, Adriana Arellana Cruz came home and ate dinner with her kids. For a moment, that's all that mattered.

* * *

We had come close in the legislature. Adriana had gone home. And yet for two years running ICE was able to use the two largest jails in Las Vegas to suck people into its deportation pipeline. Every time a police officer in Las Vegas arrested and booked an immigrant, whether for an unpaid ticket or a violent crime, the officer was effectively working for ICE and potentially breaking up a family. Our initial attempts to pass legislation to stop this had been swatted away. When Democrats pulled the transparency measure from consideration in 2019 Jon Ralston, the founder of the *Nevada Independent* and the state's leading political journalist, lamented: "This is who we are." Against the escalating attacks on immigrants from the Trump administration, we couldn't get the Democratic-led Nevada legislature or governor to take even the most moderate steps.[7]

This is why Bliss Requa-Trautz told me we need to be able to drive in more than one lane. And we were. We were driving in several lanes, actually, and settling in for a long campaign to pinch the Las Vegas deportation pipeline where it started, in the jails. In February 2019, just as the legislature was opening its session, ¡Arriba! staged a protest outside police headquarters against the sheriff's cooperation with ICE. In attendance was a newly elected county commissioner, Tick Segerblom, one of seven commissioners on whom the sheriff depended for his budget. Later in the year, representatives of Mi Familia Vota, Progressive Leadership Alliance of Nevada, and Make the Road had meetings with other county commissioners about police cooperation with ICE. In July 2019, another new commissioner, Justin Jones, threatened to oppose future staffing for the jail unless the police gave more information about the actual criminal records of the people they were handing over to ICE. Jones said: "As we speak, ICE agents are out raiding people's houses. ICE agents are holding people in cages at the direction of, frankly, a president who has weaponized an organization. And Metro has decided to re-up with ICE in that regard, and I have issues with that."[8]

Sheriff Lombardo had publicly promised to limit cooperation with ICE to people with more serious records. We knew from the cases coming into the UNLV Immigration Clinic that he hadn't implemented his promise. He had also not released any new operating procedures for the jail. But we could see that he was feeling far more pressure than in the past.

Meanwhile, dirty immigration lawyers were at work. As I described in chapter 6, the UNLV Immigration Clinic and the National Immigration Law Center had come very close to suing the sheriff to stop him from holding people in jail for ICE back in 2014. In 2018 and 2019, Mayra Salinas-Menjivar spent late afternoons and some evenings visiting ICE detainees in the Henderson Detention Center. She provided legal consults, and she quietly fed these cases to lawyers at NILC and the ACLU. Paloma Guerrero, who was still a law student, went with me and with some of the outside lawyers as an interpreter to do the same thing. ¡Arriba! sent cases, too, and Bliss kept the pressure on the lawyers to move the process along. We were plaintiff-hunting, getting ready to go to court to challenge cooperation between the police and ICE, even as the legislature debated the issue, even as the sheriff faced tougher questions on the county commission and mounting media scrutiny. Driving in multiple lanes.

On October 11, 2019, the ACLU of Nevada sent Sheriff Lombardo a letter demanding that he stop holding people in jail for ICE after they would otherwise be released. The letter repeated arguments that we had made back in 2014—that ICE detainers violate the U.S. Constitution because they aren't based on a sufficient finding of probable cause. In the United States, the police should not be able to lock a person up by just checking a box on a form, giving no evidence, and without having a judge review it.[9]

Now, in 2019, the ACLU had a new argument. Even if holding immigrants in a county jail was legal under federal law (which it likely isn't), local police didn't have authority to do it under Nevada law. That's because local police only have the power given to them by the state legislature. Nevada, like many states, has limited the police to criminal matters. This is important. I might be getting audited by the IRS, or I might have an ongoing lawsuit with a bank over an unpaid debt. Those are civil matters, and they aren't the business of the local police department. Likewise, immigration—and specifically deportation—is civil. That's important to ICE. That's why they don't have to take immigrants to a real federal court. It's also why the government doesn't provide lawyers to people facing deportation, which makes it much easier for ICE to get quick deportation orders against them. But for the same reason—because deportation is civil, not criminal—Sheriff Lombardo does not have any authority to detain someone just because ICE might want to deport that person. This argument had been gaining traction in courts around the United States, and in September 2019 it was endorsed by a federal district court in California.[10]

The ACLU gave the sheriff two weeks to respond. Litigation seemed inevitable. I hoped that finally, after years of collecting and sorting potential plaintiffs, a federal case might finally start, maybe the week of October 28, after the ACLU's deadline passed. I knew that the case would then drag on. But there were good legal arguments against the way people were being handed over to ICE in Las Vegas, and at last they would be before a judge. At a minimum, litigation would keep the pressure on, with the risk of financial liability, which might give the county commission or the state legislature a reason to take firmer action to rein in the sheriff.

On October 23, I was at the University of Michigan giving a lecture. It was an escape from the trench warfare back home—and, frankly, a chance to collect my thoughts. I had been looking forward to it for weeks. I turned my phone off during my lecture. I'd often had a problem when teaching back in UNLV with my now teenage daughter calling me in the middle of classes, demanding to know who would pick her up or pressuring me to give her more Internet access or order her food on Postmates. The Michigan lecture was going to be recorded on video, and I didn't want a buzzing phone to distract me. I put it in my bag on the side of the room.

Sure enough, when I'd finished the Q&A and thanked my hosts, my phone screen had alerts all over it. I sighed and braced myself. I thought it was my daughter. That's how things were going at home. And I did have a message or two from her. But that wasn't the main thing. The big news was that Sheriff Lombardo had suspended the 287(g) Program. His department issued a statement: "Until the uncertainty in the law is clarified, it must cease honoring ICE detainers." The next day, October 24, the City of Las Vegas announced that it, too, would stop honoring ICE detainers at the city jail—the jail that had turned Fernando over for deportation after his unpaid brake light ticket.[11]

I have learned not to get too excited at small pieces of good news. In this situation, there was still so much more that needed to happen. These changes had come about because the sheriff and the City of Las Vegas were cornered. They might slide back into the arms of ICE, just as they had before. We needed to get a more definitive legal decision to prevent this from happening again.

I also knew that ICE would regroup and attack again. Most likely, they would conduct a greater number of high-visibility arrests in the community. No longer able to rely on the local jails to hand people over, ICE officers would have to go out and arrest more on their own. The number of people who would be deported would probably be lower—that seems to be what has happened in other cities. But the community would likely be terrified by a more visible ICE presence. ICE promises as much. At the end of September, ICE issued a press statement about having made eighty arrests in the New York City area. That's not a particularly large number for one of the most densely populated regions of the country. But ICE meant it to send a message: "Any local jurisdiction thinking that refusing to cooperate with ICE will result in a decrease in local immigration enforcement is mistaken. Local jurisdictions that choose to not cooperate with ICE are likely to see an increase in ICE enforcement activity." With statements like this, ICE menaces and bullies local communities the way an abusive husband terrorizes his spouse. You made me hit you, they seem to be saying.[12]

But that's on them.

We knew pretty fast when Sheriff Lombardo failed to implement the promises he'd made at the Mexican restaurant back in the spring of 2019. But this time, it looked like the public statements promising a suspension of the 287(g) Program were being implemented at the Clark County Detention Center and at the Las Vegas City Jail. Overnight, the number of people being transferred from the local jails to ICE custody went way down, at least for the first weeks.

For a moment, people were just a little more protected. This protection didn't mean anything dramatic. There were no speeches, no rallies, no parades, no swelling music. What it meant was this: Somewhere in Las Vegas, as Thanksgiving and Christmas approached at the end of 2019, a father came home to his kids. He might be a model parent who helped his kids with math homework, or he might struggle to be patient enough, like many of us do. He might work too much, or he might struggle with unemployment. He might have had an unpaid ticket. Or maybe he'd done something else he shouldn't have, like peeing on the sidewalk or arguing with a police officer. A few months earlier his little mistake would have been the end. He would have been detained by ICE and processed for deportation. He would have become absent from his children's lives. A tragedy. A statistic. An empty chair at the family table. That's what would have happened in 2017, and in 2018, and for most of 2019. But instead, this man went home. That's all. For a moment, it would have to be enough.

10

The Coming Battle

THERE IS SO much to fear. At the end of the summer in 2019, the *Las Vegas Review-Journal* ran a long interview with Dana Fishburn, then the top ICE official in Nevada. In the interview, she complained that it takes too long to deport people. "Those individuals that are not in custody—say, one of the mothers that's not committed a crime, but she's here illegally—she's not going to court for three or four years right now. Who knows what could happen in those three years? She could have three more babies."[1]

By this point, it was no surprise that ICE wanted to deport mothers with no criminal record. In his first weeks in office, President Trump repealed the enforcement priority system that would have prevented that. But here was a federal official, in an on-the-record interview, invoking an ethnic stereotype, the immigrant woman who just keeps having babies. Fishburn seemed to be saying that she saw it as her mission to *prevent* immigrants from having babies. That's an invocation of white supremacist thinking—the idea that the purpose of immigration restrictions is to prevent the non-white population from growing. That's why ICE needs to deport people faster, so they don't reproduce, she seemed to be saying. By late 2019, this kind of talk was normal.

I am disturbed by more minor conversations, too, that maybe I should not think about so much. I had a conversation with a tow truck driver late one night when my car had a flat tire. He had bad news: because of the late hour, he told me, "all the tire shops are closed." And then he added: "But there are some Mexican tire shops that are open twenty-four hours." When I told the tow truck driver I would go to the shop that was open, he asked me for confirmation.

"You want to go to the Mexican tire shop?"

"Yes. The Mexican shop." Did I have to show more explicit, informed consent before being taken to such a place? I just needed the tire fixed.

Busy Bee Tire Shop, where the driver took me, is open twenty-four hours a day, while Firestone two doors down closes at 6 p.m. Unlike Firestone, Busy Bee was not well lit. There was a thin layer of grime on everything. There were lots of guys standing around the place, and it felt like they all knew each other. It was hard to tell who worked for the shop, who was a customer, and who was just hanging out. And they were all speaking in Spanish. But they switched to English when I approached, told me a price, and in ten minutes my Elantra was back on the road. That's all I cared about. That's what mattered.

I wonder: Why was the tow truck driver so unsure if I would be willing to go to this "Mexican" place, when it was the only place open? It was as if that tow truck driver was asking me for consent to enter another world, as if I did not already live in it, as if I had a choice. We too often treat our neighbors as expendable, optional, and invisible.

At best, we are stuck in some kind of stalemate. Many of my neighbors may be forced to live with ever-present fear for the foreseeable future. What toll will this take on people—on their health, on their families, on their kids' ability to learn? And of course, there is the real danger that some people may be taken away by the government. Families will be broken. People will be exposed to harm. Some already have been.

If I step back into my role as a professor, I can find theoretical cause for optimism. Immigration lawyers know that the machinery of cruelty was built into immigration law more than a century ago and was never taken out. In some ways, Donald Trump has helped many people to see the nature of the deportation and exclusion regime that we have constructed in this country. He makes little effort to blunt its cruelty, because, as others have written about his immigration policy, "the cruelty is the point." When the federal government was led by individuals who were more fundamentally decent and free of abject bigotry, the arbitrariness and often discriminatory nature of immigration law were harder for the general public to see. Previous administrations would often use their discretion to blunt the most severe applications of the legal tools they held in their hands. Now it is easier to see that these tools are dangerous.[2]

According to polls, Americans have actually grown more favorable to immigrants during the Trump presidency, at least in terms of willingness to offer legalization to undocumented immigrants already here and willingness to agree that immigrants benefit the country. In June 2018, 75 percent of adults told Gallup that "immigration is a good thing" for the country. In August 2019, the number of Americans who supported allowing refugees at the southern border into the country stood at 57 percent—a clear majority, and an increase of six points from the previous December. After the 2018 midterms, a majority of voters in key swing districts—including a majority of independents—thought that President Trump was "playing politics" by talking up the threat of migrant caravans, rather than acting out of "genuine concern" for the country. However, I also know that the way people answer pollsters on specific issues does not always correspond to the candidates they vote for. I fear that there is a small but pivotal group of voters who know President Trump is racist, don't really like the harshness and bombast of his immigration policy, but also don't see these as deal-breakers. I also know that there are many voters who dislike Trump but also dislike Democrats. We're on a razor's edge. As Cecia Alvarado told me, "It feels like this is just the beginning. They're not done with us."[3]

For the immediate future, much depends on the outcome of the 2020 elections. I make no predictions. Even if the Democrats win in 2020, it is not at all clear what they would do. Cecia told me that even if Trump is out in 2021, there would be a need for a concerted effort at healing wounds and restoring trust between the Latino community and the government. Her message to the community is to not rely on Washington, no matter who is in power.

In very brief terms, I would recommend four general steps to change immigration policy. The good news is that three of them are quite popular. The bad news, for Democrats, is that one necessary step will require going out on a limb politically.

First, embrace our undocumented neighbors. A CNN poll taken in June 2019 asked this question:

> In dealing with immigrants already living in the U.S. illegally, should the government's top priority be:
>
> - Deporting all people living in the U.S. illegally
> - Developing a plan to allow some people living in the U.S. illegally to become legal residents
> - No opinion

Only 15 percent supported deporting everyone who is living in the country illegally. Equally striking, only 4 percent said they have no opinion. This is a question on which Americans have made up their minds. In a July 2019 Marist poll, 64 percent of Americans favored "a pathway to citizenship for immigrants who are in the U.S. illegally"—about the same number who favored legalizing marijuana. A pathway to citizenship would require an act of Congress. However, a new president could at least prevent ICE from trying to deport most undocumented immigrants, essentially by improving on policies that came into force in the last years of the Obama administration. ICE can be transformed into an agency that focuses on serious criminals and leaves other people alone.[4]

Second, fix the administration of immigration laws. I talked to Nevada senator Catherine Cortez Masto, who was elected in 2016 on the same day as Donald Trump. When I'd heard her campaign in 2016, she hit the usual Democratic talking points: pass the DREAM Act, establish a path to citizenship, comprehensive immigration reform. But later she told me that before she was in the Senate, "I knew we had a broken system at the federal level. I didn't know the extent that we were underfunding the administration [of the law]." She gave the example of backlogged Immigration Courts, which had more than 1 million cases pending by the end of August 2019. "That gets lost. It's all about the process. A fair and equitable process. This administration has taken advantage of it." U.S. Citizenship and Immigration Services must process applications promptly. It should never take the government years to just read an application for a legal program. If we want people to follow the laws, the laws have to be administered in a way that makes following them possible. Congress should make the Immigration Courts an independent part of the judicial branch, and the judges should be given broad jurisdiction so that they have discretion when deportation would cause disproportionate harm. We should use the same checks and balances that we all learn about in grade school to help us make immigration policy fair. Even if this can't be passed through Congress, the attorney general can do a great deal single-handedly to improve the Immigration Courts. President Obama's attorneys general—Eric Holder and Loretta Lynch—failed to do that. That mistake can't happen again.[5]

Third, we should have a controlled and ordered border. This is popular. Large majorities want border security enhanced. Given a choice between "basically open borders" and "secure borders," secure borders wins 79 to 21 percent. We should be clear, though, that the poll questions on this are extremely superficial. Of course people should want "secure borders." No one should like a system where large numbers of people walk through a dangerous desert, escorted by criminals. All government programs should operate in an orderly way, governed by law. This doesn't mean we need to be cruel to anyone at the border. This doesn't mean we should lose a sense of proportionality. A person who crosses a border illegally has not committed a major crime, and she may have done so for sympathetic reasons. She may have done so out of necessity. Treat her accordingly.[6]

The real question is who should be allowed to enter legally. And that's where things get difficult politically. We have to actually welcome immigrants. Too much of immigration policy is built on the assumption that migration is a problem to be managed, like carbon emissions. It's considered a success when fewer people try to come to the United States. That's wrong. Our legal immigration system will be far more orderly if we start from the premise that migration is good, and that it's good when we are the kind of country to which people want to come. To migrate is human. It is part of how we survive in a difficult and unfair world. People do it because they have hope, because they have ambition to make things better, because they love their kids, because they want to escape harm. Migrants should be welcomed like people, not restricted like pollution or removed like trash.

The politics are difficult, which is why you don't see too many Democratic politicians saying they want more legal immigration. When asked in a January 2018 Harvard-Harris Poll how many legal immigrants should be allowed into the United States each year, the most popular answer was "1 to less than 250,000." In reality, the actual annual rate of legal immigration has not been below 250,000 since 1955. Only 19 percent in the Harvard-Harris Poll favored allowing more than 1 million people to immigrate legally. That's alarming, because the United States already grants legal permanent residency to around 1.1 million people each year. A Democrat running in a swing district is going to be reluctant to call for an increase in the level of legal immigration.[7]

Part of the problem is that people who have a loud voice in politics have spent several decades peddling myths about the immigration system. For several decades, proponents of immigration reform would say that undocumented immigrants "should go to the back of the line." President Barack Obama said this in 2013, trying to promote a comprehensive immigration reform bill:

> This bill would provide a pathway to earned citizenship for the 11 million individuals who are in this country illegally, a pathway that includes passing a background check, learning English, paying taxes and a penalty, and then going to the back of the line behind everyone who's playing by the rules and trying to come here legally.[8]

Obama made a mistake by talking that way, a mistake he inherited from a long line of politicians in his party. He implied that undocumented immigrants haven't been paying taxes. But they have been. He implied that they need a law to tell them to learn English. They don't. Worst of all, he told them to go to the back of the line. He should have helped educate the public by explaining clearly that there is no line. We can't fault people for not "playing by the rules" if the rules don't allow them to play at all. President Obama should have said: Our laws must allow for a fair chance for good people, and they don't right now. Change the law, not the people.

Media advisors will train candidates to avoid answering questions about whether they support more legal immigration. They will say, "I think the real issue is that we should not separate families and put kids in cages." And then they'll pivot to protecting people with preexisting medical conditions and opposing tax cuts for the wealthy. That's fine. It's part of how the game is played. Yet at some point Democrats will no longer be able to avoid the issue of opening the country to more legal immigration, for a couple of reasons.

The first reason is policy. If you don't address why people enter the country illegally—by giving them a way to enter legally—then it will keep happening. You'll end up promising the American public that you're fixing the immigration system, and then sooner or later chaotic scenes at the border will show everyone that you failed. We already have a system that self-evidently doesn't work. Our law makes groups of people theoretically eligible to immigrate legally, and then tells them to wait a decade or more to do so. We say that we have an asylum system to shelter the persecuted, and then the government fights asylum applications by rape victims because they weren't raped for the right reasons. That's a broken system. The public has a general sense that it's broken, too. Only 14 percent of Americans in swing states think the immigration system is working well. In the same poll, 86 percent supported "creating new laws to make our legal immigration system work better so that there is a working process for people to legally enter the country." Two other choices— reducing the waiting period to immigrate legally, and creating "a more fair and efficient process for those seeking asylum to the US at the border"—won the support of 71 and 78 percent, respectively. The argument that we need to be open to more legal immigration can be won, but people running for office will have to do a bit of work to explain to people why the system isn't working, and why we have to make it more open to fix it.[9]

The second reason Democrats have to embrace more legal immigration is that if they don't, voters will rightly think they're not quite playing straight. Most mainstream Democrats now support letting most undocumented immigrants stay in the United States. It now seems fairly comfortable for an elected official to declare that our immigrant neighbors are our friends, we should not deport them, that sort of thing. But there's a problem. You can't say,

I like immigrants, and then say, Please keep the number of new immigrants small. Voters may not fully understand why our immigration system is broken. But when a politician says, I would embrace the undocumented immigrants in the country, and then advocates guarding the border so that no more of them come, voters can tell that something doesn't quite fit. Democrats will end up taking relatively popular positions on immigration and yet will not be fully trusted on the issue, which gives demagogues an opening. So, just say it: We welcome immigrants. Period.

Still, for me, engaging in this kind of thought about what should be done if the 2020 elections go well feels like escapism. Everything that has happened in the first three years of the Trump administration feels like a prelude to something much worse. The immigration enforcement system in the United States was always a complicated, illogical contraption, the result of a century of struggle between America's xenophobic tendencies and our equally genuine commitments to respect families and minimize human suffering. This administration knows how to work inside the machine. They've removed the safety valves, the control panels, and the brakes, and as a result the machine can increasingly only do one thing. It removes people.

The number of new deportation cases in the Las Vegas Immigration Court keeps going up, at least through the summer of 2019. In fiscal year 2017, it averaged 231 a month. Then 275 in 2018, and just short of 400 a month in 2019. These cases don't always lead to speedy deportations because the Immigration Courts are so slow. For many years before President Trump, Congress pumped more and more money into border enforcement but did not increase funding for the Immigration Courts at a similar pace. In August 2019, Las Vegas immigration judges were scheduling hearings for June 2021. Nationally in 2019, the immigration courts took on average 962 days to complete a case. The Trump administration clogged its own deportation machine, in a sense, by trying to ram more and more deportation cases through the Immigration Courts. Yet they have been hiring more immigration judges. There were 46 percent more immigration judges working in April 2019 than in September 2016. The Department of Justice says that the pace of adjudication is picking up. Most important, no matter how slowly this pipeline flows, they are putting more people into it. If no one stops it, eventually most of them will be ordered removed.[10]

It's likely to get worse. The administration issued a rule to allow expedited removal, avoiding immigration court entirely. That's been challenged in court and initially blocked, but as I am writing this I do not know what the eventual outcome will be. The administration recently issued a rule that legal residency would not be available to people who might use government benefits to which they are legally entitled. This is known as the public charge rule. There is a court challenge pending there, too, also with an uncertain outcome. DACA is hanging by a thread. It could be dead before this book is published. For TPS, the same. Nearly a million people who are now protected could be exposed to deportation, and stripped of legal employment in the meantime.

Right now, my real message is that we have to care. By "we," I mean people like me. People who do not have to live in fear. People who can live among immigrants without really seeing them, much less the challenges they overcome just to get home to their children. In July 2018, the *Washington Post* asked voters what they thought the most important issue is. This was in the middle of the family separation crisis, when the Trump administration was ripping children away from parents. Immigration was one of voters' top three concerns—19 percent said it was their top concern, only 5 percent fewer than the number who picked "the economy and jobs." Yet the people who said immigration was the most important issue for them favored Republicans 47 to 40 percent. In other words, immigration is more important to people who support Trump than it is to the people who oppose how he treats immigrants. We can't continue that way. We have to take sides on this. We have to make our neighbors a priority.[11]

We've had some victories. We've kept some families safe, at least for a time. But on most days I read my email and I know: we're losing. At best we're buying time. Time has value, for sure. It means more days when kids get to be taken to school by their dad. Time means more nights when Mom is there to help with homework. Time means a chance for this country to choose another path. Yet I once told a student group that we needed to keep working until good people no longer need to be afraid. That feels like it will be a very long time from now. The people who make Las Vegas run day and night, the people who inhabit neighborhoods in Spring Valley and East Las Vegas, are a community under siege. I know we are building stronger defenses. But I know that the other side is getting even stronger and more efficient all the time. The other side is the federal government.

Yet people are still here, even when we don't always see them. Along Charleston Boulevard in Selena Torres's assembly district, there's a wonderful Central American bakery. It offers cakes piled high in the display cases, and a choice of Salvadoran- or Mexican-style tamales. It's a little place, and it's in a strip mall, of course, next to Tacos El Compita, which is usually packed at lunch. Drivers along Charleston don't always see this strip mall, and I suspect many people who commute along this artery from the suburban homes in Summerlin don't even know that it's there. From the road, you can only see a car wash, a fried chicken place, and a Subway—all with signs in English. The bakery and the taco shop and the *tienda de segunda* (secondhand store) are in a row behind, not easily visible from the main road. These are the layers of our country, those we see and those we don't.

In late summer 2019, a white supremacist massacred Latino shoppers in El Paso, Texas, followed a few days later by one of the largest immigration raids in recent history in Mississippi, followed immediately by the ubiquitous image on television of a hysterical eleven-year-old girl crying that her daddy is not a criminal. But still, the shops on Charleston opened. The car wash was running. Subway made sandwiches. And behind it, on the side of the parking lot that not everyone can see, the lunch crowd waited for their tacos. Kids begged their moms for sweets at the bakery. People were still out, even amid all the fear. Most of them didn't have a choice, of course. They had to work. They had to eat. And also, this is their home. It is the city we share.

While he waited for his deportation case in court, I met Fernando Gonzalez at a McDonald's. He has to make payments to his lawyer every month, but he's got a steady income now. His wife, Reina, also is working, at one of the fancier resorts on the Strip. She's getting Culinary Workers Union health insurance, and Fernando is hoping it will help him, too. He has a broken upper tooth that he could never afford to fix before. They moved to a smaller apartment to save money. He's paying off all his debts to all the people who lent them money when he was locked up. Most important, their baby, Diamond, is healthy—though she makes a mess everywhere, he told me with a smile. I know Fernando is worried. But he still drives his truck. He still goes to work. He posted photos on Facebook of himself taking his older daughter on a boat ride one weekend. They smiled together. Just like Elvis said, a strong heart and a nerve of steel.

Rebeca, the daughter of the house cleaner who bought her mom a house, sent me a photo of the guava tree that she and her mom had planted, the tree that I had doubted would grow in Las Vegas. It bore ripe fruit. Manuela and Olivero are still cooking in some of the best restaurants we have. Come visit my town; you may get the chance to eat their food. Their oldest daughter, Adelina, is studying for the LSAT and planning to apply to law school. She tells me she's doing well on the practice exams. Maybe she'll be in my class in a few years. I would really like that.

Danger looms over many. This may be a very long fight. But it's worth it. This is a town that lives on the edge, pushes its luck, puts on a show, and then goes home to the kids. As long as that can happen, this is not over. These are my neighbors, and I want them to stay.

Viva Las Vegas.

Acknowledgments

THIS BOOK COULD NOT HAVE been written if neighbors of mine in Las Vegas had not opened their life stories and their homes to me. I can't name all of these people. Some are in the book and some are not. I will remember the hours I spent at your kitchen tables and on your sofas. I often interviewed whole families together, and some of the moments I will remember most were when kids learned things about their parents that they did not know. The greatest pieces of encouragement I received were from teenagers who thanked me for telling their parents' stories. My greatest worry is whether I've done them justice. It has been a humbling experience to understand how fiercely some people have had to struggle to get their kids to school, go to work, and feel secure that they will be allowed to do the same thing again the next day. I hope more people come to understand that struggle, and to respect it.

I asked for interviews with officials of the City of Las Vegas, Las Vegas Metro, and Immigration and Customs Enforcement (ICE) for this book. A spokesperson for Metro sent me an email asking for clarification about what I wanted to talk about. Other than that, none of them got back to me. Astrid Silva declined to be interviewed for this book as well.

Although all errors in this book are mine, I thank Michelle Kagan Gaines, Mayra Salinas-Menjivar, Josh Gupta-Kagan, and Cathryn Humphris for excellent and necessary feedback. I owe special gratitude to Bliss Requa-Trautz, Bethany Khan, Cecia Alvarado, Hardeep "Dee" Sull, and Leo Murrieta, who were indispensable allies, facilitators, and counselors, in addition to being willing to be interviewed. The ¡Arriba! Las Vegas Workers Center did essential public records work to discover connections between the City of Las Vegas and ICE. Thank you to Assemblywoman Selena Torres and her dad, and to

Senator Catherine Cortez Masto for making time for me. Michael Lyle gave me a useful tip.

My agent, Barbara Braun, saw promise in this project from an early stage. Alrica Goldstein believed in the book and in my ability to meet deadlines. I thank Clark Whitehorn for pushing this toward the finish line.

My spouse and my best friend, Cindy Johnston, put up with a lot during the battles described in this book. She told me to keep going, even when that was difficult, and she also told me when to stop. I am forever grateful. I love you. Also, Cindy is the toughest editor on this planet.

My older daughter, Maya, has been my conscience more than she realizes. Thank you, Maya. You will lead us to better. I know it. My younger daughter, Tesi, asked me on election night in 2016, "Daddy, why did the bully win?" I know you deserve an answer. It worries me, too. We will make a world worthy of both of you.

Thank you to my father-in-law, Dan Johnston, for being a strong keel in rocky seas. I thank my late grandparents, Millie, Arthur, Fred, and Rhoda, and my late mother-in-law, Jan. I would have liked them to read this, and it saddens me that they can't.

Dean Dan Hamilton and Associate Dean Rebecca Nathanson were rock-solid supporters of the UNLV Immigration Clinic during the period I write about here. There were many times when Dean Hamilton would have had good cause to just say no to my ideas. Instead, he said, "Let's keep talking." Good things came from that, I think. I thank Alissa Cooley and Katelyn Leese, who inspired me by their example to climb back into the trenches. I thank Martha Arellano, the soul of the UNLV Immigration Clinic, for reminding us always of the humanity of our clients, and for keeping the ship afloat generally. To Laura Barrera—on paper I was supposed to be your mentor, but I think you taught me more often. I'm grateful. And a second thank you to Mayra Salinas-Menjivar, who changed the law in Nevada, helped dozens, and never took a vacation.

Finally, thank you to my parents, Laura and Richard Kagan. I grew up comfortably in the suburbs in upstate New York. But my parents made sure I knew that I also come from a scared little girl hiding in an oven during a pogrom and from an exhausted mother and father running a laundry in Brooklyn. I carry them with me, always.

Glossary

Government Agencies and Laws

Customs and Border Protection (CBP): A branch of the Department of Homeland Security (DHS), CBP is responsible for patrolling the borders of the United States. They are also the folks who check your passport at airports when you return from a foreign trip.

Immigration and Customs Enforcement (ICE): Also a branch of DHS, ICE is a police department that enforces immigration laws inside the United States. It includes multiple divisions, including Homeland Security Investigations (HSI), which investigates human trafficking, money laundering, and other serious transnational crimes, and Enforcement and Removal Operations (ERO), which enforces routine immigration laws. ICE-ERO is the source of most controversy involving ICE.

Immigration and Nationality Act (INA): The primary law governing immigration and citizenship in the United States. It has its origins in the late nineteenth century, but the basic form of the current law was introduced in 1952 with the McCarran-Walter Act. Promoted by Nevada senator Walter McCarran for explicitly anti-Communist, anti-Semitic, and xenophobic purposes, it includes the provision that President Trump used to ban migration from certain Muslim countries. In 1965, the law was amended to add an anti-discrimination provision and to remove the 1924 national origin quotas that had blocked most immigration from Eastern and Southern Europe. Together the 1952 and 1965 laws opened the country up to more legal immigration but failed to cure many of the structural failures of our immigration system.

Immigration and Naturalization Service (INS): The old INS included the functions of our current ICE, CBP, and USCIS. It was abolished with the creation of the Department of Homeland Security in 2003.

Immigration Courts: Adjudication bodies that decide whether to issue orders of removal at the request of ICE. The Immigration Courts are built to function somewhat like regular courts, but they are not part of the judicial branch. The Immigration Courts are instead part of the Department of Justice, which normally plays the role of prosecutor and defender of the government in other areas of law. Immigration judges are employees of the attorney general, who can change the procedures of the Immigration Courts and the interpretation of immigration law. In general, immigration judges' decisions may be appealed to the **Board of Immigration Appeals (BIA)**, which is also under the attorney general. Although they can grant asylum, the Immigration Courts have only limited authority to grant legal residency to immigrants.

U.S. Citizenship and Immigration Service (USCIS): The branch of the Department of Homeland Security that processes most applications for legal residency, other forms of legal immigration, and naturalization. Although designed as a "service" agency that could say yes to immigrants, it has increasingly been brought into immigration enforcement. In February 2018, USCIS changed the mission statement on its website so that it no longer includes the phrase "America's promise as a nation of immigrants."

Important Concepts

Birthright citizenship: A colloquial term describing how people obtain U.S. citizenship by being born in the United States. Often disputed by anti-immigrant politicians, including President Trump, this is the form of citizenship with the most explicit basis in the U.S. Constitution.

Deferred action: A policy and practice dating back at least to the 1970s by which the federal government decides not to pursue deportation against a non-citizen because doing so would be inhumane, inefficient, or generally not in the country's best interest. By regulation issued during the Reagan administration, an immigrant with deferred action is eligible to apply for employment authorization.

Deferred Action for Childhood Arrivals (DACA): A program launched by President Obama in 2012 to give two-year reprieves from deportation, plus employment authorization, to people who (among other things) came to the United States before they were sixteen, were under age thirty-one in 2012, had no criminal record, and were unlawfully present in 2012. The Trump administration has been trying to end DACA since September 2017, but people who already had the permits have been allowed to apply for renewals because of injunctions issued by federal courts. The Supreme Court will likely decide the fate of the program in 2020.

Entry without inspection (EWI): The act of crossing the border at an unauthorized location. Immigrants who are EWI are generally blocked (though there are some exceptions) from adjusting their status inside the United States, even if they marry a citizen. Also known as improper entry by an alien, which is criminalized as a misdemeanor at Section 1325 of Title 8 of the U.S. Code.

Legal permanent residency (LPR): Known colloquially as a "green card," this is the best legal status that an immigrant can obtain in the United States, other than naturalization as a citizen. Legal permanent residency can be lost by being convicted of certain crimes. A person with LPR status will be issued an identity card about the size of a driver's license. The cards have often been green in color, which is where the phrase "green card" originated.

Mixed family: A household in which family members have different immigration statuses, including at least one person who is undocumented. In a common situation, one or both parents may be undocumented and thus in danger of being deported, their oldest child may have DACA, and the youngest children may be U.S. citizens.

Misdemeanor: Generally in American law, a minor crime (but still a crime). In federal law a **felony** is a crime punishable by more than a year in prison, while a misdemeanor is punishable by less than a year in prison. In federal law, improper entry is a misdemeanor, while reentry after having already been removed is a felony. In Nevada, speeding, failing to stop at a crosswalk, using a cellphone while driving, and other minor traffic offenses are classified as misdemeanors.

Naturalization: The process by which a non-citizen becomes a citizen, if the person was not a citizen at birth.

Temporary protected status (TPS): A legal immigration status in which the Secretary of Homeland Security allows a class of non-citizens to stay,

for renewable periods, because there is an armed conflict that would
threaten their personal safety if they were to return to their home country,
or a natural disaster that substantially disrupts living conditions. People
can apply for TPS only if they are already here. They can't apply for a visa
to come to the United States under the TPS program. The Trump administration has tried to end the protection for six nationalities benefiting
from TPS.

Removal: The term used in the INA for deportation.

Unlawfully present: The condition of being in the United States without
legal authorization, some because they entered illegally, and others
because they overstayed their visas. While crossing the border without
permission can be a crime, being unlawfully present in the United States
is not. However, ICE may target any unlawfully present person for
removal. A person who has been unlawfully present for a year or more will
be generally barred from legally immigrating for ten years. Roughly 11
million people are in this situation.

Key Government Officials

Jeff Sessions: President Trump's first attorney general. He aggressively used
his powers as head of the Department of Justice to narrow interpretations
of immigration law and to limit opportunities in Immigration Court for
immigrants to avoid deportation. He had been the most stridently
anti-immigrant member of the United States Senate. He resigned in
November 2018 and was eventually replaced by **William Barr.**

Kirstjen Nielsen: Donald Trump's second Secretary of Homeland Security,
from December 2017 to April 2019. Preceded by **John Kelly.**

Stephen Miller: Senior advisor to President Trump. A former aide to Jeff
Sessions, Miller is often described as the driving force in the White House
behind anti-immigrant policies.

Wilbur Ross: President Trump's Secretary of Commerce. He ordered steps
to add questions about citizenship to the 2020 census, which generated
fears that the census would undercount Latino and Asian families.

Notes

Preface

1. Immigration and Nationality Act, 8 U.S.C. § 1101(a)(15).
2. Immigration and Nationality Act, 8 U.S.C. § 1101(a)(3).
3. "Illegal," Merriam-Webster.com.

Introduction

1. Maria Sacchetti, "ACLU: US Has Taken Nearly 1,000 Child Migrants from Their Parents Since Judge Ordered Stop to Border Separations," *Washington Post*, July 30, 2019; Jean Guerrero (interview), "Migrant Seeking Asylum Says His Toddler Was Taken Away at the U.S. Border," *PBS NewsHour*, December 22, 2017.
2. Diane Bernard, "The Time a President Deported 1 Million Mexican Americans for Supposedly Stealing U.S. Jobs," *Washington Post*, August 13, 2018; Bernard, "The Time a President Deported 1 Million."
3. Emanuella Grinberg and Konstantin Toropin, "A US-Born Citizen Who Was in Immigration Detention for Three Weeks Has Been Released," CNN.com, July 25, 2019; Mary Papenfuss, "Immigration Officials Snatch 9-Year-Old U.S. Citizen Heading to School, Hold Her for 2 Days," *HuffPost*, March 23, 2019.
4. Immigration and Customs Enforcement Arrests," Transactional Records Access Clearinghouse, Syracuse University, data through May 2018, https://trac.syr.edu /phptools/immigration/arrest; United States Census Bureau, American Community Survey 2012–2016, https://www.census.gov/acs/www/data/data-tables-and-tools/data -profiles/2016; "U.S. Unauthorized Immigrant Population Estimates by State, 2016," Pew Research Center, February 5, 2019, https://www.pewresearch.org/hispanic /interactives/u-s-unauthorized-immigrants-by-state; "Mapping the USA's Diversity 1960–2060," *USA Today*, October 21, 2014, https://www.usatoday.com/story/news /nation/2014/10/21/diversity-map/17657485.

Chapter 1
The Graveyards of Nevada

1. American Community Survey 2012–2016, ZCTA5 89115; "Sandy Searles Miller Elementary School," GreatSchools.org, last accessed August 20, 2019.
2. Beth Lew-Williams, *The Chinese Must Go* (Cambridge, MA: Harvard University Press, 2018), 44; Edan Strekal, "Chinatown (Site)," RenoHistorical.org, last accessed August 21, 2019, http://renohistorical.org/items/show/173; Lew-Williams, *The Chinese Must Go*, 3, 98–102.

Chapter 2
Plan B

1. Todd Miller, "Over 7,000 Bodies Have Been Found at the US-Mexican Border Since the '90s," *The Nation*, April 24, 2018.
2. *Border Security Metrics Report*, Department of Homeland Security, February 26, 2019, 10.
3. "U.S. Unauthorized Immigrant Population Estimates by State, 2016," Pew Research Center, February 5, 2019, https://www.pewresearch.org/hispanic/interactives/u-s-unauthorized-immigrants-by-state.
4. "Fact Sheet: Immigrants in Nevada," American Immigration Council, October 6, 2017, https://www.americanimmigrationcouncil.org/research/immigrants-in-nevada.
5. Tal Kopan, "ICE Director: Undocumented Immigrants 'Should Be Afraid,'" CNN.com, June 16, 2017.
6. Catalina Gonella, "Visa Overstays Outnumber Illegal Border Crossings, Trend Expected to Continue," NBCNews.com, March 7, 2017; Robert Warren, "US Undocumented Population Continued to Fall from 2016 to 2017, and Visa Overstays Significantly Exceeded Illegal Crossings for the Seventh Consecutive Year," Center for Migration Studies of New York, January 16, 2019; "Of the estimated 515,000 arrivals in 2016, a total of 320,000, or 62 percent, were overstays and 190,000, or 38 percent, were EWIs." Warren, "US Undocumented Population Continued to Fall."
7. Warren, "US Undocumented Population Continued to Fall."
8. Warren, "US Undocumented Population Continued to Fall"; "Fast Facts: United States Travel and Tourism Industry 2016," National Travel and Tourism Office, November 2017, https://travel.trade.gov/outreachpages/download_data_table/Fast_Facts_2016.pdf; Maria Sacchetti and Kevin Uhrmacher, "Nations Targeted by U.S. for High Rates of Visa Overstays Account for Small Number of Violators," *Washington Post*, April 24, 2019.

Chapter 3
The Cleaners

1. Jerry Markon, "Can a 3-Year-Old Represent Herself in Immigration Court? This Judge Thinks So," *Washington Post*, March 5, 2016.
2. Interview with Bethany Khan, director of communications for Culinary Workers Local 226, July 24, 2019.
3. "Immigrate," Merriam-Webster.com, last accessed July 30, 2019.

4. Immigration and Nationality Act, 8 U.S.C. § 1254a.

5. "Fact Sheet: Temporary Protected Status in the United States—Beneficiaries from El Salvador, Honduras and Haiti," American Immigration Council, October 23, 2017.

6. "Fact Sheet: Temporary Protected Status in the United States."

7. "TPS Holders in Nevada," Center for American Progress, October 23, 2017.

8. *Ramos v. Nielsen*, Order Granting Plaintiffs' Motion for Preliminary Injunction, No. 18-cv-01554-EMC, N.D. Cal., October 3, 2018.

9. Tom K. Wong, Sanaa Abrar, Tom Jawetz, Ignacia Rodriguez Kmec, Patrick O'Shea, Greisa Martinez Rosas, and Philip E. Wolgin, "Amid Legal and Political Uncertainty, DACA Remains More Important than Ever," Center for American Progress, August 15, 2018.

10. Barack Obama, Facebook post, September 5, 2017 ("Immigration can be a controversial topic . . ."), www.facebook.com/barackobama/posts/10155227588436749; Rep. Steny Hoyer, "Press Release: A Look at H.R.6, the Dream and Promise Act of 2019," March 12, 2019; . A. Crunden, "DREAMers Face Anxiety, Terror amid Back-and-Forth on DACA," ThinkProgress.org, September 18, 2017; David Bacon, "Undocumented Youth Are Here Through No Fault of Their Own. But It's Not Their Parents' Fault, Either," InTheseTimes .com, November 5, 2015.

Chapter 4
The Unaccompanied

1. Immigration and Nationality Act, 8 U.S. Code § 1229a; "Remove," Merriam-Webster .com, last accessed July 30, 2019.

2. *United States v. Peralta-Sanchez*, Oral Argument, 2016 WL 3232805, May 4, 2016 ("For those individuals providing a right to counsel would take a procedure that is intended by Congress to be expeditious and make it entirely unexpeditious").

3. Illegal Immigration Reform and Immigrant Responsibility Act of 1996 (IIRIRA), 110 Stat. 3009-546; Immigration and Nationality Act, 8 U.S.C. § 1182(9)(B); Jennifer Lee Koh, "Removal in the Shadows of Immigration Court," *Southern California Law Review* 90 (2017): 181–236.

4. Designating Aliens for Expedited Removal, 69 Fed. Reg. 48877, 48880–81, August 11, 2004; Koh, "Removal," 235.

5. Immigration and Nationality Act, 8 U.S.C. § 1225(b)(1)(A)(iii)(II); Executive Order No. 13767, Border Security and Immigration Enforcement Improvements, 82 Fed. Reg. 8793 (January 25, 2017).

6. "Fact Sheet: A Primer on Expedited Removal," American Immigration Council, July 22, 2019.

7. Immigration and Nationality Act, 8 U.S.C. § 1101(a)(42).

8. *Perez-Zenteno v. U.S. Attorney General*, 913 F.3d 1301 (11th. Cir 2019).

9. *Perez-Zenteno v. U.S. Attorney General*, 913 F.3d at 1304.

10. Immigration and Nationality Act, 8 U.S.C. § 1101(a)(42).

11. "Asylum Decisions and Denials Jump in 2018," Transactional Records Access Clearinghouse, Syracuse University, November 29, 2018, https://trac.syr.edu/immigration /reports/539.

12. Matter of L-E-A-, 27 I&N Dec. 581, 582 (A.G. 2019).

13. Jaya Ramji-Nogales, Andrew I. Schoenholtz, and Philip G. Schrag, "Refugee Roulette: Disparities in Asylum Adjudication," *Stanford Law Review* 60 (November 2007): 330.

14. "Asylum Decisions by Custody, Representation, Nationality, Location, Month and Year, Outcome and More," Transactional Records Access Clearinghouse, Syracuse University, last accessed August 21, 2019, https://trac.syr.edu/phptools/immigration/asylum; Judge Munish Sharda, Transactional Records Access Clearinghouse, Syracuse University, last accessed August 21, 2019, https://trac.syr.edu/immigration/reports/judgereports /00474LVG/index.html; Gabriel Thompson, "Your Judge Is Your Destiny," Topic.com, July 2019.

15. "The Attorney General's Judges: How U.S. Immigration Courts Became a Deportation Tool," Innovation Law Lab and Southern Poverty Law Center, June 2019, 6, 22; Thompson, "Your Judge Is Your Destiny."

16. Beth Fertig, "Presiding Under Pressure," WNYC News, May 21, 2019; Julia Preston, "Is It Time to Remove Immigration Courts from Presidential Control?," The Marshall Project, August 28, 2019.

17. Brad Heath, "As Feds Focused on Detaining Kids, Border Drug Prosecutions Plummeted," *USA Today*, October 10, 2018.

18. Melissa del Bosque, "The Case That Made an Ex-ICE Attorney Realize the Government Was Relying on False 'Evidence' Against Migrants," ProPublica, August 13, 2019; John Washington, "Bad Information," The Intercept, August 11, 2019.

19. Matter of Castro-Tum, 27 I&N Dec. 271 (A.G. 2018).

Chapter 5
Two Arrests

1. Dan Whitcomb, "Nevada Has Highest Proportion of Illegal Immigrants in U.S.: Study," Reuters.com, November 18, 2014.

2. "Fact Sheet: Immigrants in Nevada," American Immigration Council, October 6, 2017; Hugo Bachega, "Trump Immigration: The Effects of a Raid on One Tiny Town," BBC .com, July 2, 2018.

3. "Details on Deportation Proceedings in Immigration Court," Transactional Records Access Clearinghouse, Syracuse University, last accessed November 30, 2019, https://trac.syr .edu/phptools/immigration/nta (Las Vegas Immigration Court, Initial Filings, September 2019).

4. "Secure Communities: A Fact Sheet," American Immigration Council, November 29, 2011.

5. "Secure Communities: A Fact Sheet"; César Cuauhtémoc García Hernández, *Crimmigration Law* (Chicago: ABA Publishing, 2015), 258–59.

6. Hernández, *Crimmigration Law*; "Secure Communities," National Conference of State Legislatures, July 26, 2012.

7. "Secure Communities," 148; Jennifer M. Chacón, "Overcriminalizing Immigration," *Journal of Criminal Law and Criminology* 102 (Summer 2012): 615, 640–47; César Cuauhtémoc García Hernández, "Deconstructing Crimmigration," *U.C. Davis Law Review* 52 (2018): 200; Doris Marie Provine, Monica W. Varsanyi, Paul G. Lewis, and Scott H. Decker, *Policing Immigrants: Local Law Enforcement on the Front Lines* (Chicago: University of Chicago Press, 2016), 149; Juliet Stumpf, "The Crimmigration Crisis: Immigrants,

Crime, and Sovereign Power," *American University Law Review* 56 (2006): 367–419; Hernández, *Crimmigration Law.*

8. *Border Security Metrics Report*, Department of Homeland Security, February 26, 2019, 10.

9. Barack Obama, "Remarks by the President in Address to the Nation on Immigration," November 20, 2014.

10. Doyle Murphy, "ICE Raid Nets Estimated 300 Workers in Greeley Plant," *Greeley Tribune*, December 12, 2006; Stewart M. Powell, "Bush Administration Steps Up Immigration Raids," *San Francisco Chronicle*, June 1, 2008.

11. Jeh Johnson, "Memorandum: Policies for the Apprehension, Detention and Removal of Undocumented Immigrants," Department of Homeland Security, November 20, 2014.

12. Marc R. Rosenblum, "Understanding the Potential Impact of Executive Action on Immigration Enforcement," Migration Policy Institute, July 13, 2015; Julia Preston, "Most Undocumented Immigrants Will Stay Under Obama's New Policies, Report Says," *New York Times*, July 23, 2015.

13. Executive Order No. 13768, Enhancing Public Safety in the Interior of the United States, 82 Fed. Reg. 8799 (January 25, 2017); Esther Yu Hsi Lee, "'No Population Is Off the Table': Data Shows Increase in Immigrants Arrests Inside U.S.," ThinkProgress.org, December 5, 2017; Ed Kilgore, "ICE Has Tripled the Number of Undocumented Immigrants Without Criminal Records It Arrests," NYMag.com, August 13, 2018; Josh Bowden, "ICE Arrests of Immigrants with No Criminal Convictions Rises: Report," *The Hill*, May 18, 2018.

14. Shoba Sivaprasad Wadhia, *Banned: Immigration Enforcement in the Time of Trump* (New York: NYU Press, 2019), 41–42, 43; Andrea Castillo, "'Collateral Arrests' by ICE Amount to Racial Profiling, Violate Immigrants' Rights, Lawyers Say," *Los Angeles Times*, February 4, 2018.

15. Kristen Bialik, "Most Immigrants Arrested by ICE Have Prior Criminal Convictions, a Big Change from 2009," Pew Research Center, February 15, 2018.

16. Guillermo Cantor, Emily Ryo, and Reed Humphrey, "Changing Patterns of Interior Immigration Enforcement in the United States 2016–2018," American Immigration Council, July 1, 2019, 2; Bialik, "Most Immigrants"; Cantor et al., "Changing Patterns," 19; "ICE Detains Fewer Immigrants with Serious Criminal Convictions Under Trump Administration," Transactional Records Access Clearinghouse, Syracuse University, December 6, 2019, https://trac.syr.edu/immigration/reports/585.

17. Alan Gomez, "ICE Sets Record for Arrests of Undocumented Immigrants with No Criminal Record," *USA Today*, March 21, 2019; "ICE Focus Shifts Away from Detaining Serious Criminals," Transactional Records Access Clearinghouse, Syracuse University, June 25, 2019, https://trac.syr.edu/immigration/reports/564; "ICE Focus Shifts Away from Detaining Serious Criminals."

18. *Arizona v. United States*, 567 U.S. 387, 396 (2012)

Chapter 6
Psychological Warfare

1. Scott Bixby, "ICE Told Agents 'Happy Hunting' as They Prepped for Raid," *Daily Beast*, July 3, 2019.

2. A. C. Thompson, "Inside the Secret Border Patrol Facebook Group Where Agents Joke About Migrant Deaths and Post Sexist Memes," ProPublica.com, July 1, 2019; Lauren Frias, "Border Patrol Chief Who Was Member of Secret Facebook Group Said She Didn't Realize 'Highly Offensive' Posts Were Being Shared Until ProPublica Report," *Business Insider*, July 26, 2019.

3. Catherine E. Shoichet, "A Father and Daughter Drowned Crossing the Rio Grande. Here's How Their Journey Began," CNN.com, June 26, 2019.

4. Nick Miroff, "ICE Raids Targeting Migrant Families Slated to Start Sunday in Major U.S. Cities," *Washington Post*, June 21, 2019; Julia Ainsley and Jacob Soboroff, "ICE to Launch Mass Raids Targeting Undocumented Families on Sunday," NBCNews.com, June 21, 2019.

5. Josh Wingrove, Billy House, and Margaret Talev, "Trump Delays Raids on Migrants, Cites Democrats' Requests," Bloomberg.com, June 22, 2019; Camilo Montoya-Galvez, "Top Immigration Official Says ICE Is Willing to Deport 1 Million Undocumented Immigrants," CBS News, July 7, 2019; Miriam Jordan, "More than 2,000 Migrants Were Targeted in Raids. 35 Were Arrested," *New York Times*, July 23, 2019.

6. "Trump Accused of 'Deporting Kids with Cancer' After the Administration Reportedly Ends Medical Deferral Program," TheWeek.com, August 26, 2019.

7. Brenda Eskenazi, Carolyn A. Fahey, and Katherine Kogut, "Association of Perceived Immigration Policy Vulnerability with Mental and Physical Health Among US-Born Latino Adolescents in California," *JAMA Pediatrics* 173, no. 8 (2019): 744–753; Kara Manke, "Deportation Worries Fuel Anxiety, Poor Sleep, Among U.S.-Born Latinx youth," *Berkeley News*, June 24, 2019; Alison Gemmill, Ralph Catalano, Joan A. Casey, et al., "Association of Preterm Births Among US Latina Women with the 2016 Presidential Election," *JAMA Network Open* 2, no. 7 (2019): e197804.

8. Caitlin Oprysko, "Trump Talks Up Success of Raids, Despite Little Evidence of Widespread Deportations," Politico.com, July 15, 2019.

9. Elliott Spagat, "Making an Immigration Arrest Requires Hours of Surveillance," Associated Press, July 16, 2019.

10. Guillermo Cantor, Emily Ryo, and Reed Humphrey, "Changing Patterns of Interior Immigration Enforcement in the United States 2016–2018," American Immigration Council, July 1, 2019, 22.

11. Cantor, Ryo, and Humphrey, "Changing Patterns," 22.

12. "Immigration and Customs Enforcement Arrests," Transactional Records Access Clearinghouse, Syracuse University, last visited July 19, 2019, https://trac.syr.edu /phptools/immigration/arrest (data through May 2018; TRAC lists 133 arrests as "located," as in located by ICE).

13. "Immigration and Customs Enforcement Arrests."

14. "Immigration and Customs Enforcement Arrests"; "Ten-Fold Difference in Odds of ICE Enforcement Depending upon Where You Live," Transactional Records Access Clearinghouse, Syracuse University, April 11, 2019, https://trac.syr.edu/immigration /reports/555/#f1.

15. Christianne Klein, "Mayor Says Las Vegas Isn't Sanctuary City," 8NewsNow.com, January 26, 2017; City of Las Vegas, COR 5962, Arrest and Detention of Foreign Nationals, May 2017, available at http://arribalasvegas.org/wp-content/uploads/2019/03/COR -5962-Arrest-and-Detention-of-Foreign-Nationals.pdf.

16. Wayne A. Logan, "Criminal Law Sanctuaries," *Harvard Civil Rights–Civil Liberties Law Review* 38 (2003): 323–24.

17. Sophie H. Pirie, "The Origins of a Political Trial: The Sanctuary Movement and Political Justice," *Yale Journal of Law and the Humanities* 2 (1990): 381–416; John Morton, Director, U.S. Immigration and Customs Enforcement, Memorandum on Enforcement Actions at or Focused on Sensitive Locations from to Field Office Directors, Special Agents in Charge, and Chief Counsel, 2011.

18. "Sanctuary City Ordinance," City and County of San Francisco, Office of Civic Engagement and Immigrant Affairs, https://sfgov.org/oceia/sanctuary-city-ordinance-0, last visited August 3, 2019; S.F. Admin Code § 12H.1.

19. Carrie Kaufman, "Will UNLV Become a Sanctuary Campus?" KNPR Nevada Radio, December 1, 2016; Jason A. Cade, "Immigration Equity's Last Stand: Sanctuaries and Legitimacy in an Era of Mass Immigration Enforcement," *Northwestern University Law Review* 113, no. 3 (2017): 441, 484, 494–497.

20. Executive Order No. 13768; Immigration and Nationality Act, 8 U.S.C. 1373.

21. For a more complete taxonomy, see Christopher N. Lasch, R. Linus Chan, Ingrid V. Eagly, Dina Francesca Haynes, Annie Lai, Elizabeth M. McCormick, and Juliet P. Stumpf, "Understanding 'Sanctuary Cities,'" *Boston College Law Review* 59 (2018): 1703–1774; S.F. Admin Code § 12H.2.

22. S.F. Admin Code § 12I.3.

23. According to Syracuse University's TRAC program in a 2019 report ("Ten-Fold Difference"), the willingness of different local police departments to cooperate with ICE is one of the main reasons the chances of an undocumented person being arrested and deported are quite different in different locations. "Ten-Fold Difference"; "Immigration and Customs Enforcement Arrests."

24. City of Las Vegas, COR 5962, Arrest and Detention of Foreign Nationals.

Chapter 7
How to Talk to Your Neighbors About Immigration

1. Thomas B. Edsall, "How Immigration Foiled Hillary," *New York Times*, October 5, 2017.

2. "Mapping the USA's Diversity from 1960–2060," USAToday.com, October 21, 2014.

3. Edsall, "How Immigration Foiled Hillary."

4. Stanley Greenberg and Nancy Zdunkewicz, "Macomb County in the Age of Trump," Democracy Corps and Roosevelt Institute, March 9, 2017.

5. Josh Dawsey and Nick Miroff, "The Hostile Border Between Trump and the Head of DHS," *Washington Post*, May 25, 2018.

6. *Justice Manual*, U.S. Department of Justice 9-28.300, November 2015.

7. Hunter Hallman, "How to Undocumented Immigrants Pay Federal Taxes? An Explainer," Bipartisan Policy Center, March 28, 2018.

8. Timothy Kane, "The Economic Effect of Immigration," Hoover Institution, February 17, 2015.

9. Michael Greenstone and Adam Looney, "What Immigration Means for U.S. Employment and Wages," The Hamilton Project, May 4, 2012.

10. Rakesh Kochhar, C. Soledad Espinoza, and Rebecca Hinze-Pifer, "After the Great Recession: Foreign Born Gain Jobs; Native Born Lose Jobs," Pew Research Center, October 29, 2010; Kochhar, Espinoza, and Hinze-Pifer, "After the Great Recession."

11. Kochhar, Espinoza, and Hinze-Pifer, "After the Great Recession."

12. Kochhar, Espinoza, and Hinze-Pifer, "After the Great Recession."

13. "Results from Tom K. Wong et al., 2017 National DACA Study," Center for American Progress, October 7, 2017, https://cdn.americanprogress.org/content/uploads/2017/11 /02125251/2017_DACA_study_economic_report_updated.pdf; Tom K. Wong, Greisa Martinez Rosas, Adam Luna, Henry Manning, Adrian Reyna, Patrick O'Shea, Tom Jawetz, and Philip E. Wolgin, "DACA Recipients' Economic and Educational Gains Continue to Grow," Center for American Progress, August 28, 2017, https://www .americanprogress.org/issues/immigration/news/2017/08/28/437956/daca-recipients -economic-educational-gains-continue-grow.

14. Doris Marie Provine, Monica W. Varsanyi, Paul G. Lewis, and Scott H. Decker, *Policing Immigrants: Local Law Enforcement on the Front Lines* (Chicago: University of Chicago Press, 2016), 29.

15. Colton Lochhead, "Suspected Undocumented Immigrant Pawned Jewelry After Northern Nevada Killings, Police Say," *Las Vegas Review-Journal*, January 23, 2019; Samuel Chamberlin, "Illegal Immigrant Accused in Nevada Killings Charged with 4 Counts of Murder," FoxNews.com, January 28, 2019.

16. Alex Nowrasteh, "Criminal Immigrants in Texas in 2017: Illegal Immigrant Conviction Rates and Arrest Rates for Homicide, Sex Crimes, Larceny, and Other Crimes," CATO Institute, August 27, 2019.

17. Michael T. Light and Ty Miller, "Does Undocumented Immigration Increase Violent Crime?," *Criminology* 56 (2018): 370–401.

18. "Shifting Public Views on Legal Immigration into the U.S.," Pew Research Center, June 28, 2018.

19. SSRS/CNN Poll conducted June 28–30, 2019, July 2, 2019, https://cdn.cnn.com/cnn /2019/images/07/02/rel8b.-.trump,.immigration.pdf.

20. Patrick Ruffini, "Far From Settled: Varied and Changing Attitudes on Immigration in America," Democracy Fund Voter Study Group, October 2018.

21. Laura Hill, "Just the Facts: English Proficiency of Immigrants," Public Policy Institute of California, March 2011.

22. Hill, "Just the Facts."

23. Ken Stone, "No Speaking Spanish to Shoppers? San Carlos Albertsons Sued by Feds," *Times of San Diego*, May 3, 2018.

24. Monthly Harvard-Harris Poll, January 2018, http://harvardharrispoll.com/wp-content /uploads/2018/01/Final_HHP_Jan2018-Refield_RegisteredVoters_XTab.pdf, last accessed August 5, 2019.

25. Julie Hirschfeld Davis, Sheryl Gay Stolberg, and Thomas Kaplan, "Trump Alarms Lawmakers with Disparaging Words for Haiti and Africa," *New York Times*, January 11, 2018; Sasha Ingber and Rachel Martin, "Immigration Chief: 'Give Me Your Tired, Your Poor Who Can Stand on Their Own 2 Feet,'" NPR.org, August 13, 2019; Sarah Ruiz-Grossman, "Ken Cuccinelli: Statue of Liberty Poem About 'People Coming from Europe,'" HuffPost .com, August 14, 2019.

Chapter 8
The Strip Mall Resistance

1. Dara Lind, "Donald Trump Tried to Sue a Nevada County That Let Polls Stay Open So People Could Vote," Vox.com, November 8, 2016.
2. Lind, "Donald Trump Tried to Sue a Nevada County."
3. Nevada Legislature, 79th (2017) Session, S.B. 223.
4. Thomas Mitchell, "Bill Proposes to Turn Nevada into a Sanctuary State," *Ely Times*, March 10, 2017.
5. Jonathan Easley, "Poll: Americans Overwhelmingly Oppose Sanctuary Cities," *The Hill*, February 21, 2017; Louis Jacobson, "Anatomy of a Statistic: Do 80 Percent of Americans Oppose Sanctuary Cities?" Politifact, February 24, 2017 (emphasis added).
6. SSRS/CNN poll conducted June 28–30, 2019, released July 2, 2019.
7. Amanda Sakuma, "Astrid Silva: Obama Lifts One Immigrant's Story Out of the Shadows," MSNBC.com, November 21, 2014.
8. Laura Myers, "Reid: Hispanics Playing Bigger Political Role in Nevada, West," *Las Vegas Review-Journal*, October 16, 2011; Andrew Prokop, "Harry Reid Choked a Man for Trying to Bribe Him, and 10 More Facts About the Senate Leader," Vox.com, March 27, 2015; Michelle L. Price, "Nevada Democrats Hope Latinos Can Propel Them to Victory," USNews.com, August 16, 2018; Steve Phillips, "Latinos Are the Key to Taking Back the Senate in 2018," *The Nation*, January 31, 2018.
9. U.S. Constitution, Article I, Section 2, Clause 3.
10. *Kravitz et al. v. U.S. Dept. of Commerce et al.*, Third Amended Complaint, 2018 WL 8647607 (D. Md. 2018), para. 81; American Community Survey 2013–2017.
11. Tierney Sneed, "Census Bureau Study Ups the Estimate for Non-Response Due to Citizenship Question," TalkingPointsMemo.com, June 24, 2009.
12. Hansi Lo Wang, "More than 2 Dozen States, Cities Sue to Block Census Citizenship Question," NPR.org, April 3, 2018.
13. *Kravitz et al. v. U.S. Dept. of Commerce et al.*, Third Amended Complaint, 2018 WL 8647607 (D.Md. 2018), para. 22.
14. Kelly Percival, "What the Blockbuster Documents Uncovered This Week Mean for the Census Citizenship Case at the Supreme Court," Brennan Center for Justice, May 31, 2019.
15. *Dep't of Commerce v. New York*, No. 18-966, June 27, 2019 (U.S.).
16. Matthew Choi, "Trump Wants Census to Find Out Who Is 'an Illegal,'" Politico, July 1, 2019.
17. Shoba Sivaprasad Wadhia, *Banned: Immigration Enforcement in the Time of Trump* (New York: NYU Press, 2019), 29.
18. Lesley Marin and Joe Bartels, "Mother Who Claimed She Was Assaulted During ICE Detainment Wants Records in Case," KTNV.com, April 5, 2018; Chris Kudialis, "Las Vegas Family Hoping for Release of Detained Immigrant Mom," *Las Vegas Sun*, April 5, 2018.
19. Marin and Bartels, "Mother." Kudialis, "Las Vegas Family."

Chapter 9
Dirty Immigration Lawyers

1. Jefferson Sessions, "Remarks to the Executive Office for Immigration Review," October 12, 2017.

2. Ingrid Eagly and Steven Shafer, "Access to Counsel in Immigration Court," American Immigration Council, September 28, 2016.

3. "Details on Deportation Proceedings in Immigration Court," Transactional Records Access Clearinghouse, Syracuse University, last accessed November 30, 2019, https://trac .syr.edu/phptools/immigration/nta (Las Vegas Immigration Court, Initial Filings, September 2019).

4. Nevada Legislature, 80th (2019) Session, A.B. 376.

5. Nevada Legislature, 80th (2019) Session, A.B. 376.

6. Nevada Legislature, 80th (2019) Session, A.B. 275.

7. Jon Ralston, Twitter, @RalstonReports, May 26, 2019, 3:29 p.m.

8. Jennifer Solis, "Segerblom, Advocates Tell Metro to Come Clean About ICE," *Nevada Current*, February 8, 2019; Michelle Rindels, "Commissioners Question Police Cooperation with ICE, as They Approve More Staff for Jail Where Collaboration Takes Place," *Nevada Independent*, July 17, 2019.

9. Mark Hernandez, "ACLU of Nevada Calls on Metro to Stop Honoring ICE Detainers, Says They Constitute Warrantless Arrest," *Nevada Independent*, October 12, 2019; Michael Kagan, "Immigration Law's Looming Fourth Amendment Problem," *Georgetown Law Journal* 104 (2015): 125–70.

10. *Gonzalez v. Immigration and Customs Enforcement*, Findings of Fact and Conclusions of Law, Case No 2:12-cv-09012-AB (C.D. Cal 2019).

11. Michelle Rindels, "Metro Suspending Controversial 287g Collaboration with ICE; Federal Agency Says Public Safety Will Be Compromised," *Nevada Independent*, October 23, 2019; "LVMPD Will No Longer Detain Persons on Federal Immigration Holds; 287(g) Program Suspended," Las Vegas Metropolitan Police Department, press release, October 23, 2019; Michael Lyle, "Following Metro, Las Vegas Ends Its 287(g) Agreement," *Nevada Current*, October 24, 2019.

12. "ICE Arrests More than 80 During 5-Day Enforcement Action in New York City, the Hudson Valley, and Long Island," Immigration and Customs Enforcement, press release, September 26, 2019.

Chapter 10
The Coming Battle

1. Arthur Kane, "Top Las Vegas ICE Official Discusses Flood of Undocumented Criminals," *Las Vegas Review-Journal*, August 28, 2019.

2. Adam Serwer, "A Crime by Any Name," *The Atlantic*, July 3, 2019.

3. Geoffrey Skelly, "Can Democrats Win on Immigration Policy in 2020?," FiveThirtyEight .com, April 30, 2019; "Immigration and the 2020 Elections," Immigration Hub, June 2019, https://static1.squarespace.com/static/5b60b2381aef1dbe876cd08f/t/5d38b9c91a39bc 0001416ecd/1563998672198/Hub+-+GSG+-+2020+Immigration+Survey+-+Analysis+ FINAL.pdf, 7; Justin McCarthy, "Support for Allowing Border Refugees into U.S. Edges Up," Gallup.com, August 13, 2019.

4. SSRS/CNN Poll conducted June 28–30, 2019, released July 2, 2019; NPR/PBS News-Hour/Marist Poll, July 15–17, 2019, http://maristpoll.marist.edu/wp-content/uploads /2019/07/NPR_PBS-NewsHour_Marist-Poll_USA-NOS-and-Tables_1907190926 .pdf, 13.

5. "Immigration Court's Active Backlog Surpasses One Million," Transactional Records Access Clearinghouse, Syracuse University, September 18, 2019, https://trac.syr.edu /immigration/reports/574.

6. Immigration Court's Active Backlog Surpasses One Million"; Harvard-Harris Monthly, January 2018, http://harvardharrispoll.com/wp-content/uploads/2018/01/Final_HHP _Jan2018-Refield_RegisteredVoters_XTab.pdf, 70.

7. Harvard-Harris Monthly, January 2018, 68; *2017 Yearbook of Immigration Statistics*, Department of Homeland Security, updated September 12, 2019, Table 1: Persons Obtaining Lawful Permanent Resident Status: Fiscal Years 1820 to 2017.

8. "Obama Weekly Address: Illegal Immigrants Must Go to Back of the Line for Citizenship," RealClearPolitics.com, June 8, 2013.

9. "Immigration and the 2020 Elections," 15, 18.

10. "New Deportation Proceedings Filed in Immigration Court," Transactional Records Access Clearinghouse, Syracuse University, last accessed August 10, 2019, https://trac.syr .edu/phptools/immigration/charges/deport_filing_charge.php; "Empty Benches: Underfunding of Immigration Courts Undermines Justice," American Immigration Council, June 17, 2016; "Trump Tried to Deport People Faster. Immigration Courts Slowed Down Instead," The Marshall Project, July 16, 2019. ("With more judges, more cases are being resolved. Between last October [2018] and May [2019], the courts completed more cases than they did in each of the last three full years under Obama, said Kathryn Mattingly, a Justice Department spokeswoman.")

11. Dan Balz and Scott Clement, "Most Americans Oppose Key Parts of Trump Immigration Plans, Including Wall, Limits on Citizens Bringing Family to U.S., Poll Says," *Washington Post*, July 6, 2018.

Bibliography

"Asylum Decisions and Denials Jump in 2018." Transactional Records Access Clearinghouse, Syracuse University, November 29, 2018, https://trac.syr.edu/immigration/reports/539.

"Asylum Decisions by Custody, Representation, Nationality, Location, Month and Year, Outcome and More." Transactional Records Access Clearinghouse, Syracuse University, last accessed August 21, 2019, https://trac.syr.edu/phptools/immigration/asylum.

"Details on Deportation Proceedings in Immigration Court." Transactional Records Access Clearinghouse, Syracuse University, last accessed November 30, 2019, https://trac.syr.edu/phptools/immigration/nta (Las Vegas Immigration Court, Initial Filings, September 2019).

"Empty Benches: Underfunding of Immigration Courts Undermines Justice." American Immigration Council, June 17, 2016.

"Fact Sheet: A Primer on Expedited Removal." American Immigration Council, July 22, 2019.

"Fact Sheet: Immigrants in Nevada." American Immigration Council, October 6, 2017, https://www.americanimmigrationcouncil.org/research/immigrants-in-nevada.

"Fact Sheet: Temporary Protected Status in the United States—Beneficiaries from El Salvador, Honduras and Haiti." American Immigration Council, October 23, 2017.

"Fast Facts: United States Travel and Tourism Industry 2016." National Travel and Tourism Office, November 2017, https://travel.trade.gov/outreachpages/download_data_table/Fast_Facts_2016.pdf.

"ICE Arrests More than 80 During 5-Day Enforcement Action in New York City, the Hudson Valley, and Long Island." Immigration and Customs Enforcement, press release, September 26, 2019.

"ICE Detains Fewer Immigrants with Serious Criminal Convictions Under Trump Administration." Transactional Records Access Clearinghouse, Syracuse University, December 6, 2019, https://trac.syr.edu/immigration/reports/585.

"ICE Focus Shifts Away from Detaining Serious Criminals." Transactional Records Access Clearinghouse, Syracuse University, June 25, 2019, https://trac.syr.edu/immigration/reports/564.

"Immigration and Customs Enforcement Arrests." Transactional Records Access Clearinghouse, Syracuse University, data through May 2018, https://trac.syr.edu/phptools/immigration/arrest.

"Immigration and Customs Enforcement Arrests." Transactional Records Access Clearinghouse, Syracuse University, last visited July 19, 2019, https://trac.syr.edu/phptools
/immigration/arrest (data through May 2018; TRAC lists 133 arrests as "located," as in located by ICE).

"Immigration and the 2020 Elections." Immigration Hub, June 2019, https://static1.squarespace
.com/static/5b60b2381aef1dbe876cd08f/t/5d38b9c91a39bc0001416ecd/1563998672198
/Hub+-+GSG+-+2020+Immigration+Survey+-+Analysis+FINAL.pdf.

"Immigration Court's Active Backlog Surpasses One Million." Transactional Records Access
Clearinghouse, Syracuse University, September 18, 2019, https://trac.syr.edu/immigration
/reports/574.

"LVMPD Will No Longer Detain Persons on Federal Immigration Holds; 287(g) Program
Suspended," Las Vegas Metropolitan Police Department, press release, October 23, 2019.

"Mapping the USA's Diversity 1960–2060." USA Today, October 21, 2014, https://www
.usatoday.com/story/news/nation/2014/10/21/diversity-map/17657485.

"New Deportation Proceedings Filed in Immigration Court." Transactional Records Access
Clearinghouse, Syracuse University, last accessed August 10, 2019, https://trac.syr.edu
/phptools/immigration/charges/deport_filing_charge.php.

"Obama Weekly Address: Illegal Immigrants Must Go to Back of the Line for Citizenship."
RealClearPolitics.com, June 8, 2013.

"Of the estimated 515,000 arrivals in 2016, a total of 320,000, or 62 percent, were overstays
and 190,000, or 38 percent, were EWIs." Warren, "US Undocumented Population Continued to Fall."

"Results from Tom K. Wong et al., 2017 National DACA Study." Center for American
Progress, October 7, 2017, https://cdn.americanprogress.org/content/uploads/2017/11
/02125251/2017_DACA_study_economic_report_updated.pdf.

"Sanctuary City Ordinance." City and County of San Francisco, Office of Civic Engagement
and Immigrant Affairs, https://sfgov.org/oceia/sanctuary-city-ordinance-0, last visited
August 3, 2019.

"Sandy Searles Miller Elementary School." GreatSchools.org, last accessed August 20, 2019.

"Secure Communities." National Conference of State Legislatures, July 26, 2012.

"Secure Communities: A Fact Sheet." American Immigration Council, November 29, 2011.

"Shifting Public Views on Legal Immigration into the U.S.," Pew Research Center, June 28,
2018.

"Ten-Fold Difference in Odds of ICE Enforcement Depending upon Where You Live." Transactional Records Access Clearinghouse, Syracuse University, April 11, 2019, https://trac
.syr.edu/immigration/reports/555/#f1.

"The Attorney General's Judges: How U.S. Immigration Courts Became a Deportation Tool."
Innovation Law Lab and Southern Poverty Law Center, June 2019, 6.

"TPS Holders in Nevada." Center for American Progress, October 23, 2017.

"Trump Accused of 'Deporting Kids with Cancer' After the Administration Reportedly Ends
Medical Deferral Program." TheWeek.com, August 26, 2019.

"Trump Tried to Deport People Faster. Immigration Courts Slowed Down Instead," The Marshall Project, July 16, 2019.

"U.S. Unauthorized Immigrant Population Estimates by State, 2016." Pew Research Center,
February 5, 2019, https://www.pewresearch.org/hispanic/interactives/u-s-unauthorized
-immigrants-by-state.

2017 Yearbook of Immigration Statistics. Department of Homeland Security, updated September 12, 2019, Table 1: Persons Obtaining Lawful Permanent Resident Status: Fiscal Years 1820 to 2017.

"U.S. Unauthorized Immigrant Population Estimates by State, 2016." Pew Research Center, February 5, 2019, https://www.pewresearch.org/hispanic/interactives/u-s-unauthorized-immigrants-by-state.

Ainsley, Julia, and Jacob Soboroff. "ICE to Launch Mass Raids Targeting Undocumented Families on Sunday." NBCNews.com, June 21, 2019.

American Community Survey 2012–2016, ZCTA5 89115.

American Community Survey 2013–2017.

Arizona v. United States, 567 U.S. 387, 396 (2012)

Bachega, Hugo. "Trump Immigration: The Effects of a Raid on One Tiny Town." BBC.com, July 2, 2018.

Bacon, David. "Undocumented Youth Are Here Through No Fault of Their Own. But It's Not Their Parents' Fault, Either." InTheseTimes.com, November 5, 2015.

Balz, Dan, and Scott Clement, "Most Americans Oppose Key Parts of Trump Immigration Plans, Including Wall, Limits on Citizens Bringing Family to U.S., Poll Says." *Washington Post,* July 6, 2018.

Barack Obama, Facebook post, September 5, 2017 ("Immigration can be a controversial topic . . ."), www.facebook.com/barackobama/posts/10155227588436749.

Bernard, Diane. "The Time a President Deported 1 Million Mexican Americans for Supposedly Stealing U.S. Jobs." *Washington Post,* August 13, 2018.

Bialik, Kristen. "Most Immigrants Arrested by ICE Have Prior Criminal Convictions, a Big Change from 2009." Pew Research Center, February 15, 2018.

Bixby, Scot.t "ICE Told Agents 'Happy Hunting' as They Prepped for Raid." *Daily Beast,* July 3, 2019.

Border Security Metrics Report. Department of Homeland Security, February 26, 2019, 10.

Bowden, Josh. "ICE Arrests of Immigrants with No Criminal Convictions Rises: Report," *The Hill,* May 18, 2018.

Cade, Jason A. "Immigration Equity's Last Stand: Sanctuaries and Legitimacy in an Era of Mass Immigration Enforcement." *Northwestern University Law Review* 113, no. 3 (2017): 441, 484, 494–497.

Cantor, Guillermo, Emily Ryo, and Reed Humphrey. "Changing Patterns of Interior Immigration Enforcement in the United States 2016–2018." American Immigration Council, July 1, 2019, 2.

Castillo, Andrea. "'Collateral Arrests' by ICE Amount to Racial Profiling, Violate Immigrants' Rights, Lawyers Say." *Los Angeles Times,* February 4, 2018.

Chacón, Jennifer M. "Overcriminalizing Immigration." *Journal of Criminal Law and Criminology* 102 (Summer 2012): 615, 640–47.

Chamberlin, Samuel. "Illegal Immigrant Accused in Nevada Killings Charged with 4 Counts of Murder." FoxNews.com, January 28, 2019.

Choi, Matthew. "Trump Wants Census to Find Out Who Is 'an Illegal.'" Politico, July 1, 2019.

City of Las Vegas. COR 5962, Arrest and Detention of Foreign Nationals, May 2017, available at http://arribalasvegas.org/wp-content/uploads/2019/03/COR-5962-Arrest-and-Detention-of-Foreign-Nationals.pdf.

Crunden, E. A. "DREAMers Face Anxiety, Terror amid Back-and-Forth on DACA." Think-Progress.org, September 18, 2017.

Dawsey, Josh, and Nick Miroff, "The Hostile Border Between Trump and the Head of DHS." *Washington Post*, May 25, 2018.

del Bosque, Melissa. "The Case That Made an Ex-ICE Attorney Realize the Government Was Relying on False 'Evidence' Against Migrants." ProPublica, August 13, 2019.

Dep't of Commerce v. New York. No. 18-966, June 27, 2019 (U.S.).

Designating Aliens for Expedited Removal. 69 Fed. Reg. 48877, 48880–81, August 11, 2004.

Eagly, Ingrid, and Steven Shafer. "Access to Counsel in Immigration Court." American Immigration Council, September 28, 2016.

Easley, Jonathan. "Poll: Americans Overwhelmingly Oppose Sanctuary Cities." *The Hill*, February 21, 2017.

Edsall, Thomas B. "How Immigration Foiled Hillary." *New York Times*, October 5, 2017.

Eskenazi, Brenda, Carolyn A. Fahey, and Katherine Kogut. "Association of Perceived Immigration Policy Vulnerability with Mental and Physical Health Among US-Born Latino Adolescents in California." *JAMA Pediatrics* 173, no. 8 (2019): 744–753.

Executive Order No. 13767. Border Security and Immigration Enforcement Improvements, 82 Fed. Reg. 8793 (January 25, 2017).

Executive Order No. 13768. Enhancing Public Safety in the Interior of the United States, 82 Fed. Reg. 8799 (January 25, 2017).

Fertig, Beth. "Presiding Under Pressure." WNYC News, May 21, 2019.

Frias, Lauren. "Border Patrol Chief Who Was Member of Secret Facebook Group Said She Didn't Realize 'Highly Offensive' Posts Were Being Shared Until ProPublica Report." *Business Insider*, July 26, 2019.

Gemmill, Alison, Ralph Catalano, Joan A. Casey, et al., "Association of Preterm Births Among US Latina Women with the 2016 Presidential Election." *JAMA Network Open* 2, no. 7 (2019): e197804.

Gomez, Alan. "ICE Sets Record for Arrests of Undocumented Immigrants with No Criminal Record." *USA Today*, March 21, 2019.

Gonella, Catalina. "Visa Overstays Outnumber Illegal Border Crossings, Trend Expected to Continue." NBCNews.com, March 7, 2017.

Gonzalez v. Immigration and Customs Enforcement. Findings of Fact and Conclusions of Law, Case No 2:12-cv-09012-AB (C.D. Cal 2019).

Greenberg, Stanley, and Nancy Zdunkewicz. "Macomb County in the Age of Trump." Democracy Corps and Roosevelt Institute, March 9, 2017.

Greenstone, Michael, and Adam Looney. "What Immigration Means for U.S. Employment and Wages." The Hamilton Project, May 4, 2012.

Grinberg, Emanuella, and Konstantin Toropin. "A US-Born Citizen Who Was in Immigration Detention for Three Weeks Has Been Released." CNN.com, July 25, 2019.

Hallman, Hunter. "How to Undocumented Immigrants Pay Federal Taxes? An Explainer." Bipartisan Policy Center, March 28, 2018.

Harvard-Harris Monthly. January 2018, http://harvardharrispoll.com/wp-content/uploads/2018/01/Final_HHP_Jan2018-Refield_RegisteredVoters_XTab.pdf, 70.

Heath, Brad. "As Feds Focused on Detaining Kids, Border Drug Prosecutions Plummeted." *USA Today*, October 10, 2018.

Hernández, César Cuauhtémoc García. "Deconstructing Crimmigration." *U.C. Davis Law Review* 52 (2018): 200.

Hernández, César Cuauhtémoc García. *Crimmigration Law.* Chicago: ABA Publishing, 2015, 258–59.

Hernandez, Mark. "ACLU of Nevada Calls on Metro to Stop Honoring ICE Detainers, Says They Constitute Warrantless Arrest." *Nevada Independent,* October 12, 2019.

Hill, Laura. "Just the Facts: English Proficiency of Immigrants." Public Policy Institute of California, March 2011.

Hirschfeld Davis, Julie, Sheryl Gay Stolberg, and Thomas Kaplan, "Trump Alarms Lawmakers with Disparaging Words for Haiti and Africa." *New York Times,* January 11, 2018.

Hoyer, Rep. Steny. "Press Release: A Look at H.R.6, the Dream and Promise Act of 2019," March 12, 2019.

Illegal Immigration Reform and Immigrant Responsibility Act of 1996 (IIRIRA), 110 Stat. 3009-546.

Immigration and Nationality Act, 8 U.S. Code § 1229a.

Immigration and Nationality Act, 8 U.S.C. § 1101(a)(42).

Immigration and Nationality Act, 8 U.S.C. § 1182(9)(B).8.

Immigration and Nationality Act, 8 U.S.C. § 1225(b)(1)(A)(iii)(II).

Immigration and Nationality Act, 8 U.S.C. § 1254a.

Immigration and Nationality Act, 8 U.S.C. 1373.

Ingber, Sasha, and Rachel Martin. "Immigration Chief: 'Give Me Your Tired, Your Poor Who Can Stand on Their Own 2 Feet.'" NPR.org, August 13, 2019.

Interview with Bethany Khan, director of communications for Culinary Workers Local 226, July 24, 2019.

ITEP website: https://itep.org/immigration.

Jacobson, Louis. "Anatomy of a Statistic: Do 80 Percent of Americans Oppose Sanctuary Cities?" Politifact, February 24, 2017.

Jean Guerrero (interview). "Migrant Seeking Asylum Says His Toddler Was Taken Away at the U.S. Border." *PBS NewsHour,* December 22, 2017.

Johnson, Jeh. "Memorandum: Policies for the Apprehension, Detention and Removal of Undocumented Immigrants." Department of Homeland Security, November 20, 2014.

Jordan, Miriam. "More than 2,000 Migrants Were Targeted in Raids. 35 Were Arrested." *New York Times,* July 23, 2019.

Justice Manual, U.S. Department of Justice 9-28.300, November 2015.

Kagan, Michael. "Immigration Law's Looming Fourth Amendment Problem." *Georgetown Law Journal* 104 (2015): 125–70.

Kane, Arthur. "Top Las Vegas ICE Official Discusses Flood of Undocumented Criminals." *Las Vegas Review-Journal,* August 28, 2019.

Kane, Timothy. "The Economic Effect of Immigration." Hoover Institution, February 17, 2015.

Kaufman, Carrie. "Will UNLV Become a Sanctuary Campus?" KNPR Nevada Radio, December 1, 2016.

Kilgore, Ed. "ICE Has Tripled the Number of Undocumented Immigrants Without Criminal Records It Arrests." NYMag.com, August 13, 2018.

Klein, Christianne. "Mayor Says Las Vegas Isn't Sanctuary City." 8NewsNow.com, January 26, 2017.

Kochhar, Rakesh, C. Soledad Espinoza, and Rebecca Hinze-Pifer. "After the Great Recession: Foreign Born Gain Jobs; Native Born Lose Jobs." Pew Research Center, October 29, 2010.

Koh, Jennifer Lee "Removal in the Shadows of Immigration Court." *Southern California Law Review* 90 (2017): 181–236.

Kopan, Tal. "ICE Director: Undocumented Immigrants 'Should Be Afraid.'" CNN.com, June 16, 2017.

Kravitz et al. v. U.S. Dept. of Commerce et al. Third Amended Complaint, 2018 WL 8647607 (D. Md. 2018), para. 81.

Kravitz et al. v. U.S. Dept. of Commerce et al. Third Amended Complaint, 2018 WL 8647607 (D.Md. 2018), para. 22.

Kudialis, Chris. "Las Vegas Family Hoping for Release of Detained Immigrant Mom." Las Vegas Sun, April 5, 2018.

Lasch, Christopher N., R. Linus Chan, Ingrid V. Eagly, Dina Francesca Haynes, Annie Lai, Elizabeth M. McCormick, and Juliet P. Stumpf. "Understanding 'Sanctuary Cities.'" Boston College Law Review 59 (2018): 1703–1774.

Lew-Williams, Beth. The Chinese Must Go. Cambridge, MA: Harvard University Press, 2018, 44.

Light, Michael T., and Ty Miller, "Does Undocumented Immigration Increase Violent Crime?" Criminology 56 (2018): 370–401.

Lind, Dara. "Donald Trump Tried to Sue a Nevada County That Let Polls Stay Open So People Could Vote." Vox.com, November 8, 2016.

Lo Wang, Hansi. "More than 2 Dozen States, Cities Sue to Block Census Citizenship Question." NPR.org, April 3, 2018.

Lochhead, Colton. "Suspected Undocumented Immigrant Pawned Jewelry After Northern Nevada Killings, Police Say." Las Vegas Review-Journal, January 23, 2019.

Logan, Wayne A. "Criminal Law Sanctuaries." Harvard Civil Rights–Civil Liberties Law Review 38 (2003): 323–24.

Lyle, Michael. "Following Metro, Las Vegas Ends Its 287(g) Agreement." Nevada Current, October 24, 2019.

Manke, Kara. "Deportation Worries Fuel Anxiety, Poor Sleep, Among U.S.-Born Latinx youth." Berkeley News, June 24, 2019.

Marin, Lesley, and Joe Bartels. "Mother Who Claimed She Was Assaulted During ICE Detainment Wants Records in Case." KTNV.com, April 5, 2018.

Markon, Jerry. "Can a 3-Year-Old Represent Herself in Immigration Court? This Judge Thinks So." Washington Post, March 5, 2016.

Matter of Castro-Tum, 27 I&N Dec. 271 (A.G. 2018).

Matter of L-E-A-, 27 I&N Dec. 581, 582 (A.G. 2019).

McCarthy, Justin. "Support for Allowing Border Refugees into U.S. Edges Up." Gallup.com, August 13, 2019.

Miller, Todd. "Over 7,000 Bodies Have Been Found at the US-Mexican Border Since the '90s." The Nation, April 24, 2018.

Miroff, Nick. "ICE Raids Targeting Migrant Families Slated to Start Sunday in Major U.S. Cities." Washington Post. June 21, 2019.

Mitchell, Thomas. "Bill Proposes to Turn Nevada into a Sanctuary State." Ely Times, March 10, 2017.

Monthly Harvard-Harris Poll, January 2018, http://harvardharrispoll.com/wp-content/uploads/2018/01/Final_HHP_Jan2018-Refield_RegisteredVoters_XTab.pdf, last accessed August 5, 2019.

Montoya-Galvez, Camilo. "Top Immigration Official Says ICE Is Willing to Deport 1 Million Undocumented Immigrants." CBS News, July 7, 2019.

Morton, John, Director. U.S. Immigration and Customs Enforcement, Memorandum on Enforcement Actions at or Focused on Sensitive Locations from to Field Office Directors, Special Agents in Charge, and Chief Counsel, 2011.

Murphy, Doyle. "ICE Raid Nets Estimated 300 Workers in Greeley Plant." *Greeley Tribune,* December 12, 2006.

Myers, Laura. "Reid: Hispanics Playing Bigger Political Role in Nevada, West." *Las Vegas Review-Journal,* October 16, 2011.

Nevada Legislature, 79th (2017) Session, S.B. 223.

Nevada Legislature, 80th (2019) Session, A.B. 275.

Nevada Legislature, 80th (2019) Session, A.B. 376.

Nowrasteh, Alex. "Criminal Immigrants in Texas in 2017: Illegal Immigrant Conviction Rates and Arrest Rates for Homicide, Sex Crimes, Larceny, and Other Crimes." CATO Institute, August 27, 2019.

NPR/PBS NewsHour/Marist Poll, July 15–17, 2019, http://maristpoll.marist.edu/wp-content/uploads/2019/07/NPR_PBS-NewsHour_Marist-Poll_USA-NOS-and-Tables_1907190926.pdf, 13.

Obama, Barack. "Remarks by the President in Address to the Nation on Immigration." November 20, 2014.

Oprysko, Caitlin. "Trump Talks Up Success of Raids, Despite Little Evidence of Widespread Deportations." Politico.com, July 15, 2019.

Papenfuss, Mary. "Immigration Officials Snatch 9-Year-Old U.S. Citizen Heading to School, Hold Her for 2 Days." *HuffPost,* March 23, 2019.

Percival, Kelly. "What the Blockbuster Documents Uncovered This Week Mean for the Census Citizenship Case at the Supreme Court." Brennan Center for Justice, May 31, 2019.

Perez-Zenteno v. U.S. Attorney General, 913 F.3d 1301 (11th. Cir 2019).

Perez-Zenteno v. U.S. Attorney General, 913 F.3d at 1304.

Phillips, Steve. "Latinos Are the Key to Taking Back the Senate in 2018." *The Nation,* January 31, 2018.

Pirie, Sophie H. "The Origins of a Political Trial: The Sanctuary Movement and Political Justice." *Yale Journal of Law and the Humanities* 2 (1990): 381–416.

Powell, Stewart M. "Bush Administration Steps Up Immigration Raids." *San Francisco Chronicle,* June 1, 2008.

Preston, Julia. "Is It Time to Remove Immigration Courts from Presidential Control?" The Marshall Project, August 28, 2019.

Preston, Julia. "Most Undocumented Immigrants Will Stay Under Obama's New Policies, Report Says." *New York Times,* July 23, 2015.

Price, Michelle L. "Nevada Democrats Hope Latinos Can Propel Them to Victory." USNews.com, August 16, 2018.

Prokop, Andrew. "Harry Reid Choked a Man for Trying to Bribe Him, and 10 More Facts About the Senate Leader." Vox.com, March 27, 2015.

Provine, Doris Marie, Monica W. Varsanyi, Paul G. Lewis, and Scott H. Decker. *Policing Immigrants: Local Law Enforcement on the Front Lines.* Chicago: University of Chicago Press, 2016).

Ralston, Jon. Twitter, @RalstonReports, May 26, 2019, 3:29 p.m.

Ramji-Nogales, Jaya, Andrew I. Schoenholtz, and Philip G. Schrag. "Refugee Roulette: Disparities in Asylum Adjudication." *Stanford Law Review* 60 (November 2007): 330.

Ramos v. Nielsen, Order Granting Plaintiffs' Motion for Preliminary Injunction, No. 18-cv-01554-EMC, N.D. Cal., October 3, 2018.

Rindels, Michelle. "Commissioners Question Police Cooperation with ICE, as They Approve More Staff for Jail Where Collaboration Takes Place." *Nevada Independent*, July 17, 2019.

Rindels, Michelle. "Metro Suspending Controversial 287g Collaboration with ICE; Federal Agency Says Public Safety Will Be Compromised." *Nevada Independent*, October 23, 2019.

Rosenblum, Marc R. "Understanding the Potential Impact of Executive Action on Immigration Enforcement." Migration Policy Institute, July 13, 2015.

Ruffini, Patrick. "Far From Settled: Varied and Changing Attitudes on Immigration in America." Democracy Fund Voter Study Group, October 2018.

Ruiz-Grossman, Sarah. "Ken Cuccinelli: Statue of Liberty Poem About 'People Coming from Europe.'" HuffPost.com, August 14, 2019.

S.F. Admin Code § 12H.1.

S.F. Admin Code § 12H.2.

S.F. Admin Code § 12I.3.

Sacchetti, Maria, and Kevin Uhrmacher. "Nations Targeted by U.S. for High Rates of Visa Overstays Account for Small Number of Violators." *Washington Post*, April 24, 2019.

Sacchetti, Maria. "ACLU: US Has Taken Nearly 1,000 Child Migrants from Their Parents Since Judge Ordered Stop to Border Separations." *Washington Post*, July 30, 2019.

Sakuma, Amanda. "Astrid Silva: Obama Lifts One Immigrant's Story Out of the Shadows." MSNBC.com, November 21, 2014.

Serwer, Adam. "A Crime by Any Name." *The Atlantic*, July 3, 2019.

Sessions, Jefferson. "Remarks to the Executive Office for Immigration Review." October 12, 2017.

Sharda, Judge Munish. Transactional Records Access Clearinghouse, Syracuse University, last accessed August 21, 2019, https://trac.syr.edu/immigration/reports/judgereports /00474LVG/index.html.

Shoichet, Catherine E. "A Father and Daughter Drowned Crossing the Rio Grande. Here's How Their Journey Began." CNN.com, June 26, 2019.

Skelly, Geoffrey. "Can Democrats Win on Immigration Policy in 2020?" FiveThirtyEight.com, April 30, 2019.

Sneed, Tierney. "Census Bureau Study Ups the Estimate for Non-Response Due to Citizenship Question." TalkingPointsMemo.com, June 24, 2009.

Solis, Jennifer. "Segerblom, Advocates Tell Metro to Come Clean About ICE." *Nevada Current*, February 8, 2019.

Spagat, Elliott. "Making an Immigration Arrest Requires Hours of Surveillance." Associated Press, July 16, 2019.

SSRS/CNN Poll conducted June 28–30, 2019, July 2, 2019, https://cdn.cnn.com/cnn/2019 /images/07/02/rel8b.-.trump,.immigration.pdf.

Stone, Ken. "No Speaking Spanish to Shoppers? San Carlos Albertsons Sued by Feds." *Times of San Diego*, May 3, 2018.

Strekal, Edan. "Chinatown (Site)." RenoHistorical.org, last accessed August 21, 2019, http:// renohistorical.org/items/show/173.

Stumpf, Juliet. "The Crimmigration Crisis: Immigrants, Crime, and Sovereign Power." *American University Law Review* 56 (2006): 367–419

Thompson, A. C. "Inside the Secret Border Patrol Facebook Group Where Agents Joke About Migrant Deaths and Post Sexist Memes." ProPublica.com, July 1, 2019.

Thompson, Gabriel. "Your Judge Is Your Destiny." Topic.com, July 2019.

U.S. Constitution, Article I, Section 2, Clause 3.

United States Census Bureau, American Community Survey 2012–2016, https://www.census .gov/acs/www/data/data-tables-and-tools/data-profiles/2016.

United States v. Peralta-Sanchez, Oral Argument, 2016 WL 3232805, May 4, 2016.

Wadhia, Shoba Sivaprasad. *Banned: Immigration Enforcement in the Time of Trump*. New York: NYU Press, 2019.

Warren, Robert. "US Undocumented Population Continued to Fall from 2016 to 2017, and Visa Overstays Significantly Exceeded Illegal Crossings for the Seventh Consecutive Year." Center for Migration Studies of New York, January 16, 2019.

Washington, John. "Bad Information," The Intercept, August 11, 2019.

Whitcomb, Dan. "Nevada Has Highest Proportion of Illegal Immigrants in U.S.: Study." Reuters.com, November 18, 2014.

Wingrove, Josh, Billy House, and Margaret Talev. "Trump Delays Raids on Migrants, Cites Democrats' Requests." Bloomberg.com, June 22, 2019.

Wong, Tom K., Greisa Martinez Rosas, Adam Luna, Henry Manning, Adrian Reyna, Patrick O'Shea, Tom Jawetz, and Philip E. Wolgin, "DACA Recipients' Economic and Educational Gains Continue to Grow." Center for American Progress, August 28, 2017, https://www .americanprogress.org/issues/immigration/news/2017/08/28/437956/daca-recipients -economic-educational-gains-continue-grow.

Wong, Tom K., Sanaa Abrar, Tom Jawetz, Ignacia Rodriguez Kmec, Patrick O'Shea, Greisa Martinez Rosas, and Philip E. Wolgin, "Amid Legal and Political Uncertainty, DACA Remains More Important than Ever." Center for American Progress, August 15, 2018.

Yu Hsi Lee, Esther. "'No Population Is Off the Table': Data Shows Increase in Immigrants Arrests Inside U.S." ThinkProgress.org, December 5, 2017.

Index

About the Author

Michael Kagan is the director of the UNLV Immigration Clinic, which defends children and families fighting deportation in Las Vegas, and is Joyce Mack Professor of Law at the University of Nevada, Las Vegas. He was a plaintiff in one of the lawsuits that prevented the Trump administration from adding a question about citizenship to the 2020 census. He has written for the *Washington Post*, Salon.com, and the *Daily Beast* and is a leading national scholar of immigration and refugee law.